antennae

Beyond posthumanism®™

2022

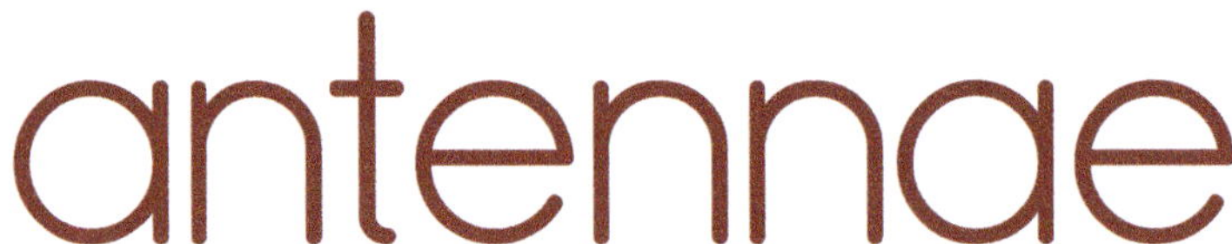

antennae

THE JOURNAL OF NATURE IN VISUAL CULTURE
edited by Giovanni Aloi

Antennae (founded in 2006) is an independent, hybrid, peer reviewed journal. We are free to the public, non-funded by institutions, and not supported by grants or philanthropists. The Journal's format and contents are informed by the concepts of 'knowledge transfer' and 'widening participation'. Independent publications share histories of originality, irreverence, and innovation and *Antennae* has certainly been an important contributor to what will be remembered as the non-human turn in the humanities. The first issue of *Antennae* coincided with the rise of human-animal studies; a field of academic inquiry now become mainstream. Our independent status has allowed us to give a voice to scholars and artists who were initially not taken seriously by mainstream presses. Through our creative approach, we have supported the careers of experimental practitioners and researchers across the world providing a unique space in which new academic fields like the environmental humanities and critical plant studies could also flourish. In January 2009, the establishment of *Antennae*'s Senior Academic Board, Advisory Board, and Network of Global Contributors has affirmed the journal as an indispensable research tool for the subject of environmental studies and visual culture. Still today, no other journal provides artists and scholars with an opportunity to publish full color portfolios of their work or richly illustrated essays at no cost to them or to readers. A markedly transdisciplinary publication, *Antennae* encourages communication and crossover of knowledge among artists, scientists, scholars, activists, curators, and students. Contact Giovanni Aloi, the Editor in Chief at: antennaeproject@gmail.com Visit our website for more info and past issues: www.antennae.org.uk

bey
posthum

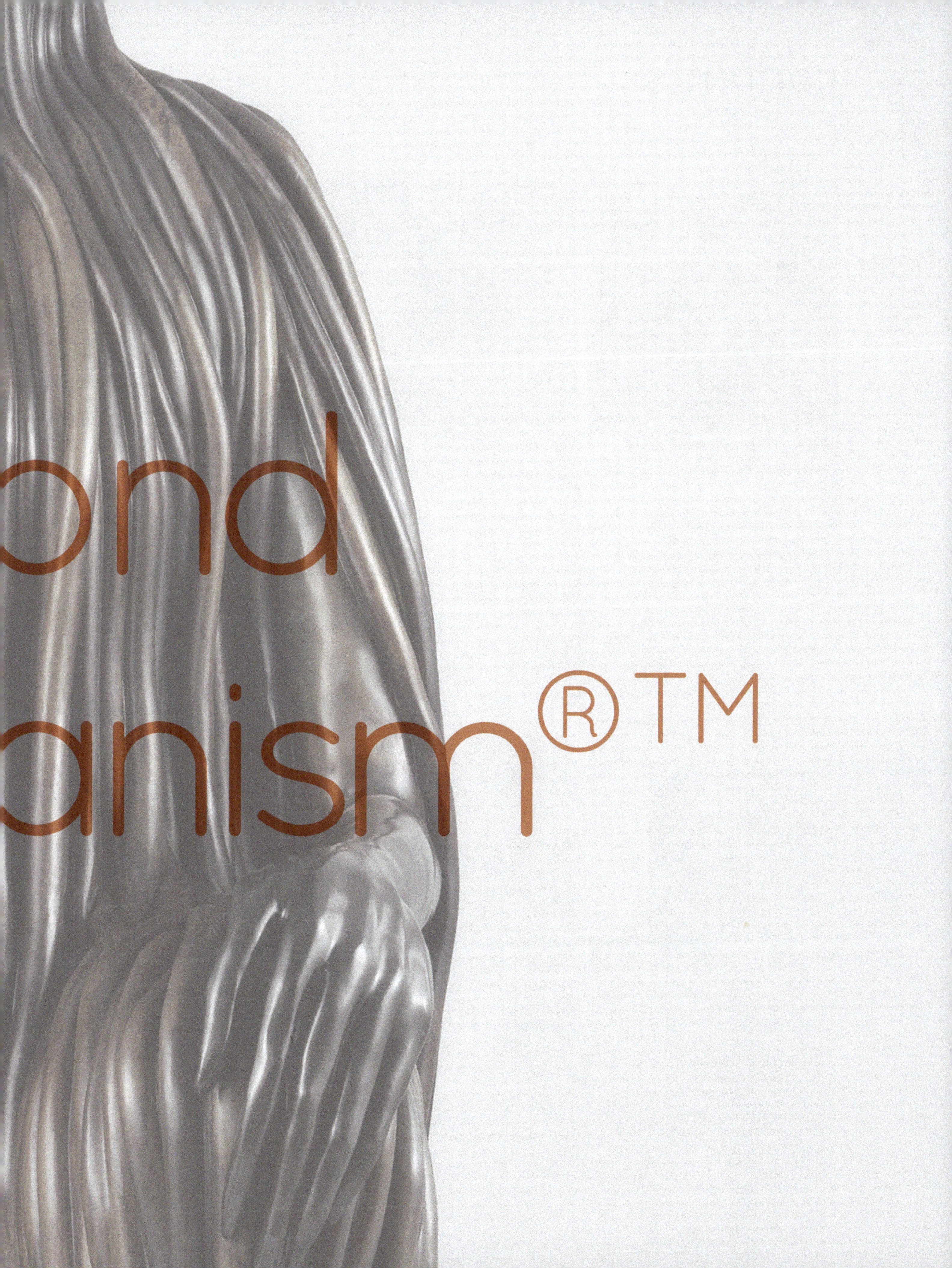
ond
anism®™

contents

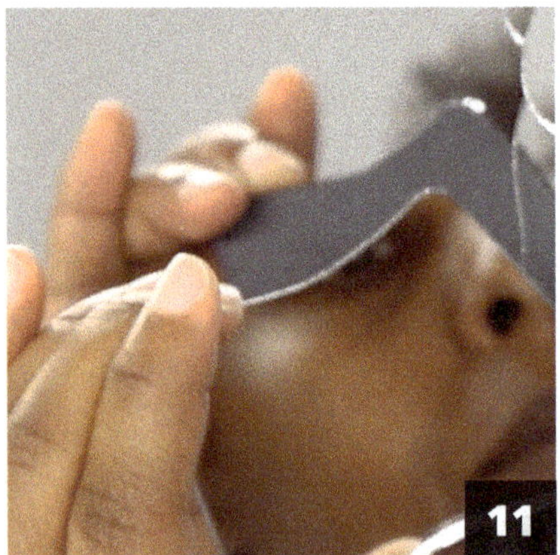

11

beyond posthumanism®TM

text and image: **Betelhem Makonnen**

IThe call for the 'Beyond posthumanism®™' issue of *Antennae* was deeply informed by the work of the black Jamaican writer and cultural theorist Sylvia Wynter who across her vast scholarship introduced perspectives and worldviews that engender "the possibility of undoing and unsettling – not replacing or occupying – Western conceptions of what it means to be human".

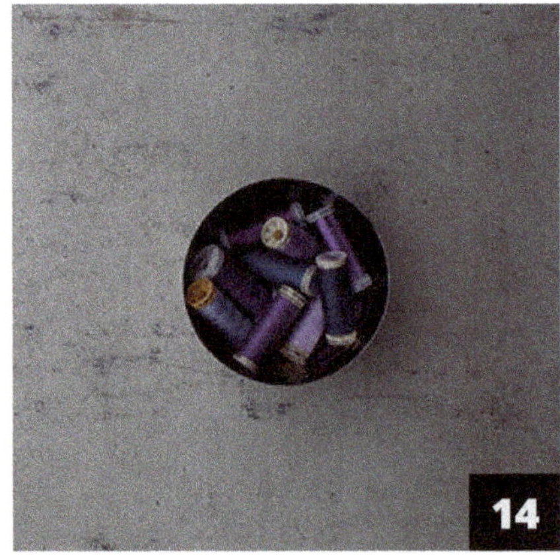

14

Demonic Grounds

in conversation: **Katherine McKittrick** and **Betelhem Makonnen**

Demonic Grounds moves between past and present, archives and fiction, theory and everyday, to focus on places negotiated by black women during and after the transatlantic slave trade. Katherine McKittrick addresses the geographic implications of slave auction blocks, Harriet Jacobs's attic, black Canada and New France, as well as the conceptual spaces of feminism and Sylvia Wynter's philosophies.

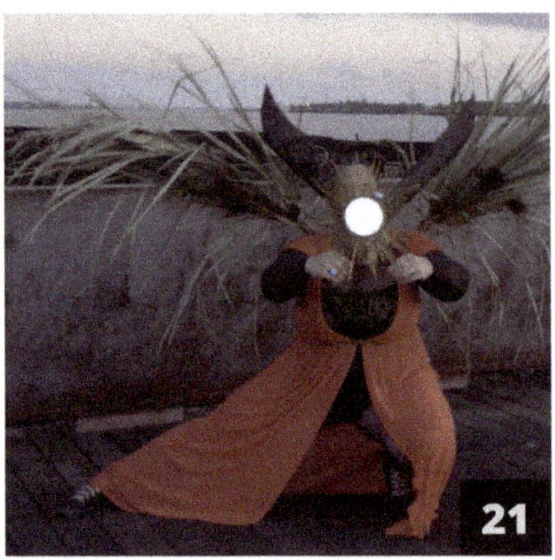

21

Socially engaged art & Wynterian ruptures

text: **Dalaeja Foreman**

This work is a theoretical analysis of socially-engaged-art practice as a political framework for grassroots organizing within communities deemed non-human by the hegemonic-white-supremacist-heteropatriarchal-colonial-capitalist gaze. Sylvia Wynter's deconstruction of the "human" after the 1492 rupture is the base for reconceptualising humanity.

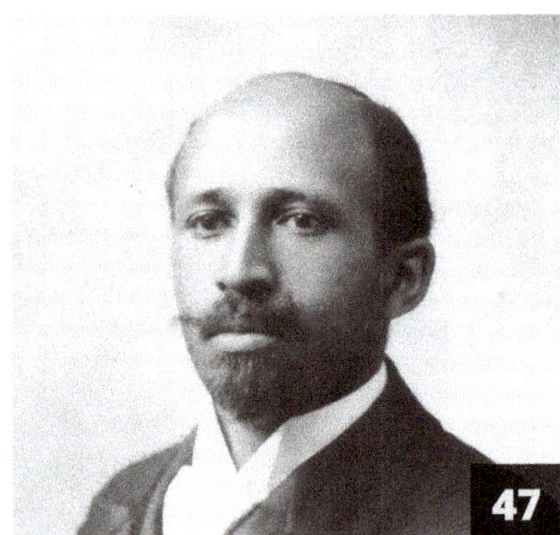

47

The posthuman racial ecology of W.E. B. DuBois

text: **Stephanie Polsky**

The article brings together the geographies, economies, and ecologies of the African American South, Wilhelmine Germany, and the Algorithmic South to illustrate how the cultivation of racial identity intersects at various points with the progress of both the Plantationocene and Anthropocene.

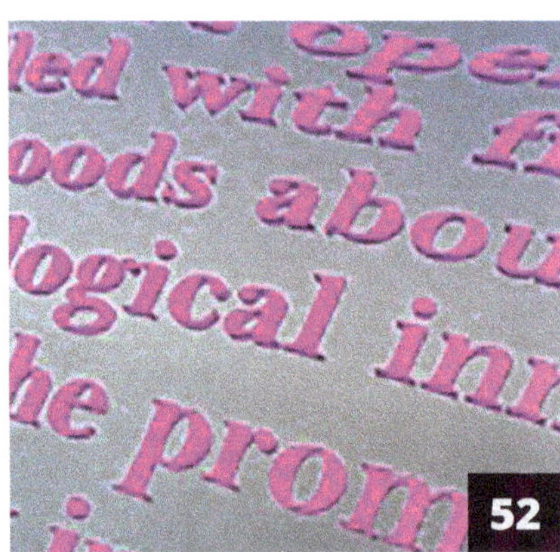

52

Workers liberation as environmental justice: beyond Amazon's Plantationocene

text: **Hiba Ali**

Hiba Ali focuses on warehouse worker leaders, Hafsa Hasan and Hibaq Mohamed, associated with Awood Center, a non-for-profit that focuses on mobilizing East African workers in Minneapolis, Minnesota.

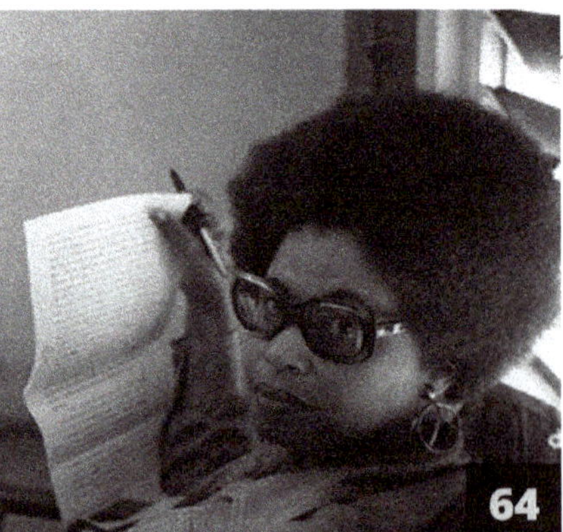

64

After Man and Nature: an ethos for the Anthropocene

text **Esther F. Jansen**

In line with the bio-evolutionary governing principles of our overrepresented order of knowledge and being, the notion of the Anthropocene is both anthropocentric and ethnocentric.

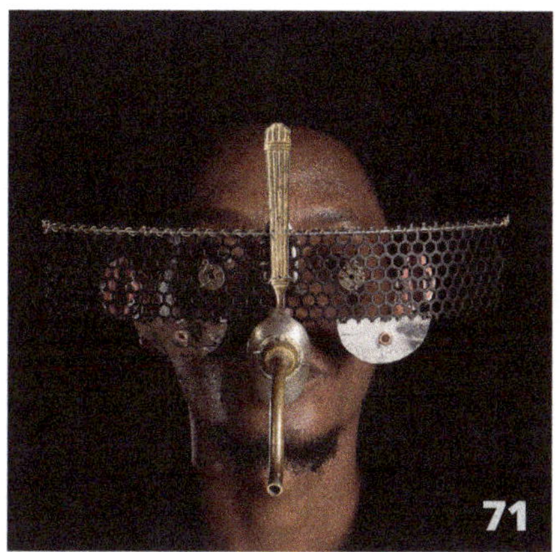

Kenyan contemporary art & the time of the posthuman

text **Joshua Williams**

This essay explores questions of form, material and time in the work of the Kenyan artists Cyrus Kabiru, Wangechi Mutu and Wanuri Kahiu. It claims that Kabiru, Mutu and Kahiu's work exists at the intersection of Afrofuturism and posthumanism.

A Billion Black Anthropocenes

in conversation: **Kathryn Yusoff and Betelhem Makonnen**

Kathryn Yusoff examines how the grammar of geology is foundational to establishing the extractive economies of subjective life and the earth under colonialism and slavery.

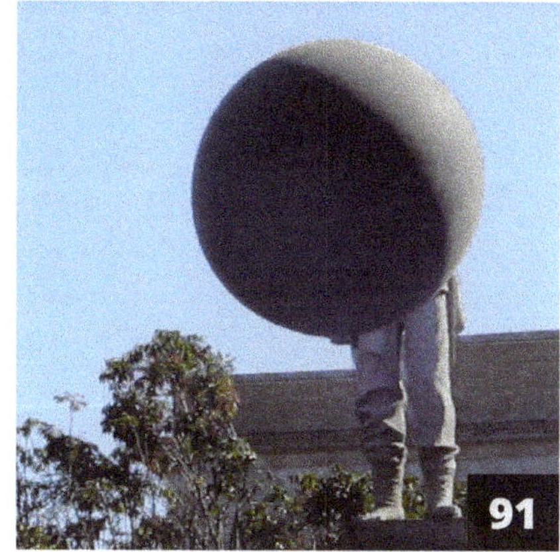

The Black tradition of forecasting

text and images **Ariel René Jackson**

Ariel René Jackson's recent work explores the term 'forecasting' as an artistic lens in social engagement via re-coding meteorological language as a means to shift perspectives of what is understood as knowable.

What if the Earth spoke to you as a black woman?

text: **Clareese Hill**

The essay seeks to explore themes of the Black female body as it equates to the poor care and condition of the Earth being thrust towards the Anthropocene.

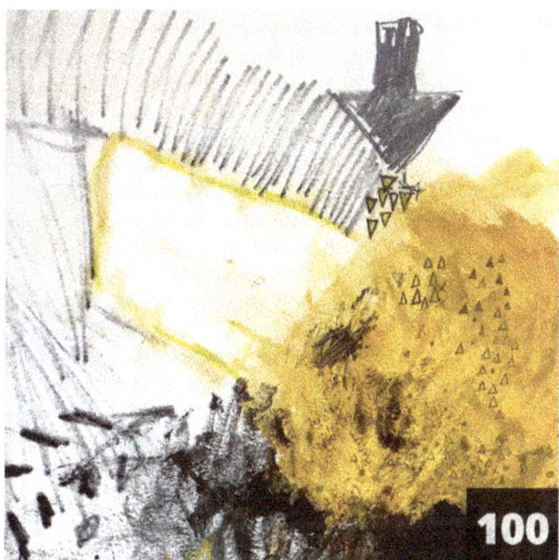

The postcollapse life

in conversation: **Ilknur Demirkoparan, Vuslat D. Katsanis, Mirela Kulović**

In this conversation piece, the authors describe "postcollapse" as a critical framework for rethinking human relationships and responsibility against the provincial identitarianism dominant in both the Anthropocene discourse and in the art world.

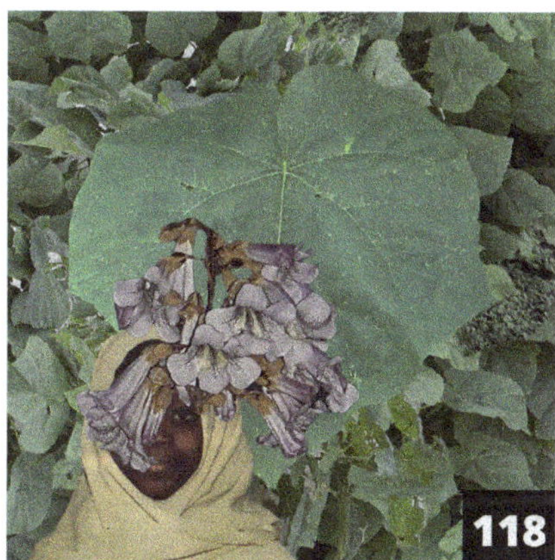

PostBroken.

text and images: **mukhtara yusuf**

In this performative multi-form text, mukhtara yusuf explores postbrokenism as an alternative model for healing the broken ontological "covenant" between human and nonhuman.

editorial

W e're in the middle of an epistemological crisis. It is written across the pages of books like *Braiding Sweetgrass* by Robin Wall Kimmerer, or Emanuele Coccia's *The Life of Plants: A Metaphysical Mixture* and in the success of Amitav Ghosh's *The Great Derangement*. Academic writing has rapidly taken a poetic turn, for the better. In part, this shift has its roots planted in our mourning—climate change and the sixth mass extinction have cast long shadows over academic discourse for over ten years, now. In their own ways, artists and scholars are implicitly, and perhaps out of necessity, looking for ways in which we can all, for better or worse, find ways to dance in the rain. My students at the School of the Art Institute of Chicago are much more receptive to set readings from *Indigo* by Catherine E. McKinley or experimental performances like *Estado Vegetal* by Manuela Infante, than academic essays. The reasons are manyfold, of course. The current epistemological crisis is different from the previous, it's deeper and more complex.

In hindsight, we can see how the rise of posthumanism and the advent of human-animal studies have wrecked the anthropocentric structures that held western philosophy together. These philosophical currents were not the first to challenge the epistemological hierarchies of the west. The cracks had begun to appear in the post-structuralism of Deleuze and Guattari, Michel Foucault, and Jacques Derrida. But despite the earthquakes, the foundations still stood in place. The self-criticality was cosmetic, not structural.

Posthumanism and human-animal studies could confidently tell apart a human from an animal. Giorgio Agamben's "anthropological machine" had made visible the processed by which the concept of the human is culturally created with and against the animal. But in animal studies circles, his argument on the animalization of Jewish prisoners in Nazi concentration camps became far too quickly embroiled in zoocentric discourses that implicitly safeguarded a white supremacist outlook. As artist and curator—as well as co-editor of this issue of *Antennae*—Betelhem Makonnen puts it "Posthumanist theory is substantially invested in notions of relationality, entanglement, and porousness, yet there remains a specter at its core that renders it largely a product of a fixed axis that overwhelmingly tethers its worlding models to Eurocentric mono-cultural constructs".

Who is the human of posthumanism, who is the *anthropos* of the Anthropocene, and where does the animal of human-animal studies begin or end? At stake in these questions is Europe's outdated idea of itself as synonymous with humanism—an isolated, self-contained, universalized truth around which all knowledge has been constructed. The colonialist blind spots that still underpin all modern, western knowledge have fostered and perpetuated a paradoxical cultural segregation deconstructing the other only so far as it was convenient.

And yet the voices could be heard. From Franz Fanon to Sylvia Wynter, the books were on the shelves, gathering dust in the libraries of many universities. They rarely made their way in the syllabi, rendered almost invisible by the same implicit, colonialist matrix that privileged white optics above all. The first part of the ontological turn in the humanities has come to an end with 2020, the global pandemic, and the rise of social justice. For some of us, the true work begins now. The scholarly essay is a trap. Its referencing system has turned into a sham. The exclusionist matrix still lives in the structure of what we say and how we are allowed to say it by the institutions that define our voices. The medium is the message. The message is still colonialist.

Indigenous knowledge, local knowledges of all kinds, erased histories, and suppressed cultures—the current epistemological crisis is long overdue and it is the result of the short-comings of western philosophy; its inability to critically competently appraise itself beyond the status quo, faster, and thoroughly enough. While the challenges ahead apply to academia as a whole, those of us researching and creating in the context of the environmental post-humanities must actively work to undo what's left of the colonialist foundations that anchor knowledge to a past that still haunts our thinking.

'Beyond posthumanism®TM' addresses these issues and more. We hope that it will provide a timely and much needed reference point for future conversations and necessary new departures. It also so happens that this ambitious project also marks *Antennae*'s 15th year of activity. 57 issues later, I ponder on the journal's future, what format it might take in order to more aptly represent and support the momentous change that pervades this field. What kind of writing, what type of formats, which structures?

Independent publications like *Antennae* share histories of originality, irreverence, and innovation. The first issue of *Antennae* coincided with the rise of human-animal studies; a field of academic inquiry now mainstream. Our independent status has allowed us to give a voice to scholars and artists who were initially dismissed by academic publishers and institutions. Our creative approach has supported the careers of experimental practitioners and research-ers across the world providing a unique space in which new academic fields like critical plant studies could also flourish.

In January 2009, the establishment of *Antennae*'s Senior Academic Board, Advisory Board, and Network of Global Contributors affirmed the journal as an indispensable research tool for the subject of environmental studies and visual culture. Still today, no other journal provides artists and scholars with an opportunity to publish full-color portfolios of their work or richly illustrated essays at no cost to them nor to the readers. Building a fairer and more inclusive system from the ground up also entails dismissing traditional pathways, ignoring the lure of institutional prestige, and pouring buckets of generosity when and where needed. I care to stress that as the editor in chief of the journal, I do not benefit from any funding or other form of support from the institutions I work for. Despite this, I consider myself lucky to have the opportunity to collaborate with the most inspirational and supportive academic board and network of volunteers I could have ever dreamt of. My gratitude is infinite. *Antennae* is a true community effort, not an academic, elitist publication hidden behind a paywall.

Every issue of this journal has been an incredibly rich opportunity to broaden my views and expand my knowledge and understanding of this deeply troubled and yet wonderful world we live in. Many kind readers and colleagues have never wasted an opportunity to remind me that *Antennae* has made a substantial difference to their work and research; and that's all we need to know.

I am also extremely grateful to Betelhem Makonnen for being a wonderful and inspira-tional co-editor, equipped with tireless determination and unflinching commitment to a radi-cal, ambitious, and yet realistic vision. My gratitude also goes to all the contributors featured in this issue as well as everyone else who, in one way or another, was involved in its making.

Giovanni Aloi

Editor in Chief of Antennae

beyond posthumanism®™

> *[T]he struggle of our new millennium will be one between the ongoing imperative of securing the well-being of our present ethnoclass (i.e., Western bourgeois) conception of the human, Man, which overrepresents itself as if it were the human itself, and that of securing the well-being, and therefore the full cognitive and behavioral autonomy of the human species itself/ourselves.[1]*
>
> --Sylvia Wynter

The ubiquity of the term posthumanism[2] within various sectors of contemporary arts and cross-disciplinary aesthetics studies is undeniable. Its deployment as the revolutionary /inclusive/heterogenic/world-envisioning framework of the Anthropocene era continues to grow across creative, philosophical, as scientific practices extend its epistemo-ontological preoccupations and iterations to territories far beyond the borders of its initial articulations. Posthumanist theory is substantially invested in notions of relationality, entanglement and porousness, yet there remains a specter at its core that renders it largely a product of a fixed axis that overwhelmingly tethers its worlding models to Eurocentric[3] monocultural constructs.

The call for the 'Beyond posthumanism®™' issue of *Antennae* was deeply informed by the work of the black Jamaican writer and cultural theorist Sylvia Wynter who across her vast scholarship introduced perspectives and worldviews that engender "the possibility of undoing and unsettling – not replacing or occupying – Western conceptions of what it means to be human," as Katherine McKittrick states in *Sylvia Wynter: On Being Human as Praxis*. I was first introduced to Wynter's expansive body of work through the above collection edited by McKittrick while doing research in grad school. My rich interview with Katherine McKittrick opens the issue.

The *human* in posthumanism is most often presented as neutral and non-subjective: a representation that ignores its structural sociohistorical entanglements with racialized European colonist projects and the corroborating philosophies, literature and science at the root of its myth. This behindhand omission correspondently perpetuates a hollow conceptualization of the universal "us" that tacitly prerequisites race as the primary immutable social ordering logic within the structures of its application. Needless to say, without unequivocal rupture from this endemic contusion of the specific with the universal, whatever anticipated paradigmatic shifts posthumanism may aspire to is critically compromised from the onset. Echoing Kathryn Yusoff,[4] echoing Dionne Brand[5] in our interview for this issue, the *human* in posthuman is not neutral. It is White and male, and it is the descendent of a traceable genealogy ideologically structured by excluding sexed and raced others in order to support its claims of superiority. This distinct human would be better articulated as human®™, to not create any confusion and inarguably distinguish it from what Sylvia Wynter calls "the referent-we of the human species itself".[6]

No human is neutral.
Wynter's work, and most expressly her text *Unsettling the Coloniality of Being/Power/ Truth/Freedom: Towards the Human, After Man, Its Overrepresentation–An Argument* not only nourishes and reinforces the foundation of my artistic practice, but also my general navigational approach to living within the contemporary configurations of this shared floating rock we call home. As a middle-aged black woman/Habesha Ethiopian, born to a Muslim Wollo mother and a Gurage Orthodox-Christian father, in Africa's last empire, on the eve of its communist birth/child immigrant/transnational/art practitioner with a eurosocialized academic education/with a white Texan life partner and two Brazilian-born children, I am grateful for the company of Sylvia Wynter's works. In spite of a heavily subsidized disenfranchising universal humanity®™ that insist to the contrary, Sylvia Wynter's life's work continually reiterates that I and others like me are not counterpoints, supporting cast members, background characters, fiction nor metaphor in the history of our world.

I am deeply grateful to each of our contributors for answering our Wynterian call to shine a "fresh source of light"[7] on the contemporary post humanism®™ discourse with methodologies, approaches, and optics that unsettle conceptions of being with broader epistemo-ontological lenses that address truly universal narratives of the Anthropocene(s). All the selections in 'Beyond Post-Humanism®™' draw from divergent scholarships, narratives and cosmologies to question, problematize and recognize fresh insights that extend beyond humanism®™ in past, present and forthcoming times. Rather than a collection of texts, I want to imagine this volume as making ceremony[8]– a ceremony among a span of contemporary thinkers, artists, and aesthetic practitioners arriving with different reads and pulses on post humanism®™ but connected by their expressed consideration of the pivotal place of subjectivity and specificity within the term's constructs and applications

Lastly, it is important to note that we realized the 'Beyond Posthumanism®™' issue of *Antennae* in a tumultuous period of severe psycho-sociopolitical rupture and upheaval across our shared world, as well as in my own personal life. I am very thankful to Giovanni Aloi, Editor of *Antennae* for his invitation to work together, for all our exciting exchanges, and his consistent concerned care throughout our many times delayed process.

Betelhem Makonnen

Endnotes

[1] (Unsettling the Coloniality of Being/Power/Truth/Freedom: Towards the Human, After Man, Its Overrepresentation–An Argument, Sylvia Wynter, CR: The New Centennial Review, Volume 3, Number 3, Fall 2003, pp. 260).

[2] I first learned of posthumanism from reading *Manifestly Haraway*, a required summer reading for all students and faculty for my first year in my SAIC Low-Residency Master of Fine Arts program, (Haraway, Donna Jeanne. 2016. *Manifestly Haraway*). In subsequent discussions we would have on the subject in class or otherwise, a lot of what was posited as posthumanism's radical emerging recognitions seemed to be conceptualizations that were always already familiar to me, not only from my own specific histo-socio-cultural background, but from the cosmologies and worlding ideas of the different Indigenous and diasporic cultures that I had learned and read with, in and outside of academia. It appeared to me that posthumanism confused epistemology with ontology, and as McKittrick states in our interview, that at its "etymological-theoretical [foundation], [it relies] on a temporal frame that cannot attend to black temporalities and black livingness—and that would include imaginative and real black geographies."

[3] Please read, Weheliye, Alexander G. *Habeas Viscus Racializing Assemblages, Biopolitics, and Black Feminist Theories of the Human*. Durham: Duke University Press, 2014. Also read , Todd, Zoe. "An Indigenous Feminist's Take on the Ontological Turn: 'Ontology' Is Just Another Word for Colonialism." speculative fictions (Dr. Zoe Todd), November 21, 2016. https://zoestodd.com/2014/10/24/an-indigenous-feminists-take-on-the-ontological-turn-ontology-is-just-another-word-for-colonialism/ and Park, Eugene Sun. "Why I Left Academia: Philosophy's Homogeneity Needs Rethinking." Hippo Reads. Accessed March 3, 2022. http://read.hipporeads.com/why-i-left-academia-philosophys-homogeneity-needs-rethinking/.

[4] "*No geology is neutral,* is a way to say that no geology is impolitic, despite Western genealogies of understanding the inhuman as an inorganic category that is separate from life and questions of subjectivity, and therefore requires no ethical or political attention," from Kathryn Yusoff 's extremely generous interview with me in this issue.

[5] Brand's *No language is neutral* (Brand, Dionne. 1998. *No language is neutral*. Toronto: McClelland & Stewar) is a work that I read and rereading since I first encountered it in graduate school. I am always renewed by Brand's poetry and her words have a deep resonance with my own diasporic consciousness, lived history and resulting conceptualizations of language, identity and belonging.

[6] McKittrick, Katherine (2015) *Sylvia Wynter: On Being Human as Praxis*. Durham and London: Duke University Press, pp. 24.

[7] "the map of spring has always to be drawn again ... the undared form ... o fresh source of light," echoing Katherine McKittrick ((2015) *Sylvia Wynter: On Being Human as Praxis*. Durham and London: Duke University Press, pp.1), echoing Sylvia Wynter (Wynter, Sylvia. "The Pope Must Have Been Drunk, The King of Castile a Madman: Culture as Actuality, and the Caribbean Rethinking Modernity." In Reordering of Culture: Latin America, the Caribbean and Canada in the Hood, edited by Alvina Ruprecht and Cecilia Taiana, 17–42, pp. 30. McGill-Queen's University Press, 1995), echoing Aimé Césaire (Césaire, Aimé, Clayton Eshleman, Annette Smith, and Aimé Césaire. 2001. *Notebook of a return to the native land*).

[8] I am thinking with ceremony as a transformational ritual experienced individually yet in concert with a collective, and also connecting to ceremony as it is considered within Wynter, Sylvia. (2015). 'The Ceremony Found: Towards the Autopoetic Turn/Overturn, its Autonomy of Human Agency and Extraterritoriality of (Self)Cognition'1. 10.5949/liverpool/9781781381724.003.0008 ,as well as in Gumbs, Alexis Pauline. Dub: Finding Ceremony. Duke University Press, 2020.

Betelhem Makonnen is an artist living in Austin, TX, with a MFA from the School of Art Institute of Chicago and a BA in History and Literature of Africa/African Diaspora from UT Austin. Her work includes photography, video, installation and text, shown nationally and internationally – including The Contemporary Austin, The Philbrook Museum of Art, Big Medium, Women & Their Work, Le Musée des Abattoirs, and The Carver Museum, with performances and screenings at The Blanton Museum, IVAHM, and Casa Daros. Her work has been featured in a variety of publications including *Artforum, NYT, Frieze, Hyperallergic, Zoetrope, O Menelick 2° Ato, Revista Lampejo, and Glasstire.* In addition to her practice she co-organizes Addis Video Art Festival, a platform for video art in Ethiopia, and is a co-founder member of the Austin-based arts collective Black Mountain Project.

Betelhem Makonnen

conjugating self, 2018

© Betelhem Makonnen

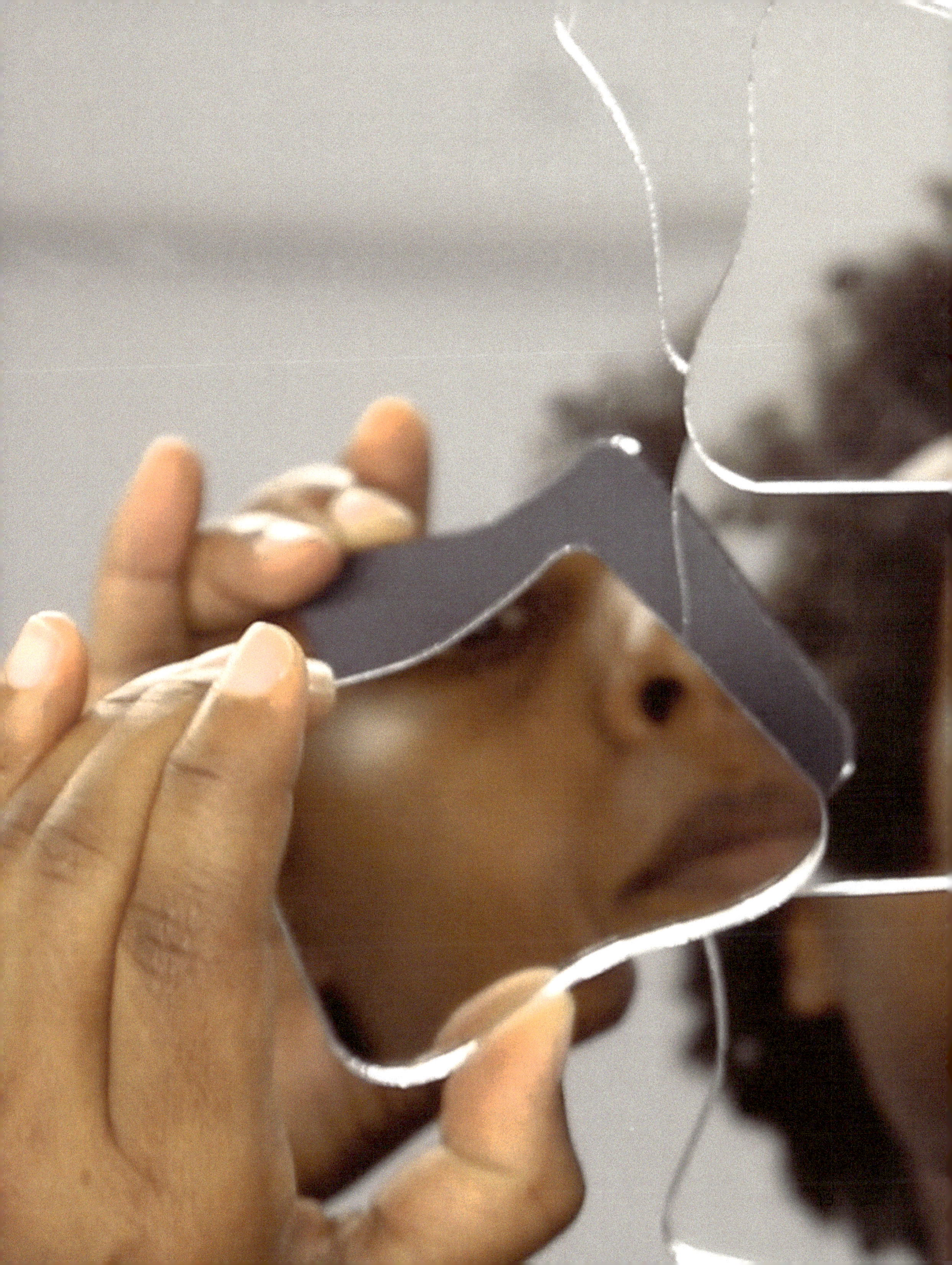

Demonic Grounds

Demonic Grounds *moves between past and present, archives and fiction, theory and everyday, to focus on places negotiated by black women during and after the transatlantic slave trade. Katherine McKittrick addresses the geographic implications of slave auction blocks, Harriet Jacobs's attic, black Canada and New France, as well as the conceptual spaces of feminism and Sylvia Wynter's philosophies.*

in conversation: **Katherine McKittrick and Betelhem Makonnen**

Betelhem Makonnen: Black and anti-colonial studies, cultural geographies, and gender studies that makes visible the links between epistemological narrative, liberation, and creative text – I am very curious as to the origins of your incredibly rich interdisciplinary practice, most especially the kinds of decisions and possibly errancy that led to your current line of transgressional philosophical inquiry?

Katherine McKittrick: I am not sure there is an origin to my thinking—I would prefer to think of all these practices and narratives and geographies, that overlap and express differential struggles against liberation, as a way of black life or black livingness. So, for me, errantry is implicit across black studies and my work is one version or one iteration of that. Interdisciplinarity opens up ways to think with, rather than solely *about* black worlds, which dislodges normative and typical approaches to studying blackness (where we, black people and our worlds, are the "objects" of study and are the "things" people do research "about"). This is moving toward a desire for expansive intellectual collaboration. I suppose, then, I would not theorize this kind of work as necessarily a philosophical inquiry, but perhaps our collective curious inquiries. Interdisciplinarity has dynamic and agentive underpinnings. I mean, this is how black people live—inventing and reinventing knowledge systems—and part of this work is learning and teaching and sharing that inventiveness and re-inventiveness. Learning and teaching and sharing is an expression of liberation. For me, engaging in this kind of intellectual work was not really an explicit decision, but instead, a way I was already living that was evidenced in what I was reading and what I continue to read and listen to and see, as well other forms of black livingness. To concretize this, there is always (still!) something exciting and new and familiar about Frantz Fanon's uses of multiple texts and ideas and stories and songs in his work; there is something meaningful about his intellectual rigor and his commitment to reading across black worlds to reimagine black worlds. The familiarity is breath-taking and the newness is jarring and I think this kind of methodology invites collaborative thinking and learning. In my work, I ask: what happens when we think about black geographies, black placemaking, and black poetry as collaborative and tightly entwined texts that are not only critiquing white supremacy but totally rethinking the production of space? What kinds of clues and stories do black intellectuals and creatives offer that interrupt and remake our worlds? This is an invitation to wonder (and wander!) for me—an invitation to enter into wonder, curiosity, and intellectual rigor.

BM: Could you please speak to Canadian Black history and its erasure as an influence on your fugitive geographical thinking?

KM: In my work, I explore black Canada through the concept of "absented presence" (which is from, if I remember correctly, one of Dionne Brand's essays in *Bread Out of Stone*) as well as the concepts of surprise and wonder. These concepts have allowed me to theorize black Canadian communities and their geographies through the complicated paradoxes that are revealed when black folks inhabit a nation that denies their histories, geographies, and experiences. You see this on multiple levels: the refusal to acknowledge that slavery happened in Canada; the wilful razing of black communities across the nation; deportations; anti-black policing and violence, including the killing (and thus elimination) of black disabled folks, black women, black men, black queers. The erasure is sweeping and intense because it is, in practice, the removal of what-who are allegedly not here! It also impacts upon every aspect of black life and livingness: it is historic erasure, discursive erasure; it is murderous; it is subtle; it is explicit; it is urbicidal. In terms of geography, this—the removal of what is not here—opens up a way to think through and map blackness in Canada without assuming blackness has a stable absolutely knowable presence or origin story. In other words, if we are "here-not-here" we are *living place* differently and we are navigating our worlds across and against (rather than totally within) the empty logics of visual surplus that so often define and delimit black life (or, we are living place differently, and we are navigating our worlds, without being beholden to elimination, abandonment, erasure, displacement, deportation). Perhaps then, we can offer new or radical ways to imagine liberation. Perhaps we can offer spatial practices that do not seek to own and totally define place, but instead are capacious, opaque, and strongly committed to undoing-refusing the violence of colonial and plantocratic place-making practices. In *Demonic Grounds* I work with surprise and wonder—the latter is indebted to Sylvia Wynter and I still use it to think through black methodologies—to notice how the impossibility of black Canada invokes curiosity rather than a knowable set of bearings or cartographies. Geography, or at least colonial and plantocratic geographic practices, tend to be tied to authenticating practices (you find space, you take space, you own place and space and property, space [property] defines who and where you are and authenticates your owning-presence which is paired accumulation-as-dispossession [this is mine, not yours, get out]). Curiosity, wonder, reorient us, and situate black geographies, and black Canadian geographies, as sites of open inquiry.

BM: How does the theory of "black human geographies" presented in your ground-breaking book *Demonic Grounds: Black Women and The Cartographies of Struggle* emerge and function as a discipline from what Sylvia Wynter's suggestion of "a third perspective," rather than an oppositionality tethered and in direct response to existing traditional geographical arrangements?

KM: The term "black human geographies" is intended to pair the discipline of human geography with black studies. It is an intervention into the assumption that human geography is, first and foremost, an academic and colonial way of knowing; it offers a somewhat clunky way (the term itself is cumbersome and imprecise to me) to centre and really contemplate these brilliant black geographic knowledges that circulate as acts of liberation and resistance. I am not abandoning geography, but instead illuminating different kinds of geographic practices that cannot be seen, or are rendered inadequate-problematic, within the context of white supremacy. I think it is important to also signal that the term is not meant to centre the human

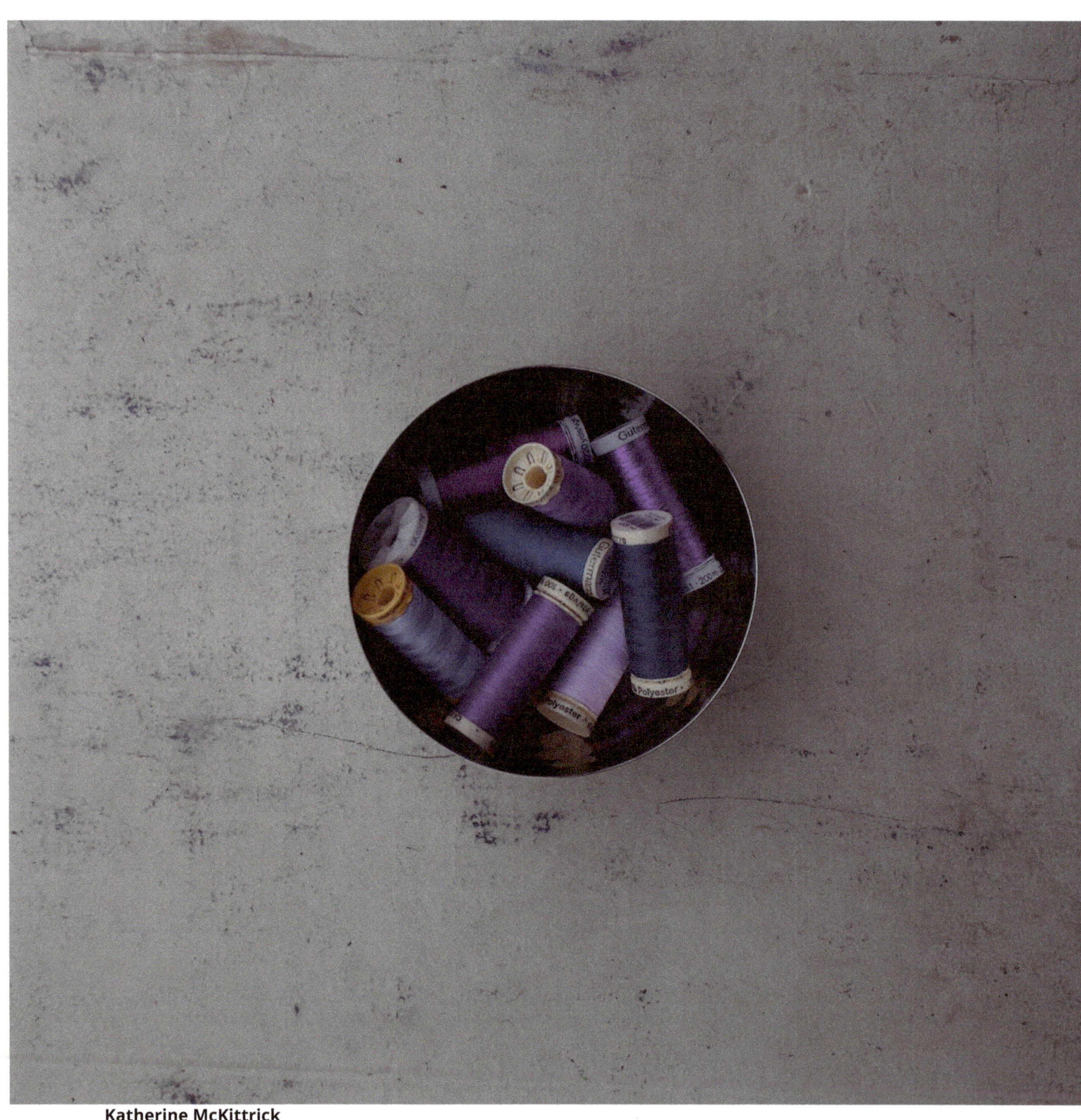

Katherine McKittrick

Worn Down (1), 2020
Worn Down (2), 2020
© Katherine McKittrick

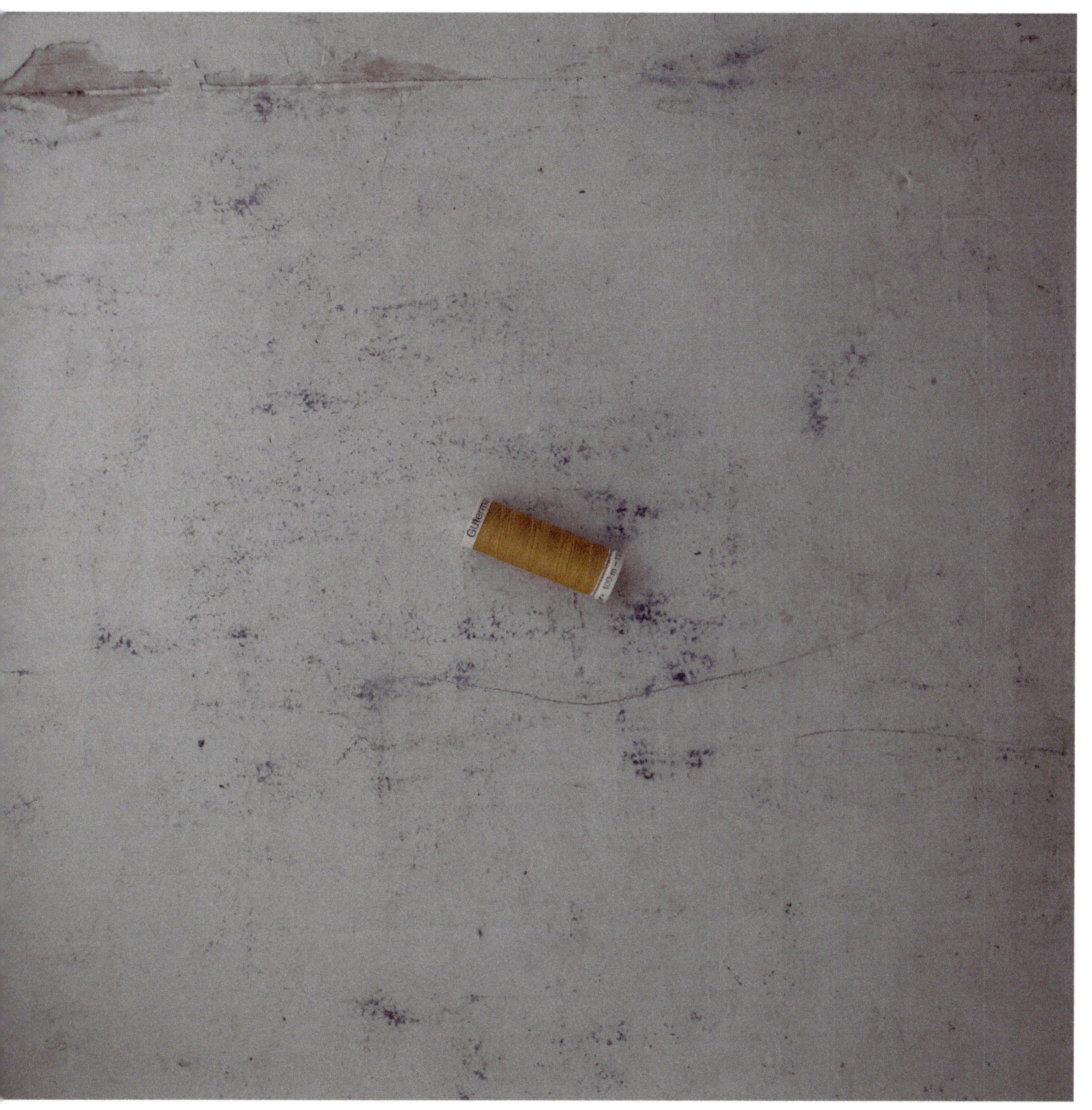

or the black human (in *Dear Science* I elaborate on the pitfalls of analytically centring "the human" in the work of Sylvia Wynter and more generally); it is, instead, an attempt to rethink and situate black geographies as robust and intricate and rebellious and creative sites of invention. I have tried to work this out through, and get some precision, in my theorization of "a black sense of place" which I position as an entangled discursive-material-imagined black methodology: a black sense of place draws attention to geographic processes that emerged from plantation slavery and its attendant racial violences yet cannot be contained by the logics of white supremacy; a black sense of place is not a standpoint or a situated knowledge (it is a location of difficult encounter and relationality); a black sense of place is not individualized knowledge—it is collaborative; a black sense of place assumes that our collective assertions of life are always in tandem with other ways of being; a black sense of place is a diasporic-plantocratic-black geography that reframes what we know by reorienting and honouring *where* we know from. For me, a black sense of place is where a third perspective can be and is engendered, because *where* is not conceptualized as insides or outsides (belonging/unbelonging inclusion/exclusion or even oppression/resistance) but is instead offering a set of conversations (not clear-cut instructions with solutions) and rebellions and curiosities and creative works that are expressing black livingness through the production of space. This is, for me, where invention and reinvention happen, and where geography, as we know it, is totally undone.

BM: What are the ways, in your opinion, that "imaginative-real black human geographies" disrupt institutionalized Post-Humanism discourses, and subsequently conceptions of the Anthropocene?

KM: I am not widely read on the posthuman or the anthropocene so I can only speak to these ideas from a distance. It seems both conceptualizations, at least in their etymological-theoretical foundations, rely on a temporal frame that cannot attend to black temporalities and black livingness—and that would include imaginative and real black geographies. Maybe that is a good thing! Even in their complexity, though, the terms are weighed down by a kind of evolutionary script (we are moving forward, we are moving away from one version of the human and toward more complex (*subsequently* more complex) human, as a species we are moving changing from this into that) that is grounded in scientific racism (that future-toward is a teleological-evolutionary projection, time-stamped with racial differentiation and punctuated by dehumanization). I realize both these concepts are more complex than this—there are backward posthuman futures and the ecological disruptions caused by anthropocentric violence are not lauded—but the weight of the linear temporality, which structures each term so poignantly, is disquieting. It is sutured to a version of time that cannot actually bear blackness and black time (black time is paused and forever and never and always and then waiting and quietly torrent). I also find that some engagements with anthropocentric moments-subjects, especially those that fold in black worlds, rely heavily on metaphor. So, the preoccupation with the future or future-present, and ecology and environmental catastrophes, gets absorbed into a framework that reduces black life—that is our books, our ideas, our livingness, our poetry, our sense of place—to a description. The engagement with black intellectual life is not analytical; rather black ideas animate an otherwise unblack story. There is a tendency to posit, for example, that vulnerable community are composed of "toxic bodies," with black people exemplifying the penultimate environmental toxicity and thus providing an ideal analytical script that proves, rather than questions, the brutality of environmental racism (this is a recitation of what we already know: the tendency to conceptualize non-white people and the land *together*, as one, is a crude and dehumanizing expression of scientific racism). When race and environmental decline *conceptually* collide, scientific racism stays in place, and we read that passive black flesh is inscribed *by or represented as* ecology or that black bodies (not people) are the receptacles of noxious substances and thus *become*, through osmosis, toxic landscapes. Here, metaphor (black elements, black toxicity, black sedimentary rocks, black cenotes) prevails and cloaks black humanity and the black experience. We witness not an assertion of capacious black livingness that is in concert with non-black communities and extra-human processes and environments, but instead the argument that black bodies are like poison, black bodies are like geology, black bodies are waste, black bodies are toxic. The preoccupation with *describing* subjugated bodies is suffocating; both the environment and the racialized body become a singular analytic site of degradation. Biological determinism (the evolutionary narrative) is normalized and spatialized and conversations (curiosities) that draw attention to relational and transnational resistances to eco-crises are foreclosed.

BM: Thinking through Chapter 5 of the book, *Demonic Grounds: Sylvia Wynter*, in what ways does Sylvia Wynter's philosophical framework relate to the geography that you are making visible? What role did her work play in your confrontation with the discourses of "normalcy" that anchor the invention of Man, essentially the Human ®™ through which the world is spatialized?

KM: I read Sylvia Wynter as an anti-colonial scholar and as a black geographic thinker who has spent considerable time thinking through the production of space. When I first engaged her work—her essay "Beyond Miranda's Meanings"—I was struck by her ability to work through the complexities of black feminism in a way that theorized black femininity and black women's knowledge both through and beyond western feminist debates. Her thinking in this essay is really brilliant because she reorients black women not as excluded from or oppositional to feminist debate (e.g. left out of feminism, counter to feminism), but rather as agentive subjects whose intellectual displacement from normative western knowledge systems provides the conditions for a completely *differen* set of political practices. She does not engage in a project that follows black women through exclusion-recovery-reclamation precisely because this kind of trajectory re-centres the infrastructures that make exclusion possible (and profit from the erasure of black thought). Instead, she formulates a totally different intellectual *place*—demonic ground. This different intellectual place is tethered to and cognizant of, but not beholden to, western discourses and literacies (what Wynter calls governing systems of meaning). This different intellectual place generates a perspective that—precisely because it is disavowed by the empowered—offers insight into the limitations of the discourses, literacies, governing systems of meaning that are underpinned by race thinking. When encountering this intricate pulling apart of feminism and black thought, I thought to myself, this is a brilliant spatial project! And I wondered: where are these demonic grounds located? From there, I studied Wynter as a geographic scholar and used her concept of demonic ground/demonic grounds to theorize the "where" of black geographies—not to pinpoint and demarcate them, but instead to work out how the production of space provides the conditions to generate the amazingly thoughtful writings, songs, places, and experiences of black intellectuals. I suppose, then, this has less to do with Man (and Man-as-human) and more to do with where black knowledge is and how, within the context of racial violence, black people understand their sense of place as one that is necessarily committed to anti-colonialism. I mean, this is one of the gifts of black studies for me—this is a very nuanced thinking through of the *where* of black liberation that overturns the terms of abandonment by positioning black thought as an agentive and ongoing (rather than absent or oppositional) process.

BM: Your work is in direct conversation with aesthetics and poetics, often interacting with and citing the perceptions and visualization brought forth via the imagination of artists. Could you talk more about your interdisciplinary relationship with knowledge making through artistic research and the possible broader contextual sense of particularities of place, purpose, and personhood that it brings into your own practice?

KM: My research on black methodologies has involved thinking about how black cultural producers and black creative texts offer analytical insights into liberation and how theory and creative narratives entwine and overlap. I am very interested in collaborative work, which not only involves sharing ideas with one another (intellectual friendships) but also pairing knowledges together (reading black music as theory as urban planning as poetics). I feel responsible for all the texts I read and hear and work with, and part of this responsibility is acknowledging that all forms of black expression (all black theories of liberation and loss, all-black stories, all-black grooves and geographies, all unspeakable archives) are, *together*, meaningful *intellectual* narratives. Applying theory to a short story, for example, makes no sense to me—because it? abandons the short story by assuming its? textuality is passive. So, I ask myself, what does this short story offer us, theoretically? How does it allow us to ask new questions? And then: what are the creative contours of this theoretical frame? So, aesthetics and poetics are, for me, theoretical and theoretical texts are creative. In terms of geography, this means black aesthetics do not only punctuate or beautify or describe or interrupt place, they actually respatialize and repoliticize our environments. How beautiful—although terrifying for some—to know that geography is alterable and that the black songwriter's sense of place is an anti-colonial and ethical reimagining of how the world is and what it can be!

BM: *Dear Science and Other Stories*, is an interdisciplinary study of Black and anti-colonial studies intersecting with Gender, Geography and Poetics. You discuss the relationality of Sylvia Wynter and electronica music! Please tell us more about this incredible project.

KM: The book is a study of black methodologies—much like the instances and ideas I have touched on throughout this interview. I think one part of the book that I have not discussed is how black theory and aesthetics move us. So, in addition to the stories and the geographies and the ecologies and collaborations and deportations and poetics (and falling in love with black electronica), in the book, I stumble through how liberation is a physiological-creative expression of black mnemonic livingness. With that in mind, I would love to end with a citational-mnemonics. Betty Davis, Frantz Fanon, Sylvia Wynter, Édouard Glissant, Prince, Nina Simone, Betelhem Makonnen, Giovanni Aloi, Frank Ocean, Sandra Brewster, Tracy Chapman, Charmaine Lurch, Paul Gilroy, Dina Georgis, Carmen Kynard, Simone Browne, Sade, Richard Iton, Drexciya, Hazel Carby, Lisa Lowe, Carole Boyce Davies, Ray Zilli, NourbeSe Philip, Kristin Moriah, Linda Peake, Nik Theodore, Alex Weheliye.

Katherine McKittrick is Canada Research Chair in black studies. She researches in the areas of black studies, anti-colonial studies, and critical-creative methodologies at Queen's University in Kingston, Canada. She authored *Demonic Grounds: Black Women and the Cartographies of Struggle*, edited *Sylvia Wynter: On Being Human as Praxis*, and co-edited, with Clyde Woods, *Black Geographies and the Politics of Place*. Her most recent monograph, *Dear Science and Other Stories* is an exploration of black methodologies.

Socially engaged art
& Wynterian ruptures

This work is a theoretical analysis of socially-engaged-art practice as a political framework for grassroots organizing within communities deemed non-human by the hegemonic-white-supremacist-heteropatriarchal-colonial-capitalist gaze. Sylvia Wynter's deconstruction of the "human" after the 1492 rupture is the base for reconceptualising of humanity. SEA becomes an approachable means of constructing humanity for hegemonically oppressed subjects, through praxis. Analyzing social practice case studies from South Africa and Palestine, it determines potentialities of this art practice as political-action to be pragmatically applied in NYC. This essay argues that a pivotal means for the oppressed to seek liberation is through continual, liminal (re)constructions of humanities.

text by **Dalaeja Foreman**

The New York City problem

What we saw was an alphabet soup of government agencies…descended on the project and the Eastchester neighborhood that was an act of state terror by the government against the people at the bottom of society.

Shannon Jones, Bronxites for Police Accountability/Why Accountability

On 21st January 2017, the day after the 45th president inauguration, the Bronx Social Center in partnership with the Incarcerated Workers Organizing Committee (IWOC)[1] NYC organized a community event entitled *Post-Inauguration Fundraiser Against Police Raids!* This community praxis included an art raffle, panel, group discussions, t-shirt screen-printing, art performances, and film screening of the catalyzing mass arrest of the BX120. The largest racialized act of terror in contemporary New York City[2] ended in indiscriminate arrests and indictment of 120 Black and Latinx young men. This neoliberal hyper-militarized surveillance, displacement, and dehumanization merger is the activator for the necessity of reimagining humanity for subjects oppressed by the 1492 modernity project.

Foreshadowed by settler-colonial projects that murdered and displaced the Lenape, Wangunk, and Quinnipiac First Nations peoples, social cleansing is neoliberal capital's homage to its colonial past in New York City. The goal being permanent de-stability of poor Black and Brown populations, the hyper-displacement exposes a wider conception of who is to be viewed by the state as Human and who is non-human.[3] While protesting the BX120 raid, Shannon Jones, a Bronx grassroots organizer in Why Accountability[4] stated, "It is about changing the scope of the city and its racial and ethnic makeup. The way to do that is to get Black and Brown folks out of public housing, through raids and convictions".[5] NYC is privatizing public assets to attract investment capital.[6] Subsequently deepening disparity for racialized poor, working-poor, non-working and working-class peoples and manufacturing atmospheres that dismantle civic responsibilities in institutions.

Neoliberal capitalist agendas are an extension of the hegemonic project; "colonial matrix of power".[7] Grassroots organizing efforts will develop fugitive means to dismantle intersectional oppressions within the "wake" of this ongoing project.[8] Exploring self-defined humanness is an essential tool while internalizing these moments as lessons to deconstruct the omnipotence of the colonial matrix of power. When racialization preempts the development of Social Consciousness across racial identifications; anti-blackness becomes the daily mode of neurophysiological being in society. Also true of other groups of people's racialized as non-white however anti-blackness is foun-

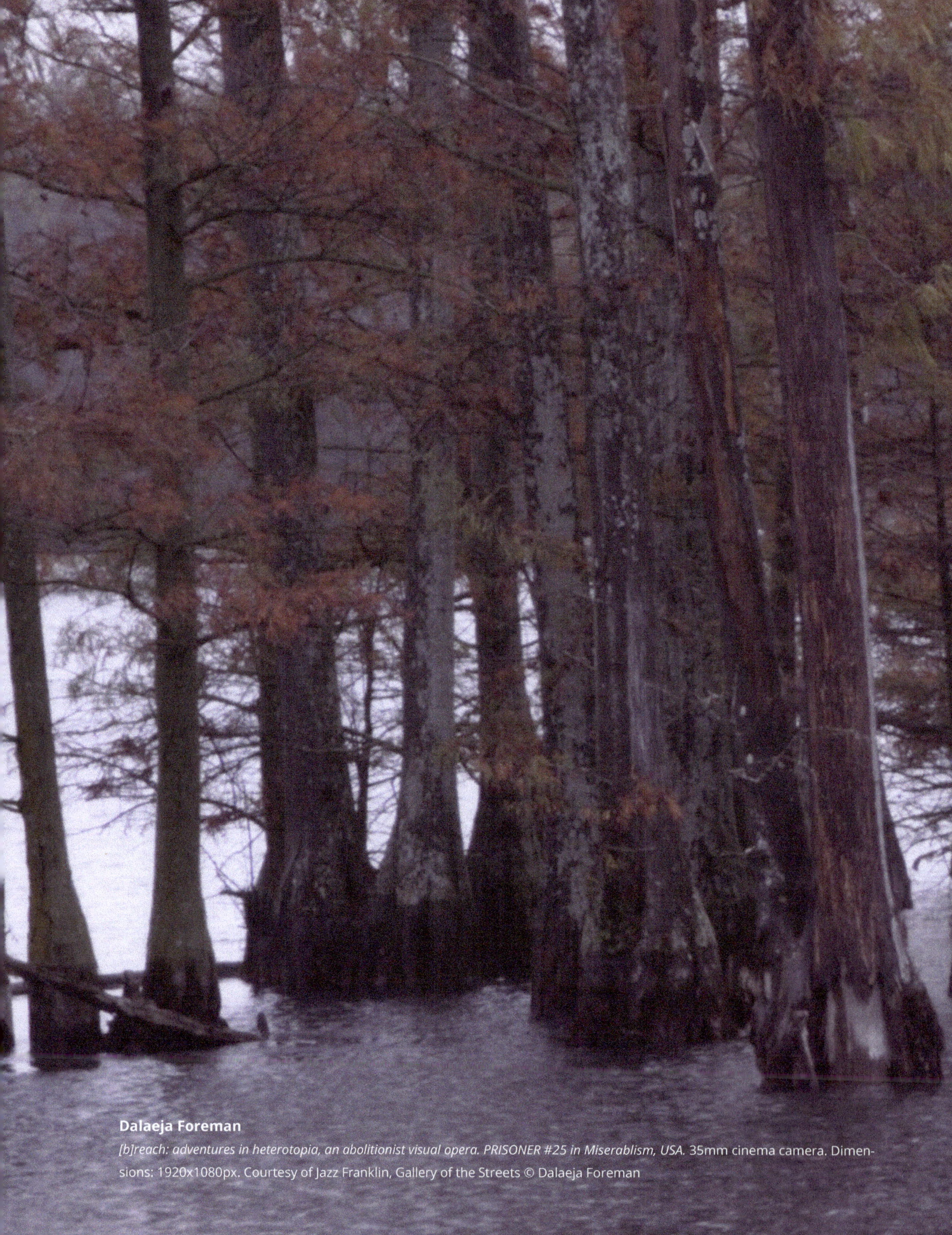

Dalaeja Foreman

[b]reach: adventures in heterotopia, an abolitionist visual opera. PRISONER #25 in Miserablism, USA. 35mm cinema camera. Dimensions: 1920x1080px. Courtesy of Jazz Franklin, Gallery of the Streets © Dalaeja Foreman

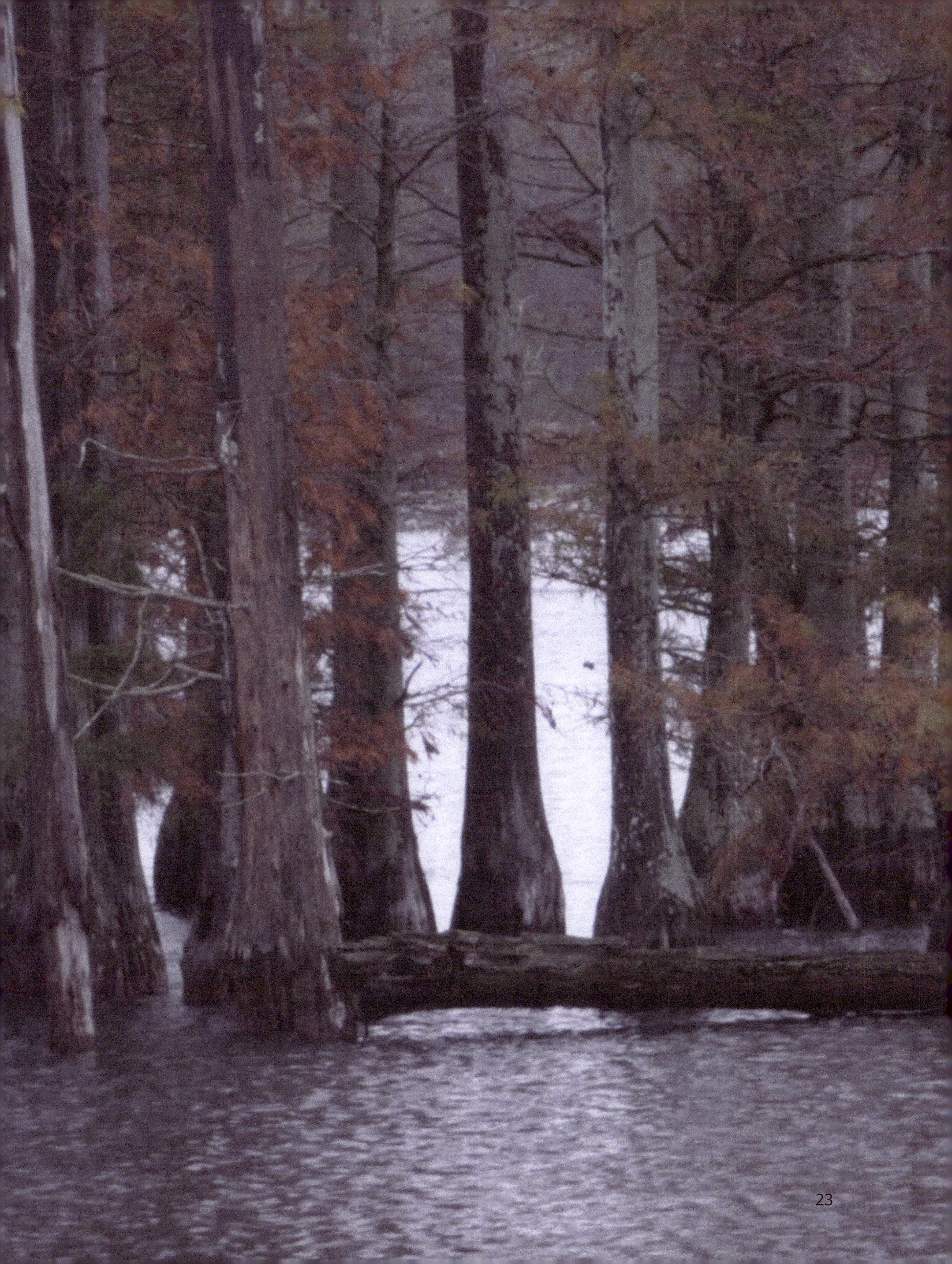

dational in this white-supremacist hegemonic super-structure. The necessity of praxis positions Socially Engaged Art[9] as means to co-create nuanced political frameworks, manifesting fulfilling humanities.

Communal knowings and actions of unity amongst oppressed peoples are transmorphing to prevail against the increasingly surveilled, co-opted, and militarized ethos of NYC. Our organizing must contribute to a methodological shift, cyclically re-examined through SEA, mobilized by learning from past moments of reactionary yet ravishing interactions. Simone Browne coined the term "dark-sousveillance" to situate the tactics of resistance of Maroons and fugitive enslaved people.[10] We must continue the legacy of using our powerful cultural production as an engagement of illegibility and counter-surveillance/dark-sousveillance. In her dissertation entitled *Maroonage As Praxis: Exploring Anti-Surveillance Tactics and Maroon Liberation During the Late 17th-Early 18th Century*, Miranda Sheffield extends Browne's term "dark-sous-veillance" to tactics used by Maroons in the USA, Haiti, and Jamaica.[11] She describes it as a means to "situate the tactics employed to render one's self out of sight, and strategies used in the fight to freedom from slavery as necessarily ones of 'under sight'".[12] While considering the possibilities of cultural production for illegibility and ungovernability, the political seldom overlaps with cultural production as intentionally as it should. Oppressed subjects exist outside of the prescribed conceptualization of Human. SEA rooted in liberation praxis will become a medium for embodying new politics of being human that center our liberation.

Sylvia Wynter and the oppressed

> Conceptualisations of the Human have been dominated in European thought by the exclusionary forms of classical order representations of 'Man'.[13]

Sylvia Wynter

Sylvia Wynter is a Black radical dramatist, critic, political activist, novelist, philosopher, and essayist born in Cuba of Jamaican parents in 1928. A post-Marxist intellectual, Wynter's work attempts to elucidate the development and maintenance of modernity and the "modern man." She interweaves science, philosophy, literary theory, and critical race theory to explain how the European man came to be considered the epitome of humanity, "Man 2".[14]

Wynterian conceptualizations of hegemonic 'Man' are separated by the identification of 'Man1' and 'Man2' to describe the concept of 'human-as-man'. 'Man1' emerged from the Renaissance as "homo politicus", and was reiterated in response to the violent European encounter with the gainfully inhabited lands of the Americas. This renaissance moment of the birth of humanism is simultaneously the initiation of Europe's colonial project.[15] During the aftermath of the 1492 rupture, this representation of human-as-religious was aligned with a secularising path to 'Man'1 as the exclusive "rational" political subject. A later revision of hegemonic humanity was conceptualized by Wynter as 'Man2', the liberal "homo oeconomicus".[16] This was formulated alongside the colonial episteme's of Darwinian malformations, divided between the naturally "selected" (Europeans) and the naturally "dysselected" (world majority). The choking caucasity of Euro-colonial-capitalist conceptualizations of human-as-man collapse other (non-white) ways of being human.[17]

Wynter's methodology interprets this narrow perception of Humanity not as an ending point but as a beginning for the possibility of creation through the queered lens of cultural production, intangibility, and the necessity of fugitiveness. Our re/birthing, with Wynterian methodology as praxis, helps us recognize imperialist Ideology as inseparably opposed to Global Indigenous histories. Disrupting vast continuums of Black and Indigenous technologies that honor care and cyclical understandings over-extraction and commodification. Wynter's "revisioned humanism depends also, *dialectically,*[18] on a reconstructed understanding of the grounds of human being, a reconstruction that entails a deeper grasp of the dimensions of human cognition and action".[19]

SEA creates praxis for this creation-as-destruction dialectic. Systematic erasure of perceptions of humanity pre-1492 rupture creates popular amnesia, making humanity that works for us and returns to alignment with all sentient beings on the planet we share a necessity.[20] Any engagement with Sylvia Wynter demands openness and is necessary for engaging in the merging politicization of grassroots organizing and social practice for the non-human.[21] Cultural production continues to be a method for the oppressed to formulate self-understanding outside of the conceptualizations of hegemony, decolonizing our imaginations. In *Social Art: A Community Approach*, Arthur Katona states "on its most intimate level, that of the community. It began to appear to us that art may become what is most significant in the meaning of the word community, namely, communal. Art becomes at its functional best a sharing, as is community living at its best; art receives inspiration from the life around it and gives its own gifts to make that life richer and more meaningful."[22] Due to our experiences as subjects deemed intrinsically inferior and undeserving of the 'protection' entrenched in humanity/whiteness, we have historically acted and mobilized communally. The colonial-capitalist-individualist means of existence can not provide conditions for our survival.

The master's tools will never dismantle the master's house and surely the master's parasitic conceptualizations of "human" will never liberate the dehumanized.[23] We must approach social practice with the intent of creating new systems of existence, not to be integrated into the systems that oppress us. In Aimé Césaire's, *Lyric and Dramatic Poetry*, the author states "Poetic knowledge is born in the great silence of scientific knowledge."[24] We must merge this with Wynter's understanding of the 'scientific' as part of the formulation of colonial rule and thus engage it critically. Social practice can become our means of poetic knowledge, in the silenced, liminal spaces of Blackness, otheredness, and non-humanness: a felt knowledge that we embrace and embraces us as a whole.

Socially Engaged Art
SEA is a form of artwork(s) wherein co-creation, process, praxis, discourse, and social interaction between humans is the artistic medium. This work spans from ephemerality to long-term projects rooted in community building, allowing for both liminal or deep-rooted formations. The processes of human interaction and social engagement not only produce this art but are the essence of the aesthetic composition of the work. SEA allows us to understand artwork outside of the confines of the art object and begin to imagine a cyclical 'praxis as outcome' approach to collective co-creation. The fluid nature and potential illegibility of this medium are one of its greatest strengths as a framework to perform new/imagined life-worlds for the non-human subject.

In Claire Bishop's *Artificial Hells: Participatory Art and the Politics of Spectatorship* the author states, "The artist is conceived less as an individual producer of discrete objects than as a collaborator and producer of situations; the work of art as a finite, portable, commodifiable product is reconceived as an ongoing or long- term project with an unclear beginning and end; while the audience, previously conceived as a 'viewer' or 'beholder', is now repositioned as a co-producer or participant".[25] This practice constructs the artist as instigator/initiator who specializes in collaboration, this democratized interpretation of the artist can speak to socialist-aspiring articulations of society as a fertile ground for co-learning, co-research, and cooperative means of engaging the material world.[26] This positioning of the artist in society allows us to make great parallels with Freire's notion of the 'student-teacher', 'teacher-student' relationship. A process in which the teacher (initiator) and student (participant) practice co-intentional education, both as subjects, in the task of unveiling and coming to know reality as well as re-creating knowledge. "As they attain this knowledge of reality through common reflection and action, they discover themselves as to its permanent re-creators. In this way, the presence of the oppressed in the struggle for their liberation will be what it should be: not pseudo-participation, but committed involvement."[27] When this art form is ethically[28] engaged, it can create space for multiple epistemological productions and embodied knowledges to have equal respect;

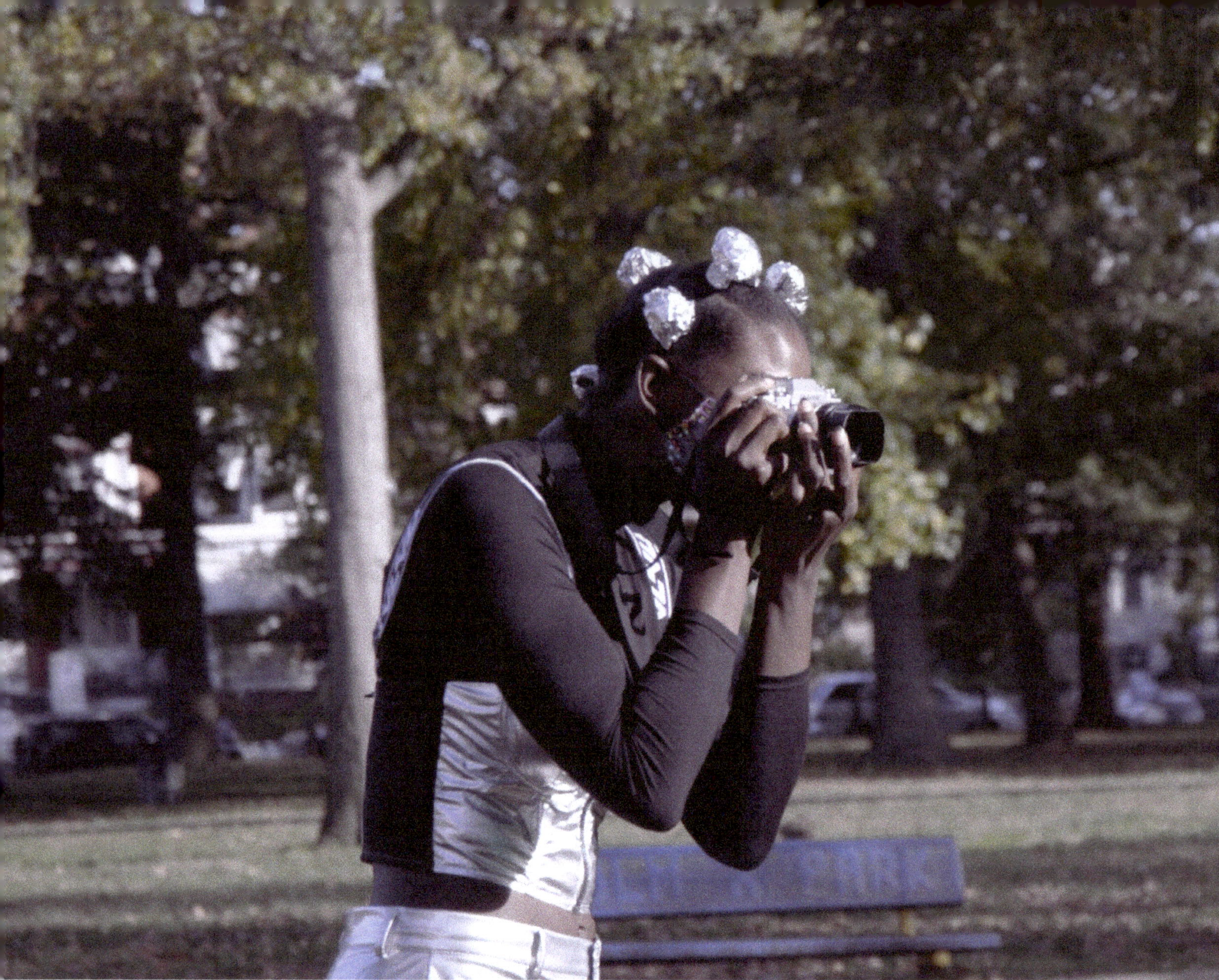

Dalaeja Foreman

[b]reach: adventures in heterotopia, an abolitionist visual opera. PRISONER #25 in Miserablism, USA. 35mm cinema camera.
Dimensions: 1920x1080px. Courtesy of Jazz Franklin, Gallery of the Streets © Dalaeja Foreman

abandoning Euro-colonial-capitalist impositions of disposability and power.

SEA is a useful framework in thinking through Wynter's conception of the (non) human because it is about art that is experienced, not art that centers on a static object. This adornment and appreciation for the process of the artwork in socially engaged art as opposed to the inanimate art object is a foreshadowing for the conceptualization of communities not as bystanders of society but as people that create it. If we communities labelled non-human were to analyze our responsibility and power as subjects, through a social practice lens, we would better understand that it is we that have the ability to actively create a society that reflects our collective interests. The necessity for active participation in SEA allows us to determine what those collective interests are, through praxis, not imposition. This ability to create a collective radical democratic public culture, allows us to articulate solutions to our problems by enacting them in unconventional ways. This artistic practice centers on dialogue, participation, and inquiry-based engagement, fundamental attributes of a truly democratic society. Not as means of social control but as open collaboration.

You know Ali, it's hard enough to start a revolution, even harder to sustain it, and hardest of all to win it. But it's only *afterward*, once we've won, that the real difficulties begin.

The Battle of Algiers, 1966

SEA's ability to pilot *the afterward* in a post-hegemonic imperialist world is its greatest strength for oppressed peoples. This process can help us transform our collective consciousness, which is a crucial step for the propagation of new ideological understandings. Understanding that leads us to cognitive shifts toward the new world(s) and new/revisited human experience(s). That is not to say this process will be easy, or all its outcomes necessarily advantageous, however, *the attempt is all we have control over*. As SEA is typically designed with a goal but no sure way to determine the outcome, this approach to our new human politic(s) allows us to find comfort in our precarity. Instead of focussing on a predetermined outcome, we collectively create a diverse vocabulary/recoding science of possibilities by attempting them and engaging the multifaceted epistemologies of our lived experiences.

Consciousness, socialty & embodied praxis

The science of the word, then, points to creative labor as recoding science through representational and biological feelings...This is an interdisciplinary and collaborative task, one that allows us to think about how the creative narrative can and does contribute to what is otherwise understood as "the laws of nature," thus creating an intellectual space to explore the worlds of those communities who are otherwise considered unscientific, scientifically inferior, endangered, and/or too alien to comprehend. This framework also points to relational and connective knowledges rather than positioning, say, science first and resistance later.[29]

Sylvia Wynter

Through the creative labor of producing new vocabularies, we collectively recode the hegemonic formations of science, history, literature, and other systems of power operating outside of these formations. Human life cannot, therefore, *pre-exist* the phenomenon of culture. Rather, it comes into being simultaneously with it.[30] This anti-modernity cultural production becomes an anti-imperialist praxis that uses creation-as-destruction.

We can create the character of our humanity through the fundamental concepts of social practice; collectivity, relationship building, and dialogue. These align with Paulo Freire's fundamentals of radical pedagogy, which are *trust, reflection, dialogue,* and *responsibility*.[31] Euro-colonial-capitalist's scientific exploration through dialogue and social interaction imposes itself as an illusory and vapid standard of human beings to strive to become. SEA allows its interlocutors to consider radical pedagogy for engaging in consciousness shift. The "naming" of oppression embodies a freedom praxis, through SEA naming becomes a tool for political education, a vital technique for opposing the constructs of power that place us outside of the "world".

As opposed to precursors of institutional tools of power, such as academic experience and access to capital, political production as cultural production has historically been an instructive space for oppressed communities. Methods in which the type of problem-solving a poor single parent or a houseless youth manifests are considered uniquely valuable and innovative. SEA will become a "crucial site of the contest out of which the human is being rewritten".[32]

In constructing our new humanity and culture, we are transcending the manufactured artworld and understanding the arts as a politic that represents our collective cyclical understanding reinterpreting history, constructing the present, and imagining the future. "Individuals start to see themselves reflected in their work and to understand their full stature as human beings through the object created, and through the work accomplished".[33] In *Representing Whiteness in the Black Imagination*, Bell Hooks explains the liminal existence for oppressed peoples living in close proximity to caucasity, through the collective experience of poor Black people in her small Kentucky town.[34] Our labor will not be synonymous with exploitation, our social duty to our communities will be fulfilled through self-expression. Social practice allows us to rethink our relationship to labor and production, "Man- as- human- and- origin fades away not to be replaced by an alternative perspective/figure who occupies that defining position".[35] Alongside counter-hegemonic cultural productions like Jazz, Salsa, and Hip Hop, social practice challenges us to question "where humanness takes place"[36] by creating a system of tools to construct humanness through action and production. Rejecting the human-as-commodity paradigm and helping us recreate the existence of the human as a social being.

Just as SEA does not create an easily profitable object, this application to the collective struggle for liberation becomes a rejection of the human-as-commodity paradigm and helps us create the existence of the human as a social being. We occupy in/outsider perspectives which become a fugitive strength for our creation-as-resistance paradigm.

Articulating a fluid politic(s)
Liminality is our central location for producing counter-hegemonic discourse that is not just found in words but habits of being.[37] The undeterminable nature of SEA doesn't boast answers to problems but provides a series of prompts that assist us in taking advantage of our oppositionality. The fluidity of SEA can demystify our sociopolitical illusions of an absolute vacuum reality and provide new poetical tactics.

Social practice can help us engage in a politic of convergence.[38] Helping us realize that most of our issues amongst one another are due to the ideological parasites we've internalized from our oppressors, necessitating community division.[39] Alongside non-carceral accountability practices and healthy conflict, the necessity for active reflection in SEA can create a culture of constant reinterpretation and purge toward our collective interests, fostering the ability to mend tensions amongst us.

In *Freedom dreams: the Black radical imagination*, Robin D. G. Kelley states "Without new visions, we don't know what to build, only what to knockdown. We not only end up confused, rudderless, and cynical, but we forget that making a revolution is not a series of clever maneuvers and tactics but a process that can and must transform us."[40] In Social Practice relationship building is the main ingredient of the work and possibly rebirth of communities based on human interaction replacing extraction. By embodying praxis' of reconstructing knowledge, we create holistic methodologies toward new grassroots organizing and guerrilla humanity(s). Participation rehumanizes a *community* [41] rendered numb and fragmented by the repressive instrumentality of capitalist production.[42]

Immateriality of Social Practice introduces subtle means of resistance and is potentially more difficult to repress and surveil (dependent upon geopolitical context) in the contemporary Global hyper-surveillance ethos. Dark-sousveillance speaks to observing those in authority (the slave patroller or the plantation overseer) and the use of keen and experimental insight of plantation surveillance in order to resist it.[43] As those deemed non-human[44], our experiences in the imperialist project as insider/outsiders create opportunities to observe gaps in oppressive rule and exploit them. These micro-actions help us imagine mobilizing and inspire liberatory educational collaboration, imagination, care, and labor amongst oppressed peoples of the world.

In the conceptions of human-as-man, the cultural production embraced by these institutions like galleries and museums are considered "logical", "neutral" and "unbiased",[45] gifting them with a cloak of implied invisibility/hypervisibility. Many institutions have transitioned their power and profit from colonialism and enslavement to environmental degradation, the weapons market, and wage-labor abuses. They have proven to be

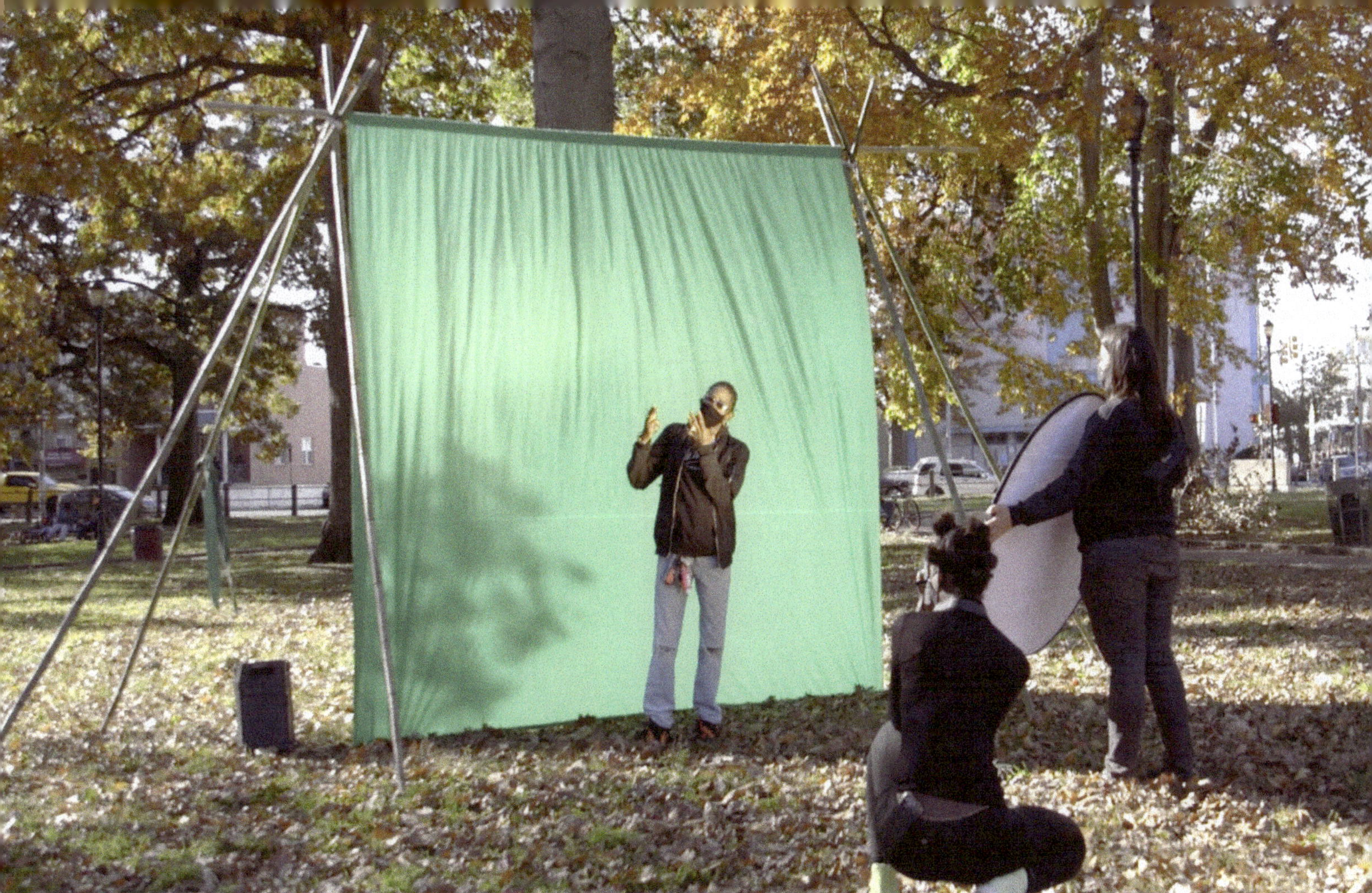

Dalaeja Foreman

[b]reach: adventures in heterotopia, an abolitionist visual opera. PRISONER #25 in Miserablism, USA. 35mm cinema camera. Dimensions: 1920x1080px. Courtesy of Jazz Franklin, Gallery of the Streets © Dalaeja Foreman

fundamentally incapable of representing our humanity. SEA has the ability to widen cracks in these intuitions, when done with the intent of oppressed people instead of trend, creating opportunities to obscure hegemony, subvert resources, and support community lead initiatives. We have consciously and unconsciously eschewed spaces designed for our dehumanization[46] while also affirming this system's validity. SEA's pliancy and ability to navigate public and nonconventional spaces allow a democratic and non-hierarchical appeal to a cocreating alternative.

Pablo Huelgera states SEA "is specifically at odds with the capitalist market infrastructure of the art world".[47] Although Social Practice may appear un-commodifiable, closer investigation exposes this farce. What can appear to be radically opposed to canonical values of art can be co-opted to represent the neoliberal mutation of capitalism. Allowing us to better create our rules of engagement amongst one another, toward shared beneficial lifeworlds, reflecting our interests. As privatization and corporatization of public services become further normalized, Social Practice must be careful to not simply become a series of shallow bandages for this festering stab wound. Co-optation may only be prevented if euro-colonial-capitalist critiques are central to the aim of a project.

Ben Davis states, "Sometimes, "social practice" can seem like little more than an aestheticized spin on typical non-profit work". Consequently, it is made vulnerable by the inherent occupational prostration of non-profit focused activism. "Having to lower one's *principles* [48] in order to please donors, mopping up the symptoms of social problems instead of going after the disease itself, and, ultimately, reducing the vital work of political organizing to a symbolic gesture—the very pitfall of political

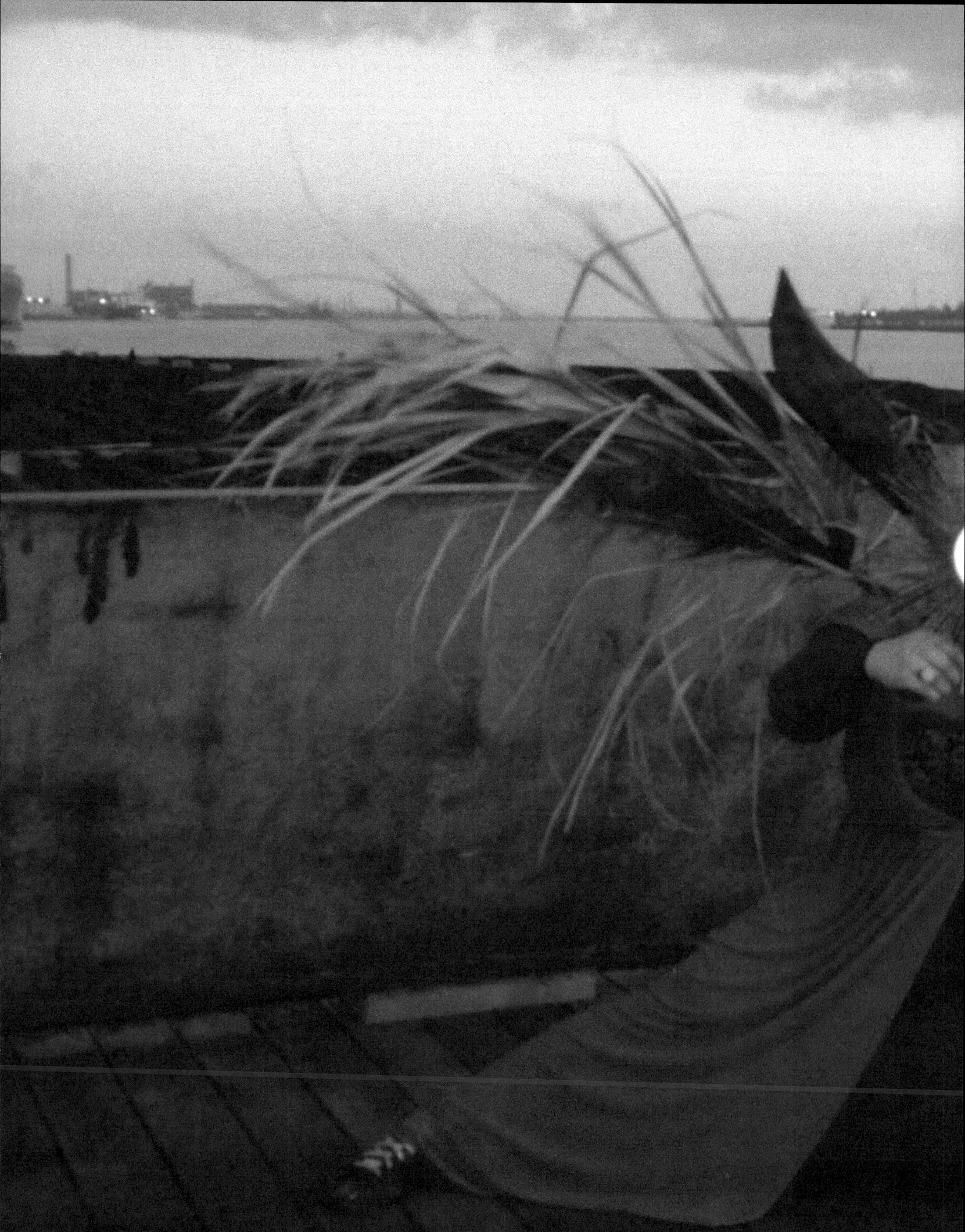

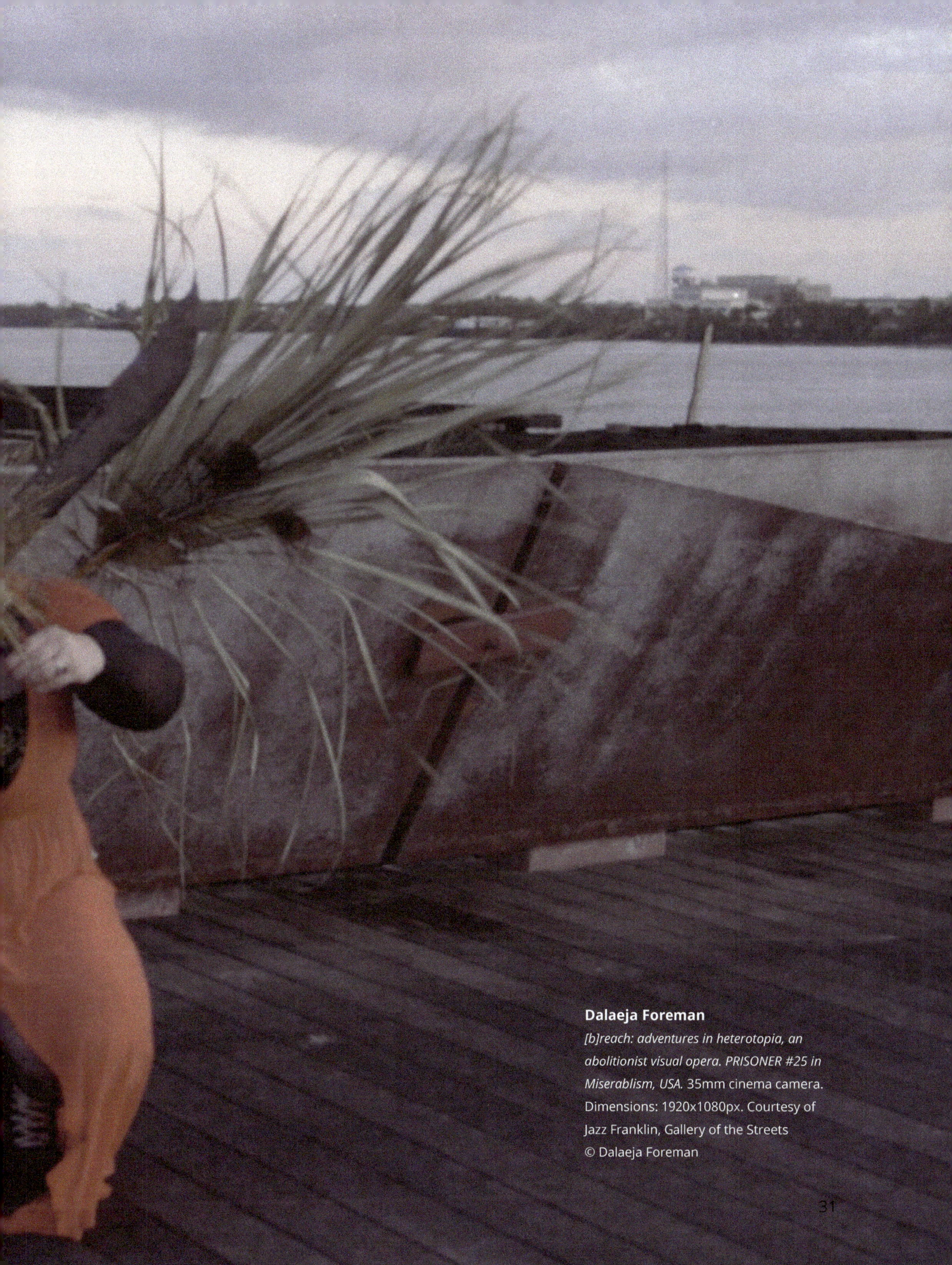

Dalaeja Foreman
[b]reach: adventures in heterotopia, an abolitionist visual opera. PRISONER #25 in Miserablism, USA. 35mm cinema camera. Dimensions: 1920x1080px. Courtesy of Jazz Franklin, Gallery of the Streets
© Dalaeja Foreman

art that political artists have always tried to escape".[49] SP's engagement outside of the cannon allows us to begin with validation of our cultural production and narratives. Reflecting upon and engaging in forms that intentionally avoid the cannon, supports movement away from neoliberal conceptualizations of being integrated into our systems of oppression. This liberatory segue imbues us with deeper understanding stepping toward a subsisting politic; taking root in our surreal gifts and abilities to thrive in spite of this oppression. This still has the potential to inflame our contradictions when needs for funding occur within capitalist infrastructure, however, SEA activates moments for critique and rethinking of our ecosystems values, beyond capital as the foundation of value. Social Practice cultural production has been used immemorially to mobilize resistance in oppressed communities, from anti-apartheid movements to AIDs activisms.

Comparative political context: South Africa and Palestine
Keteketla! Library in South Africa and the Freedom Theatre in Palestine provide examples of how Social Practice has helped mend communal ruptures enforced by the Colonial Matrix of Power. In these settler-colonial and neo-settler colonial states, cultural production is being used to defend the lives of the oppressed and create new articulations of humanities. The Global South is constantly at the forefront of the most extreme imperialist violence thus, is also in a particular position to lead struggles for Global liberation. The lessons learned from studying Keteketla! Library and Freedom Theatre offer guidance for how we can use SEA for our immediate tactics in the Global North while creating relationships to support Global South liberation. We are not free until all of us are free, and NYC must learn many lessons from these sites.

In 1948, both *the Nakba*[50] and *South African apartheid*[51] occurred.[52] Both examples of terrorist settler-colonial imposition of "whiteness" are institutionalized mechanisms of dehumanization which persist today and have intensified over time.[53] Israeli Zionists[54] and South African whites expelled most Indigenous people or imprison them. In 1947, across the Atlantic in New York, the Federal Housing Administration launched in Long Island the suburb of Levittown. Issuing affordable home loans exclusively to white returning World War II veterans.[55] Levittown went on to become and still is the home of a large Ku Klux Klan based in New York state.

Those deemed non-human in the Colonial Matrix of Power in both Palestine and South Africa[56] are connected to Euro-American maintenance of state power that has bred neo-colonial-capitalist violence. In this wake, cultural production is an accessible means of mobilizing toward liberation. Beginning in the 1960s, the academic and cultural boycott waged against the apartheid state in South Africa became one of the strongest tools of the resistance movement, viewed as an ambiguous tool of struggle.[57] The boycott called for all artists, academics, philosophers and cultural practitioners to refuse to participate in any activities in the country which was being boycotted.[58] By the late 1970s, there was popular consensus about the evil of apartheid, particularly in the U.S. and Britain. The movements for economic and military sanctions against South Africa had already succeeded in effecting an arms and oil embargo as well as a sports boycott.[59] The quintessence of the boycott allowed for cultural production to be a connector to other societal institutions, instigating thorough understandings of the interdependence of hegemonic order. In the ethos of cultural boycott, the social practice was utilized in the public sphere of Black provinces a critical pedagogical action space to instigate public discourse[60] around apartheid.[61] The success of the boycott highlights the glaring strengths of both Cultural production and Social Practice. Although the system of apartheid was discontinued in 1994, the economy still appears to work in favour of the White minority, neoliberalism in South Africa since the 1990s has maintained the economic legacy of apartheid which disadvantages the African majority.[62]

The South African Academic and Cultural boycott became one of the major influences of the Boycott Divestment and Sanctions (BDS) movement. Launched in 2005, BDS is a campaign lead by Palestinian civil-society organizations which urge international cultural workers and cultural organizations, including unions and associations, to boycott and/or work towards the cancellation of events, activities, agreements, or projects involving Israel, its lobby groups or its cultural institutions. International venues and festivals are asked to reject funding and any form of sponsorship from the Israeli government.[63] Major themes of the cultural boycott are artist-led resistance and the right to return.[64] The usurpation of sovereignty and imposition of false Indigeneity coalesce to invasively establish disharmony amongst the people and their lands; leaving them victim to unquantifiable punitive extraction[65]. The persistence and legacy of cultural boycott in both of these spaces speaks to the significance of cultural production for resistance and how it creates spaces for building solidarity amongst those rendered non-human and our accomplices.

What is Keleketla! Library? South Africa
Founded by Rangoato Hlasane and Malose Malahlela in 2008, Keleketla! Library[66] provides its community with a diasporan definition of library, as a contextual site of production rather than an infrastructure for accumulation. The project uses visionary media arts to make room for generative processes of learning and unlearning.[67] In *"Rethinking 'Aesthetics': Notes Towards a Deciphering Practice"*, Sylvia Wynter states, "the rethinking of aesthetics provides the 'ground' that can make "decipherable" the systems of meaning."[68] Keleketla!'s immaterial forms of archiving[69] and knowledge production is a means of engaging in a political praxis for redefining self and community while using embodied formations as language. These aesthetic knowledge practices parallel Freire's concept of 'naming' as an act of comprehending dehumanization and experiencing autonomy. Kelekelta! Library helps us imagine our communities as flexible and realize we harness agency over our consciousness and material conditions.

Located in the Drill Hall, a former military base, built-in 1904 for the enlistment of soldiers during World Wars One and Two, the reclamation of this large historic site by Keleketla! is a fracture to the CMP by virtue of its reclamation. Further, the 1956 Treason Trial of South Africa took place in which 156 leaders under the auspices of the Congress of the People were arrested.[70] As this project is founded and led by an intergenerational community of Black people and exists in the wake of Black struggle for liberation in South Africa, it is a bastion for a new means of engaging with the political. One that is fluid and approachable, viewing the concept of liberation outside of the linear/Euro-colonial-capitalist conception of time and space and toward cyclical/ Afro & Indigenous -diasporic concepts of time and space.

The project also engages communal politics by reassessing the concept of value and resources. During the duration of their project, Keleketla! Library has invited other cultural workers and collectives to design arts programming with their younger members. In exchange for their intellectual labor, the collectives were allowed to use the Drill Hall toward their own programs and initiatives. This illuminates how SEA can help us reimagine exchange. These networks of trust allow us to question the concept of value, what creates value, who can create it, and who doesn't. This informal value system rejects barriers created by monstrous artistic institutions that police styles of artistic practice through regulation of funding.

Keletetla! Library investigates the uses of art in life and analyzes the ways in which art actively *becomes* relevant. The organization states "We used it to address issues of heritage and the danger of one story and allow that space to be a place where multiple stories and multiple narratives can exist parallel to each other in order to challenge dominant narratives".[71] This creation of new narratives speaks to Wynter's analysis of the man-as-human by creating new humanity(s) and exploding the hegemonic ethos. In which human is a verb that is now linked to a series of actions, centering the convergent aim of liberation for those living in the wake of the Colonial Matrix of Power.

The Keleketla! After School Programme (K!ASP) was established in 2008 as a youth learning space that relates the history and contemporary issues to lived experience, "creating a community of critical thinkers".[72] The program aims to engage youth in critical analysis of contemporary socio-political and economic issues of the city, the country and the continent.[73] K!ASP is a way for youth[74] to observe the origins of content and analyze while creating space to amplify public vulnerability through socio-intellectual experiences using art and media processes.

K!ASP successfully engages in contestatory signifying practices[75] by creating an alternative means of engaging history that creates new vocabularies to connect actions of the past to the present. This rejects the dominant historical narratives by rejecting the very euro-capitalist tools of production that are imposed as the "correct" way to engage with cyclical history. Social Practice projects like K!ASP and other Keleketla! Library projects create a cross-generational dialogue with the possibility to create a consciousness shift in the community whilst creating the foundations for trust, reflection, dialogues, and responsibility.

What is Freedom Theatre? Palestine

Art, in our case, can combine and generate and mobilize other aspects of resistance

Juliano Mer Khamis, co-founder of The Freedom Theatre[76]

The Stone Theatre was founded by Arna Mer Khamis[77] during the First Intifada in the early 1990s. In 2002, during the Battle of Jenin, The Stone Theatre was destroyed by the Israel Defense Forces. In 2006 Arna's son Juliano Mer Khamis co-founded The Freedom Theatre on the site of the old Stone Theatre. Juliano served as director of the theatre until 2011 when he was assassinated.

The Freedom Theatre is based in the Jenin Refugee camp and offers a range of cultural activities, including drama workshops, theatre performances, a three-year professional theatre school, and training in stage management, photography, filmmaking, and creative writing.[78] For this essay, I will be exclusively focusing on their theatre work. Freedom Theatre travels to different Refugee camps in Palestine to help mobilize resistance in public space. The Settler-colonial Israeli state vehemently brandishes the Wynterian concept of 'human-as-man'. As the Israeli state attempts to systematically erase Palestinian peoples from their land and history; through mass murder, displacement and general theft, and denial of resources, the project of re/creating humanity is an essential necessity. Social practice disrupts this erasure, through public theatre. The accessible medium of theatre navigates and disrupts public and private spaces, raises popular consciousness and engages resistance.

In an interview entitled *"Interview with the late Juliano Mer-Khamis: 'We are freedom fighters* , Khamis states:

> You don't have to heal the children in Jenin. We didn't try to heal their violence. We tried to challenge it in more productive ways. And more productive ways are not an alternative to resistance. What we were doing in the theatre is not trying to be a replacement or an alternative to the resistance of the Palestinians in the liberation struggle. Just the opposite. This must be clear. I know it's not good for fundraising because I'm not a social worker, I'm not a good Jew going to help the Arabs, and I'm not a philanthropic Palestinian who comes to feed the poor. We are joining, by all means, the struggle for the liberation of the Palestinian people, which is our liberation struggle... We are freedom fighters. [79]

The work of Freedom Theatre uses a myriad of programs to create an ethos of solidarity that speaks to the possibility of social practice. Specifically, the Freedom Bus[80] *uses interactive theatre and cultural activism to bear witness, raise awareness, and build alliances throughout occupied Palestine and beyond.* [81]

From 2005 to at least 2011, Freedom Theatre's *Freedom Bus* was part of a weekly protest campaign in the village of Bil'in, the typical version of the Friday demonstration consists of a protest march,[82] following the midday prayer, from the mosque in the village to the Wall, a distance of a few kilometers[83]. On Friday, 17th of June 2011 a performance was put on in collaboration with a demonstration against an Israeli separation barrier that would divide the village's land in half [84.] The demonstration was performed at the gate and began with community members *taking*[85] the streets chanting "Free Palestine" amongst other phrases[86]. Even as they reach the separation barrier and are attacked unprovoked by Israeli officers with hoses, their chanting continued. Soon after, rubber-coated steel bullets were shot at the demonstrators and high-velocity tear gas canisters were deployed.[87] Once the demonstrators regained vision and covered their faces, the demonstration proceeded and the performance began. When the performance was over, the gas and bullets began again. This performance exemplifies not only the dehumanizing wanton violence imposed on Palestinian peoples by the settler-colonial Israeli State but also the threat of cultural production as a means of resistance. The public space became a stage for community alignment; forging a collective from an incident that could either be perceived as a positive-a moment of solidarity or negative-placing vulnerable populations in harm's way. The Israeli State became unintentionally center stage while exposing itself as Dehumanizer against the dehumanized; the hegemonically imperialist selected Humans vs. the deselected non-humans. Alongside their heavily funded military power from Euro-American capitalist superpowers, tying the Zionist agenda back to the ethos of the original settler-colonial experiment of 1492. This shift in gaze allows us to view cultural production as a means of galvanizing social practice as a tool for constructing our collective humanity as one by survivors, for survivors. By people who refuse to be erased, their very existence is a grand threat to the Zionist rendition of the hegemonic settler-colonialism.

Social Practice, Cross-Local Solidarities, and Pragmatic Lessons for NYC
Key methods for social practice are process, discourse, co-creation, and social interaction through ephemeral and long-term projects. The solution-oriented nature of SEA sequences imagination and performance of queered frameworks for politicizing or political education. Social practice prefaces an engagement in Freire's fundamental concepts of radical pedagogy, creating boundless opportunities for radical consciousness shift. SEA makes clear, oftentimes, it is not in the explicitly political realm that one discovers moments of contact.[88]

SP's potential is boundless for creating new frameworks, but can be starved in isolation; thus must be allowed to breathe in a multidimensional ethos of social movements. Helping us imagine alternatives and actualize them. It can be informed by grassroots organizing, indigenous practices, lived-expertise, activisms, language, and other epistemic forms of the oppressed masses.

From a radical standpoint, perspective, position, 'the politics of location' necessarily calls those of us who would participate in the formation of counter-hegemonic cultural practice to identify the spaces where we begin the process of re-vision". [89]

We must renegotiate our understanding of the systems that govern our lifeworlds. We must understand they are not negligent but are designed to dehumanize. As we come to varied understandings of this function we simultaneously create means of humanity designed For Us By Us (FUBU). By embodying experiences that recognize our full humanity we begin to illuminate the flaw of hegemonic function through reflection.

Sylvia Wynter's conceptualizations of human-as-man challenge us to dissect the confines of the western bourgeois tenet of homogeneous humanity. With Wynterian theories, the *non-human* subject engages diverse planetary concepts of humanness, harnessing universal and cosmological locale for sight beyond meaningless suffering. These ruptured encounters inform and/or make possible meaningful emancipatory moments that radically alter humanness itself.[90]

"Palestine has always occupied a pivotal place, precisely because of the similarities between Israel and the United States—their foundational settler colonialism and their ethnic cleansing processes with respect to indigenous people, their systems of segregation, their use of legal systems to enact systematic repression, and so forth".[91] Similarly, South Africa is another uniquely pivotal site of colonial terror and vast disparity, exemplary for illustrating cultural boycotts' as tools for international solidarity; and has been paid homage as such. As we live in the ripples of this homogeneous vision of

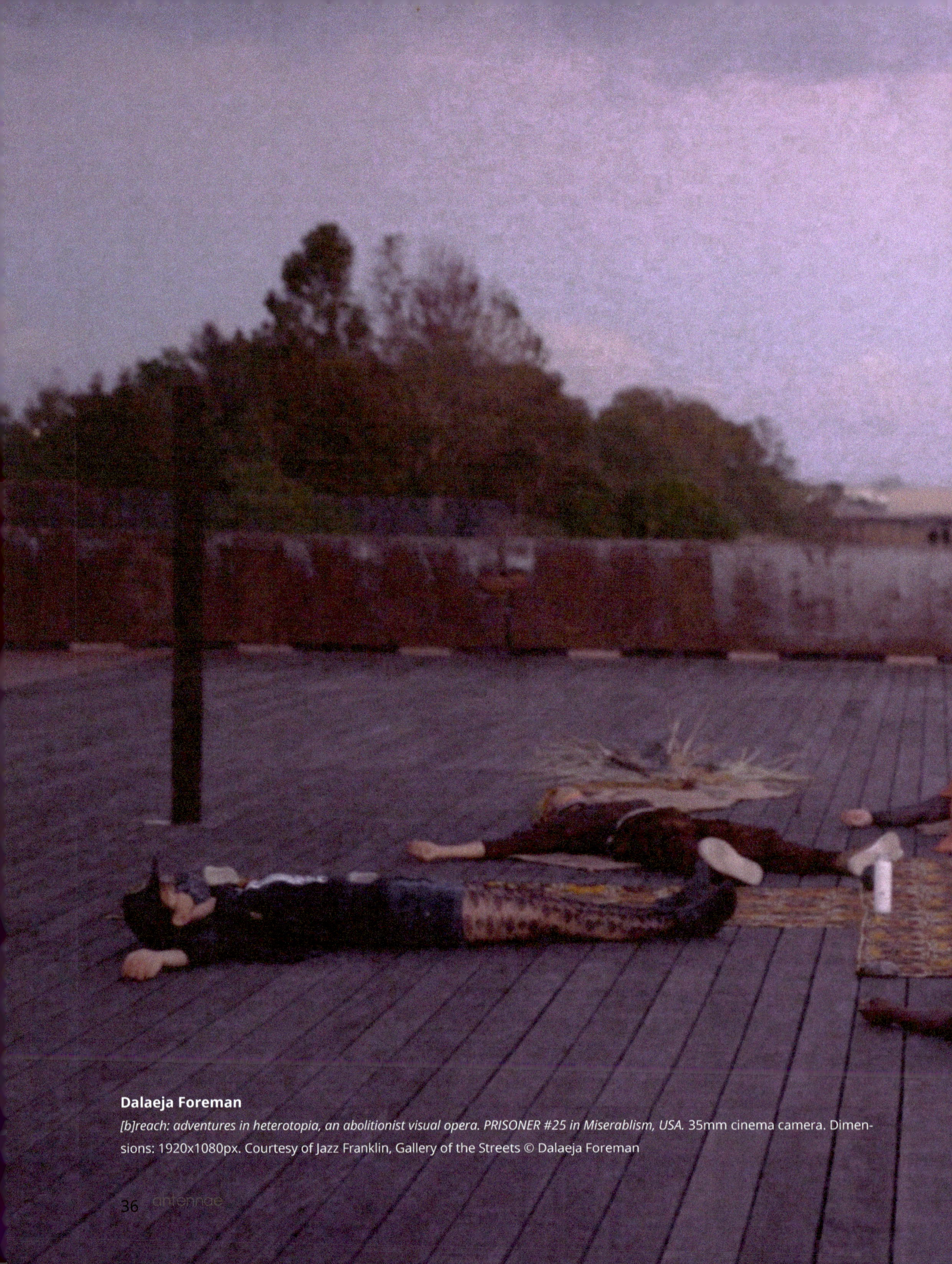

Dalaeja Foreman

[b]reach: adventures in heterotopia, an abolitionist visual opera. PRISONER #25 in Miserablism, USA. 35mm cinema camera. Dimensions: 1920x1080px. Courtesy of Jazz Franklin, Gallery of the Streets © Dalaeja Foreman

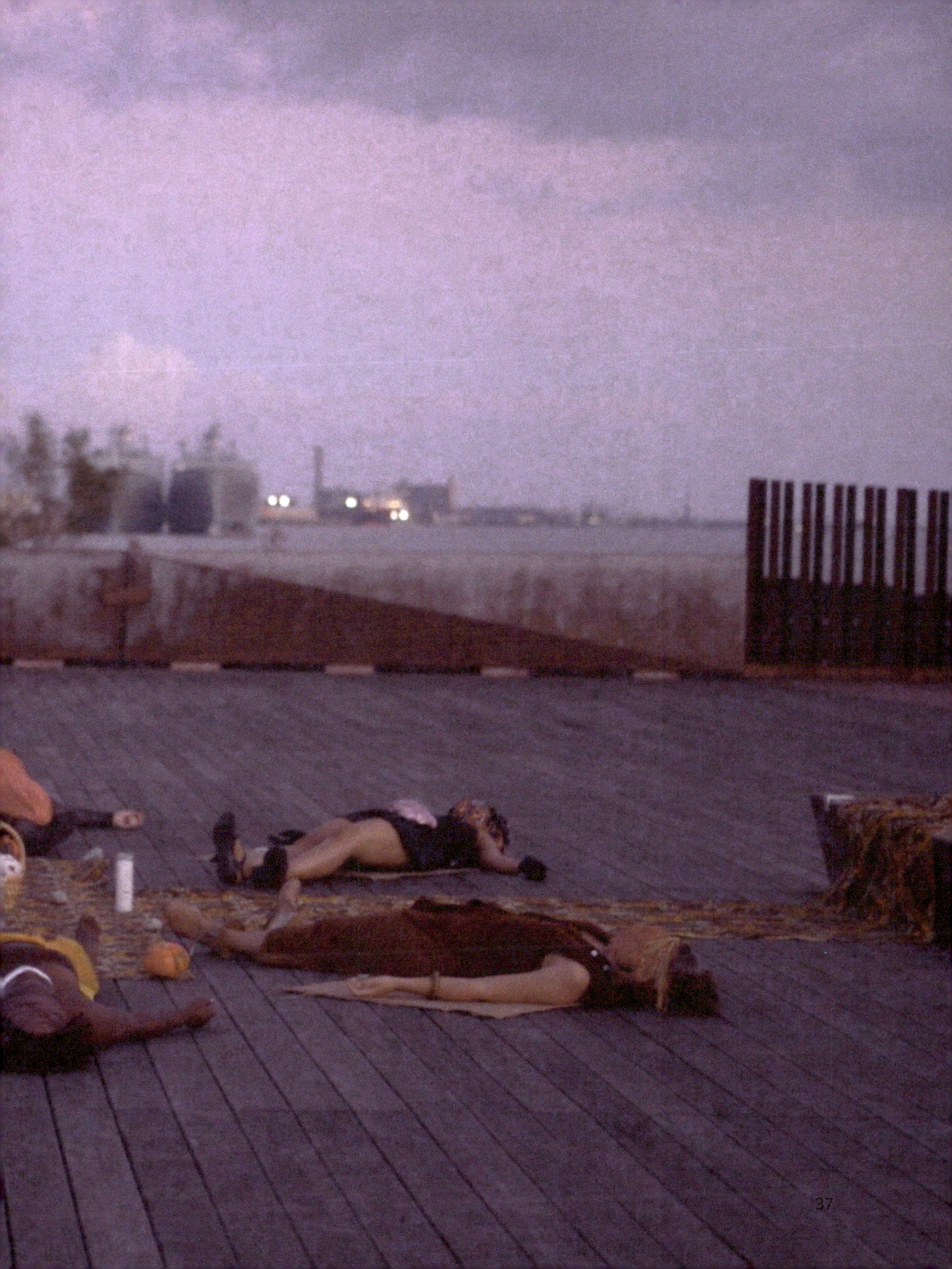

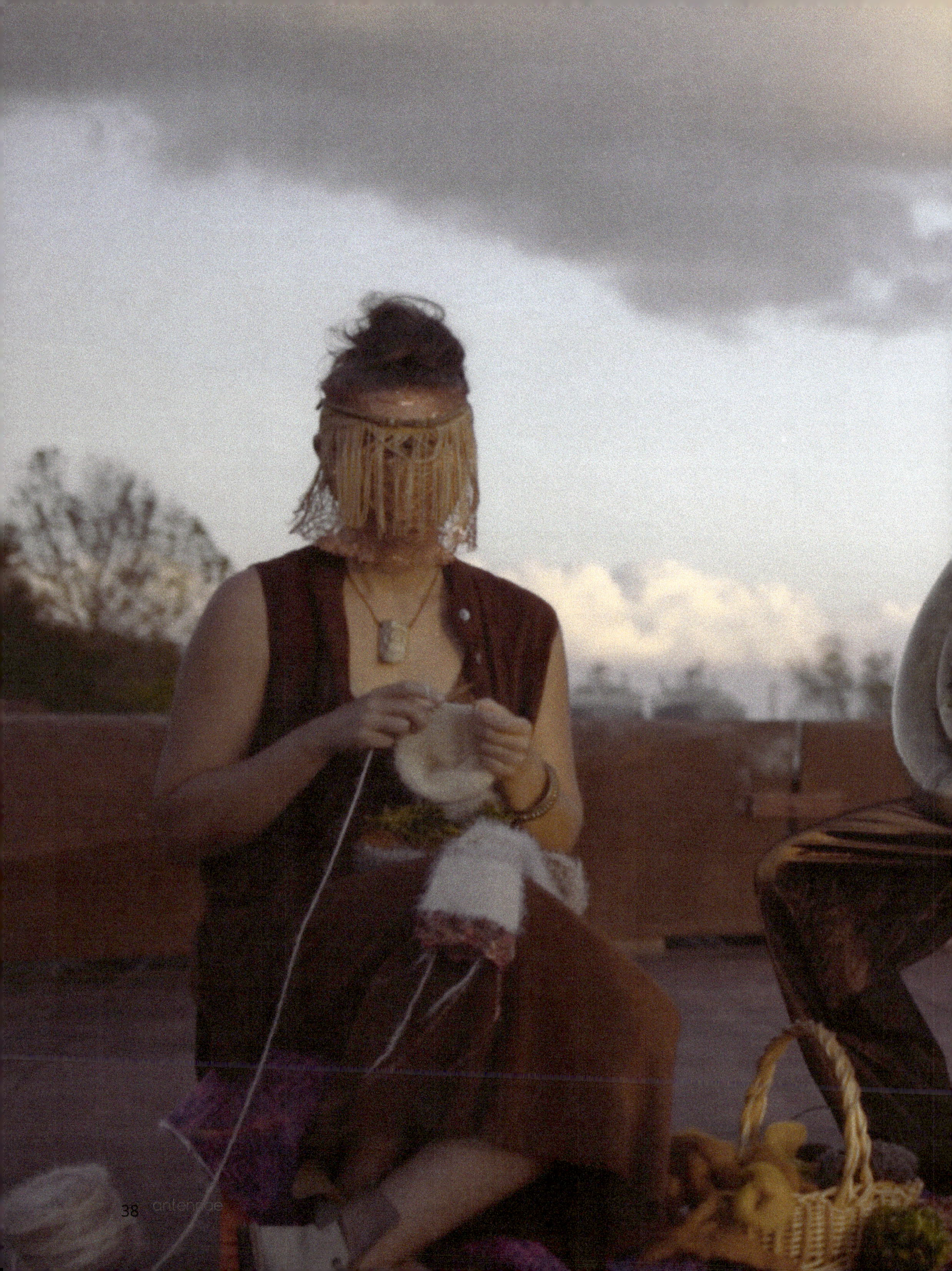

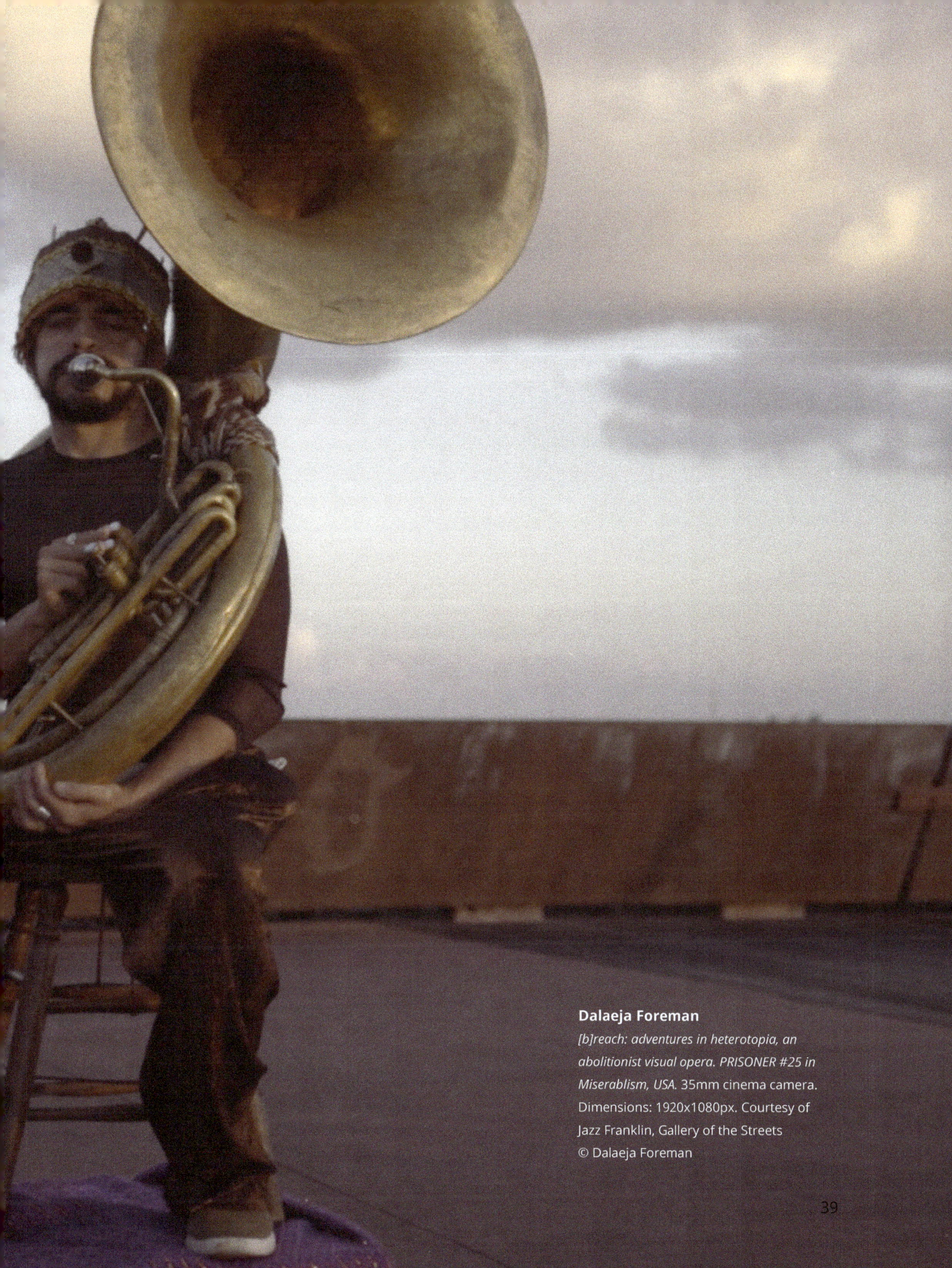

Dalaeja Foreman

[b]reach: adventures in heterotopia, an abolitionist visual opera. PRISONER #25 in Miserablism, USA. 35mm cinema camera. Dimensions: 1920x1080px. Courtesy of Jazz Franklin, Gallery of the Streets
© Dalaeja Foreman

humans that encompasses every institution in the global-north hegemonic cannon, we must dismantle the vapid and systemically materialized idea of the singular Human form. Keleketla!'s approach to social practice catalyzes the *non-human* as creating new narratives for personhood, flips the hegemonic historical gaze, emboldens and empowers critical thought and new epistemic articulations as means of smashing epistemic hierarchy. Freedom Theatre's approach to social practice centers; on the significance of cultural production as an articulation of cross-disciplinary liberation struggle, combating the persistently attempted erasure of the non-human, mobilizing global solidarities, and engaging dark-sousveillance to turn the colonial gaze on itself.

The lessons learned from The Keleketla! Library and Freedom Theatre are critical for how we re-conceptualize our approaches to organizing and mobilizing in NYC. New York City is the center of the capital in the Americas, yet it houses the poorest congressional district in the United States in the South Bronx. The social cleansing of NYC is tied up with late-stage capitalism, deindustrialization, environmental terrorism, destruction of healthcare infrastructures, neoliberalism, and rezoning. The city administration's thirst for development creates a system of corporate welfare, giving billions to corporations while its "citizenry" (workers and un/under-employed) suffer to keep roofs over their heads.[92] The mobilizations of cultural production in South Africa and Palestine succor our understanding of creating a language for our renewed existences alongside weaving our practices for the global liberation struggle. Not only as a means of demanding accountability from institutions that support oppressive forces but also as part of creating a language of the international struggle for those conceptualized as non-human, amongst ourselves, connecting our seemingly 'fixed' material conditions to the larger umbrella of oppression which connects our particular struggles.

As a revolutionist that lives and loves in The Bronx, I believe we must ensure our work to create art-making and social practice ethos' do not become absorbed by the Nonprofit Industrial complex. Nonprofit superstructures have repeatedly performed allyship while absorbing community production to maintain oppression. It becomes even more significant for us to always politically situate our social practice and art-making as anti-colonial, anti-capitalist, anti-cooptation, anti-carceral and abolitionist.

The Keleketla Library is an example of this political situating/naming Bronx movements can learn from their revelatory experiments. By reclaiming spaces that have been historically significant sites, such as the Drill Hall, we can use social practice as means of engaging in collective-community education on their local histories as well as mourning, reconciliation and reimagining liminal space. Also, their intergenerational multimedia storytelling helps us imagine new methods of communicating our stories with one another. This is particularly great potential for oppressed peoples in The Bronx because our borough is culturally diverse, in which a significant portion of the population are migrants[93] from lands violently burdened by Euro-American exploitation. These varieties of media can also help us dismantle the violence we impose on one another regarding anti-Blackness, class/non-class, gender(s), sexuality(s), ability(s), and the combinations of these. By creating living libraries of experiences and embodied theories, we create opportunities for challenging ourselves and one another to shed the violent gaze of Coloniality that we have been indoctrinated into and re/embrace iterations of our indigenous technologies and beyond.

The Freedom Theatre teaches us the significance of consistency and spectacle as means of building a culture of resistance through relationship cultivation and solidarity amongst the oppressed. By using political art embodiment as a tool we can make resistance sites visible and normalized, aesthetic and exciting. The work of the Freedom Theatre reveals to us how we can channel the traumas of our oppressions toward healthy community expression and reimagining while also using socially creative means. This FUBU training allows us to maintain control of our labor and disengage the Capitalist class, strengthening our collective autonomy through art practice. Finally, a very poignant lesson in particular from the Freedom Theatre for The

Bronx is the liberation struggle rejecting the Non-Profit Industrial Complex. The theatre would ensure that community-based artistic production is not dictated by funding nor the "easing" of oppression to make our trauma more palatable but instead is rooted in structural transformation and foundation-making, destruction-as-creation.

For those of us deemed non-human, attempting to integrate into this system is pursuing social death and acceptance into an isolated, starved, and monolithic white world view that is ideologically incapable of embracing our beings. *Believing* the system (perhaps) precludes self-expendability and or community expendability.[94] Thus we will continue to queer our methods. Our ability to remain unfixed conceptualizes lifeworlds inside and outside of hegemony, making the work of creating our own version of humanity most interesting. Gallery of the Streets (GoS) is a network of artists, activists, scholars, cultural workers, and community supporters who are committed to exploring radical possibilities within Black geographies.[95] GoS aims to "engage everyday spaces as sites of resistance" as is a fantastic example of the possibilities of an Abolition Art framework. "A Black sense of space and place, where, like Black art, Imagination is developed and practiced outside of the *rigid* borders of audience/spectator, expert/amateur, object/experience, representation/ abstraction".[96] As a network that crosses many localities, the possibilities for human re/imaginings become boundless!

As Robin Kelley puts it, "Love and imagination may be the most revolutionary impulses available to us, and yet we have failed to understand their political importance and respect them as powerful social forces...The catalyst for political engagement has never been misery, poverty, or oppression. People are drawn to the social movement because of hope: their dreams of a new world radically different from the one they inherited".[97] Social practice allows us to find love and imagination despite the suffocating non-consensual enforced violence we experience as the bastards of the hegemonic imperialist imagination. As the radical imagination force of SEA allows us to create a sustainable future, it must do so with the intent to destroy what is oppressing us. Social practice allows us to embody a blueprint for the expression of new humanities, allowing us to temporarily engage with the intangible so we can transform it into organized and tangible realities.

Endnotes

[1] In this work, *Human*, in title case will refer to the euro-colonial-capitalist conceptualization of personhood.
[2] In the early morning of 27 April 2016, 700 officers from over six law enforcement agencies plum-meted into homes in the Eastchester Gardens Public Housing complex and the Williamsbridge neigh-borhood of the Bronx with helicopters, battering rams, smoke bombs, and military arms. These include officers from the FBI, ICE, Bureau of Alcohol, Tobacco and Firearms (ATF)
[4] In this work, *Human*, in title case will refer to the euro-colonial-capitalist conceptualization of personhood.
[5] Grassroots NYC-based Police Accountability Group RT International, "Trial begins for 120 suspected NYC gang members amid protests over 'racialized terror'". 2016. Available at: https://www.rt.com/usa/363359-federal-trial-begins-bronx-120/
[6] Robin Kelley, "What is Racial Capitalism and Why Does It Matter?". Lecture, Kane Hall, University of Washington, Seattle, WA, November 7, 2017. https://www.youtube.com/watch?v=--gim7W_jQQ&ab_channel=KODXSeattle
[7] For more on the concept of the "colonial matrix of power" see Walter Mignolo and Rolando Vazquez in "Decolonial Aesthesis: Colonial Wounds/Decolonial Healings," Social Text online (2013)
[8] Throughout this text, I will be using "wake" in Christina Sharpe's concept of the afterlives/continuations of enslavement and colonial terror. See Christina Sharpe, *In the Wake: On Blackness and Being* (Durham, NC: Duke University Press, 2016)
[9] In this essay, the terms *socially engaged art*, *SEA* and *social practice* will be used interchangeably.
[10] Simone Browne, *Dark Matters: On The Surveillance of Blackness* (Durham, NC: Duke University Press, 2015)
[11] Miranda Sheffield, "Maroonage As Praxis: Exploring Anti-Surveillance Tactics and Maroon Liberation During the Late 17th-Early 18th Century" (MA diss, School of Oriental and African Studies, 2018*)*, 6
[12] Sheffield, "Maroonage As Praxis," 6
[13] Sylvia Wynter, "Unsettling the Coloniality of Being/Power/Truth/Freedom: Towards the Human, After Man, Its Overrepresentation–An Argument", CR: *The New Centennial Review*. 2003
[14] Sylvia Wynter, "Rethinking Aesthetics: Notes to a Deciphering Practice" in Exiles: Essays on Carib-bean Cinema. African World Press, 1992. 237-279
[15] David Scott, "The Re-enchantment of Humanism: An Interview with Sylvia Wynter", *Small Axe*, no. 8 (September 2000): 119–207

[16] Sylvia Wynter, "Unsettling the Coloniality of Being/Power/Truth/Freedom: Towards the Human, After Man, Its Overrepresentation–An Argument", CR: *The New Centennial Review*. 2003

[17] "Caucacity" is a term coined by the Bodega Boys podcast starring Desus Nice and the Kid Mero. A portmanteau of caucasian and audacity used to refer to objects or people in the popular culture that reflects both an origin in whiteness or white supremacy and an emboldened disregard for anything non-white. Here I am conjugating their phrase with conditions of breathing and its violent elimination that have come to the fore in generational Black uprisings against police terror. As well as an overwhelming lack of opportunity imposed in the everyday lives of oppressed peoples by hegemonic-colonial violence.

[18] Emphasis added

[19] David Scott, "The Re-enchantment of Humanism: An Interview with Sylvia Wynter", Small Axe, no. 8 (September 2000): 121

[20] See Frantz Fanon's *Black Skin, White Masks*, 1952 for more on the colonization of the dehumanized imagination.

[21] Katherine McKittrick, *Sylvia Wynter: On Being Human as Praxis* (Duke University Press, 2015)

[22] *Katona, Arthur. "Social Art: A Community Approach." The Journal of Educational Sociology 21, no. 2 (1947):* 67

[23] Audre Lorde, *The Master's Tools Will Never Dismantle the Master's House.* (London, England: Penguin Classics, 1979)

[24] Aimé Césaire, Clayton Eshleman, and Annette Smith. *Lyric and Dramatic Poetry,* 1946-82. (Charlottesville: University Press of Virginia, 1990)

[25] Claire Bishop, *Artificial Hells : Participatory Art and the Politics of Specta orship*. (London :Verso, 2012), 2

[26] When using the term *democracy*, It will be referencing this literal definition:*control of an organization or group by the majority of its member*s. This is to avoid aligning the term with the United States' conceptualization of governmental democracy.

[27] Paulo Freire, *Pedagogy of the Oppressed* (New York: Seabury Press, 1968)

[28] Ethical social practice is about mutual exchange and the process of co-learning, not about spectacle.

[29] Quoted in Katherine McKittrick, *Sylvia Wynter: On Being Human as Praxis* (Duke University Press, 2015),154-55

[30] Sylvia Wynter, "Rethinking Aesthetics: Notes to a Deciphering Practice" in *Ex-iles: Essays on Caribbean Cinema. (*African World Press,1992), 237-279

[31] Although not all socially engaged art projects adhere to these fundamentals, I believe all ethical social practice projects must

[32] Sylvia Wynter, *"Rethinking Aesthetics: Notes to a Deciphering Practice"* in *Ex-iles: Essays on Caribbean Cinema. (*African World Press,1992), 240

[33] Che Guevara, *Socialism and Man in Cuba* (first published under the title, "From Algiers, for Marcha . The Cuban Revolution Today.", March 12, 1965), 8

[34] "To be in the margin is to be part of the whole but outside the main body...We looked both from the outside in and from the inside out. We focused our attention on the center as well as on the margin. We understood both. This mode of seeing reminded us of the existence of a whole universe...This sense of wholeness, impressed upon our consciousness by the structure of our daily lives, provided us with an oppositional world-view - a mode of seeing unknown to most of our oppressors, that sustained us, aided us in our struggle to transcend poverty and despair, strengthened our sense of self and our solidarity."
bell hooks, *Representing Whiteness in the Black Imagination* (Routledge, 1997), 206

[35] Katherine McKittrick, *Sylvia Wynter: On Being Human as Praxis* (Duke University Press, 2015), 155

[36] McKittrick, *Sylvia Wynter: On Being Human as Praxis*, 155

[37] bell hooks, *Representing Whiteness in the Black Imagination* (Routledge, 1997), 206.

[38] Collective political action toward a particular goal, this concept is currently being developed by Dr. Nydia Swaby

[39] This is not to cloak internal conflicts present in oppressed communities, particularly in regards to race, class/non-class, gender, sexuality, ability, and access (and combinations of these).

[40] Robin D. G Kelley, *Freedom Dreams: The Black Radical Imagination.* (Boston: Beacon Press, 2002), xii.

[41] Emphasis added. In the original quote, the author uses the word "society".

[42] Claire Bishop, *Artificial Hells : Participatory Art and the Politics of Spectatorshi* . (London :Verso, 2012)

[43] Miranda Sheffield, "Maroonage As Praxis: Exploring Anti-Surveillance Tactics and Maroon Liberation During the Late 17th-Early 18th Century" (MA diss, School of Oriental and African Studies, 2018), 19

[44] And potentially living in the wake of Blackness

[45] More than enough scholarship has been done to expose this farce. For more on this, see the work of Decolonize This Place organizing group: http://www.decolonizethisplace.org/

[46] These include but are not limited to racism, sexism, ableism, colonialism, capitalism, homophobia, classism, colorism.

[47] Pablo Helguera, *Education for Socially Engaged Art : A Materials and Techniques Handbook*, (New York : Jorge Pinto Books, 2011), 8.

[48] Emphasis added. In the original quote, the author uses the word "rhetoric".

[49] Ben Davis, "A Critique of Social Practice Art: What does it mean to be a political artist?", International Socialist Review, Issue #90 (2013). https://isreview.org/issue/90/critique-social-practice-art

[50] The ethnic cleansing that forcibly displaced over 700,000 Palestine Arab people, 78% of historic Palestine by the Zionist Israeli state

[51] The Afrikaner National Party institutionalized racial discrimination in every aspect of the state apparatus.

[52] Aljazeera.com, *"The Nakba did not start or end in 1948",* 2017. [online] Available at: https://www.aljazeera.com/indepth/features/2017/05/nakba-start-1948-170522073908625.html.

ccal construct and tool of capitalist-colonial oppression, an extension of a militarized police state, and white supremacy as a political ethos.

[54] "Israel's regime of oppression against the Palestinian people is a special cocktail of settler-colonialism-occupation, and apartheid in which erasure of the indigenous Palestinian populations is the goal." Omar Barghouti, "The Cultural Boycott: Israel vs. South Africa", 2015 [online] Hyperallergic. Available at: https://hyperallergic.com/212014/the-cultural-boycott-israel-vs-south-africa%E2%80%A8/

[55] "The government and corporate media celebrated the town as the "model" for a new era of social stability and rising living standards. But this vision was based solidly on racism; deed restrictions, backed by New York State courts, limited the 17,400 newly constructed houses exclusively to white families".

[55] Danny Sha, "Red-lining and the historical roots of housing segregation in New York City". (July 28, 2009). [online] Available at: https://liberationschool.org/red-lining-and-the-historical-roots-of-housing-segregation-in-new-york-city/

 "The South African neo-apartheid state is still very invested in the dehumanization of Black people. With 64.2% of the African/Black population in South Africa living in poverty, there is a strong necessity to form varied identities/humanities outside of the suffocating cloud of settler-colonial rule."

[56] Kate Wilkinson," FACTSHEET: South Africa'S Official Poverty Numbers | Africa Check". Africa Check, 2018. https://africacheck.org/factsheets/factsheet-south-africas-official-poverty-numbers/.

[57] Kareem Estefan; Carin Kuoni; Laura Raicovich, *Assuming Boycott : Resistance, Agency and Cultural Production*. (New York : OR Books, 2017)

[58] South African History Online, "South Africa's Academic and Cultural Boycott", 2017 [online] Available at: https://www.sahistory.org.za/article/south-africas-academic-and-cultural-boycott

[59] Kareem Estefan; Carin Kuoni; Laura Raicovich, *Assuming Boycott : Resistance, Agency and Cultural Production*. (New York : OR Books, 2017)

[60] Particularly through public theatre in this context.

[61] Content from an interview with Ismail Mahomed, Chief Executive Director of Market Theatre Foundation. Johannesburg, SA

[62] Haydn Cornish-Jenkins," Despite The 1994 Political Victory Against Apartheid, Its Economic Legacy Persists", South African History Online, 2015. https://www.sahistory.org.za/article/despite-1994-political-victory-against-apartheid-its-economic-legacy-persists-haydn-cornish-

[63] "BDS Movement",Cultural Boycott, 2018. [online] Available at: https://bdsmovement.net/cultural-boycott

[64] The right to return is a central tool of decolonizing/un-erasing Palestinian humanity

[65] While the neo-apartheid South African state has aims for expansion of economic and political power, the non-humanity for the African subject in South Africa needs their labor to be the driving force of the maintenance of white power. While the Zionist state also exploits Palestinian labor, the core yarn for the project is to permanently disappear/erase the Palestinian African and Arab populations as the construction of the militarized state are fundamentally rooted in this erasure.

[66] Keleketla! Library is an interdisciplinary, independent library based in the Joubert Park area of inner-city Johannesburg. The project describes itself as a collection of projects that share a concern with the creation of stories through a variety of modes and media, based on a dynamic and fluid interaction between audience and storyteller – through the spoken word, music, artmaking, film, performance, writing, reading and so on. Their projects include but are not limited to; a lending and reference library, after-school programs, and experimental international and community projects.

[66] "keleketla!library – a context", 2008. https://keleketla.org/2008/09/08/keleketlalibrary-a-context/

[67] Jota Mombaça, "Sounds *That Resist Oblivion: The Golden Dreams Of Keleketla! Library* | Contemporary And. Contemporaryand.Com", 2018. https://www.contemporaryand.com/magazines/sounds-that-resist-oblivion-the-golden-dreams-of-keleketla-library/

[68] Sylvia Wynter, *Rethinking 'Aesthetics': Notes Towards a Deciphering Practice,* (Trenton, NJ : Africa World Press, 1992), 240.

[69] Such as conversations, jam sessions, DJ sets, and other gatherings

[70] The Congress of the People was a meeting held in Kliptown, South Africa on 26 June 1955 to compose the vision of the South African people. The Freedom Charter was drawn up at the gathering; this charter became the manifesto of the African National Congress and a symbol of internal apartheid. For More See:("The Congress Of The People, Kliptown 1955" 2011)

"Who We Are", Keleketla Media Arts Project, 2018. https://keleketla.org/about/

[71] "Who We Are", Keleketla Media Arts Project, 2018. https://keleketla.org/about/

[72] Statement by Rangoato Hlasane during an interview entitled "Reflections (One) - Keleketla! Library Presents 100 Meter Radius And 56 Years To The Treason Trial". 2015

[73] «education», Keleketla Media Arts Project, 2018. https://keleketla.org/education/#:~:text=The%20Keleketla!,the%20country%20and%20the%20continent.

[74] High School and Young Practitioners

[75] For more on this see: Wynter, Sylvia. 1992. "Rethinking Aesthetics: Notes to a Deciphering Practice" (pp. 237-279) in Ex-iles: Essays on Caribbean Cinema. African World Press.

[76] Maryam Monalisa Gharavi, "Interview With The Late Juliano Mer-Khamis: We Are Freedom Fighters", The Electronic Intifada, 2011. https://electronicintifada.net/content/interview-late-juliano-mer-khamis-we-are-freedom-fighters/9295.

[77] "In 1948, Arna served in the Palmach, Zionist strike force. She then joined the Communist party and married the Nazareth-born Palestinian intellectual Saliba Khamis. Arna became a human-rights activist who lived and worked among Palestinians, establishing art education centres for children in Jenin who were affected by the violence imposed on them."

Aisha Gani, "Jenin's Freedom Theatre: From Death And Destruction, A Message Of Hope", The Guardian, 2014. https://www.theguardian.com/stage/2014/mar/03/freedom-theatre-palestinian-refugee-camp-jenin-uk-tour.

[78] The Freedom Theatre, "What We Do", 2018. Web. http://www.thefreedomtheatre.org/what-we-do/
[79] Maryam Monalisa Gharavi, "Interview With The Late Juliano Mer-Khamis: We Are Freedom Fighters", The Electronic Intifada, 2011. https://electronicintifada.net/content/interview-late-juliano-mer-khamis-we-are-freedom-fighters/9295.
[80] For more on Freedom Theatre projects, see: http://www.thefreedomtheatre.org/what-we-do/
[81] The Freedom Theatre, "What We Do", 2018. Web. http://www.thefreedomtheatre.org/what-we-do/
[82] It is unclear if this still happens on a weekly basis.
[83] Jawad, Rania, *Staging Resistance in Bil'in: The Performance of Violence in a Palestinian Village*, (TDR 1988- 55, no. 4, 2011): 128-43. http://www.jstor.org/stable/41407112
[84] *Bil'in 17.6.2011- Jenin's Freedom Theatre in Bil'in*. [online] YouTube. https://www.youtube.com/watch?v=SDdtr_HQzFQ&ab_channel=DavidReeb
[85] Emphasis added. In the original quote, the author uses the word "marching through".
[86] I would have liked to be clear about what these phrases were but I don't speak Arabic
[87] During these actions, sound bombs and 0.22 caliber live ammunition were also used at times
[88] Edited by Gaye Theresa Johnson and Alex Lubin, *Futures of Black Radicalism*, (Verso Books, 2017)
[89] Bell Hooks. "CHOOSING THE MARGIN AS A SPACE OF RADICAL OPENNESS." Framework: The Journal of Cinema and Media, no. 36 (1989): 203. http://www.jstor.org/stable/44111660.
[90] Katherine McKittrick, *Sylvia Wynter: On Being Human as Praxis* (Duke University Press, 2015).
[91] Edited by Gaye Theresa Johnson and Alex Lubin, *Futures of Black Radicalism*, (Verso Books, 2017)
[92] Robin Grearson, "The Aesthetics Of Gentrification, And New York'S Top-Down Approach To Change", Hyperallergic, 2018. https://hyperallergic.com/440547/the-aesthetics-of-gentrification-and-new-yorks-top-down-approach-to-change/
[93] According to US census data, between 2014-2018, foreign-born persons were 35.4% of the Bronx population.
[94] Katherine McKittrick, *Sylvia Wynter: On Being Human as Praxis* (Duke University Press, 2015), 147.
[95] Visit galleryofthestreets.org/ for more information on Gallery of the Streets projects
[96] Emphasis added. In the original quote, the author uses the word "formal".
[97] "Gallery of the Streets", 2020. http://galleryofthestreets.org/
[98] Kelley, *Freedom Dreams*, p. xii.
[99] Gaye Theresa Johnson and Alex Lubin (eds.) *Futures of Black Radicalism*, (Verso Books, 2017)
[100] Robin Grearson, "The Aesthetics Of Gentrification, And New York'S Top-Down Approach To Change", *Hyperallergic,* 2018. https://hyperallergic.com/440547/the-aesthetics-of-gentrification-and-new-yorks-top-down-approach-to-change/
[101] According to US census data, between 2014-2018, foreign born persons were 35.4% of the Bronx population.
[102] Katherine McKittrick, *Sylvia Wynter: On Being Human as Praxis* (Duke University Press, 2015), 147.
[103] Visit galleryofthestreets.org/ for more information on Gallery of the Streets projects
[104] "Gallery of the Streets", 2020. http://galleryofthestreets.org/
[105] Kelley, Freedom Dreams, p.vxii.

Dalaeja Foreman (she/they) is a community organizer, curator, cultural worker and first-generation Caribbean-Brooklynite. As a hood-intellectual, their work focuses on political education, Black and Indigenous Autonomy, and community control through community preservation. Radical pedagogy, reclaiming public space, and liberatory action are central to Dalaeja's curatorial and organizing practices. Specifically with the goal of prototyping counter-hegemonic ideologies and actions, combating internalized misconceptions oppressed people have of ourselves and emphasizing resistance through direct action and cultural production. She is one of three founders of the wood-working cooperative, breadfruit.

The posthuman racial ecology of W.E. B. DuBois

The article brings together the geographies, economies, and ecologies of the African American South, Wilhelmine Germany, and the Algorithmic South to illustrate how the cultivation of racial identity intersects at various points with the progress of both the Plantationocene and Anthropocene. W.E.B. Du Bois acts as a modern locus for these developments through his sociobiological conceptualisation of the 'New Negro'. Through that endeavour, Du Bois prototypically casts himself as posthuman, allowing us to read his data visualisations as evidence of how he plotted a course for racial advancement through techniques of sociological reification, aesthetic rarefication, and managed development.

text by **Stephanie Polsky**

Humanity for some five centuries has positioned itself at the fulcrum of socio-political order. The posthuman is suggestive of a being capable of existing apart from that order; something situated beyond its former punitive borders of reason and sentience. Nonetheless, the posthuman, like its predecessor, has to take its place among the respective role allocation, social hierarchies, and divisions of labour that remain attendant to social being. Consequently, a coloniality of power very much persists within this redefinition of mankind and race as a technology remains both indispensable and irreplaceable to the reproduction of what qualifies as posthuman. The new paradigm of the posthuman elaborates the domination formerly expressed in terms of humanity by extending a logic that racialised others can only be assimilated into the world wide web of life and internet of things as beings granted temporary status and defined against a criterion of developmental potential that begins and ends within the contours of White masculinity. Within this context, race must be critically reassessed to plot its iteration within the post-liberal concept of the posthuman and localise its portent within the critical ecological narratives of both the Plantationocene and the Anthropocene.

The category of posthuman relies upon the being of mankind itself, in all of its "multiple self-inscripting, auto-instituting modalities".[1] Therefore, it presumes itself as the measure of the postdigital world in much the same way as its predecessor. Whilst it claims to have decentred systems of knowledge, in reality, these continue to concentrate authority by carrying out the orders of autopoiesis. Artificial intelligence and cybernetics subtly exclude the factors of race and gender and deny the emergence of multiple sites of enunciation. Posthumanism's reliance on Western exceptionalism, technological fetishism, and ableism belie its furthered commitment to a false narrative of inclusion inherent to the category of the human, which promotes on one level a superficial concept of inclusion through the lauding of the value of diversity, whilst in the same thought process failing to question the knowledge, ideologies, and privileges that subtend the very being of its sociogenic invention.

This overreliance of universal proclamation with the very term posthuman reveals a confounding in both the temporal and organic sense of what we might classify today as life. Indeed, "critical posthumanism claims to value radical inclusivity (of nature, ecovitality, and nonhuman animal life), hyper-relativity, and complexity".[2] However, in so doing, it assumes equality of interest and participation within that inclusion as the basic level of existence. It also assumes that the experience of subjectivity is one open to enhancement of a technological nature, without taking responsibility for its previous, historic role in stipulating what constitutes progress towards a shared condition of humanity, or more precisely, recognition as part of humankind by these other entities.

Within the scope of being's relativity, the figure of its others is somehow too maladaptive, or requiring of corrective to fully participate in humankind. This stance establishes a proprietary relationship from the very beginning of this project to extend humanity to others. That gesture of contemporary inclusion must necessarily imply a prior historical expulsion. It is this feature that haunts the category of the posthuman bringing it into proximity with an afterlife of anger, grief, and dispossession that is not readily absolved from memory. For this gesture to be achieved the category of humanity has to wilfully unmoor itself from its historical situation and its cultural claims to exist and to not be, in the words of Rosi Braidiotti, "'bound negatively by shared vulnerability, the guilt of ancestral communal violence, or the melancholia of unpayable ontological debts'".[3] Within Braidotti's onto-epistemological framework lurks a fundamental opacity; the inability to account for the absence of Black feeling within the structure of contemporary civil society and the purview of representation. This inability to assign humanity subjectivity, and thus positive sentience, to blackness persists as a modality of violence that continuously "produces blackness as a locus of incapacities".[4] As a consequence, "Black affective responses are only legible as signs of pathology, further reifying blackness-as-subhumanity on an "epistemic, material, metaphysical, ontological" level.[5]

Tyrone S. Palmer situates, "this inability to conceive of Black emotion, to imagine the Black as a sentient being with interiority," within "the history of racial chattel slavery;" wherein white humanness was defined by its negation within the contours of the slave body.[6] Palmer argues that "while not all 'sentient beings' are endowed with subjectivity, sentience is itself a precondition for subjectivity within the modern field of representation—the Subject has consciousness; is self-knowing, self-reflecting, and feeling. Denying and/or contesting the Black's sentience, then, has a dual function: to write Black people outside of the Human and position them as immutably affectable, unfeeling repositories for brute force".[7] The effect of this in many ways is to socially deaden them. This situation is especially significant at a time when posthumanism socially and politically advocates for the agency of nonhuman beings seemingly without regard to a world where Black bodies have yet to achieve full lively personhood.

Christina Sharpe asserts that these bodies must be conceived of through a prism of "containment, regulation, punishment, capture and captivity" as constitutive of a "total climate" through which the Black body must travel.[8] The contemporary middle passage of these bodies navigates between "ungrievable death" and "lives mean to be unliveable," and proceeds in such a way that it comes into intimate contact with the immigrant and the refugee, that is to say, stateless people who become the subject of forced movement and the object of surveillance.[9] This is indeed a form of consciousness, but one pointedly with no innate virtue. Rather, its value must be one that is externally assigned. This is not to say that there is no place where the Black body might yet thrive amidst this harsh societal atmosphere. The trick is to keep breathing, to literally maintain aspiration, within a social ecology that constricts the basic atmosphere of life. At the same time, the state concocts new modes of violence that conform with the values of a neoliberalism seeking at every point to contain resistance and promote submission, continually registering bodies within a system where nonparticipation equals death.

Environment, figures here in the formulation of the Plantationocene as an alternative reading of the Anthropocene, which stresses the centrality of slave agriculture to the formation of human-made climate change. What is important to stress here is that the "plantation isn't just a material institution that has led to the planetary catastrophes of the Plantationocene; it's also a set of ideas, archives, ideologies" that have on one hand, "become the foundation for Western capitalist endeavors at large" and on the other, have cultivated "what Vandana Shiva has called 'monocultures of the mind'" where "ideologies of the plantation ...fundamentally shape how human beings relate to each other and to the natural world".[10] Anna Lowenhaupt Tsing defines the plantation as "those ecological simplifications in which living things are transformed into resources, future assets by removing them from their life worlds".[11] Tsing defines plantations as "machines of replication", and thereafter, as "ecologies devoted to purification and the production of the same". This narrative persists online through the introduction of new algorithmic "codes that regulate, profit from, and conceptualize spaces of absolute otherness".[12]

Within this new virtual economy, marginalised communities continue to be the most heavily exploited, cultivated, and surveyed. It is, therefore, no coincidence that spaces the internet seeks to smartly regulate are disproportionately inhabited by barely surviving individuals of colour, nor that a new set of White American male masters have located novel means through which to carve out profit by manipulating their behavioural futures. Within this configuration, the plot concerns the violation of the geography of social reproduction that occurs when the Black body is coded as non-individual and as fundamentally entangled within the chain of productivity, within a monoculture of production and singular output. Therefore, it might be possible to conceive that it is not only their bodies that capitalism exploits, but equally their minds that endeavour to generate creative responses to their perpetual mistreatment, only to have had that value taken away from them by way of operative, extracting relationality.

In this scenario, blackness remains relegated to the substructure of the world and escape only is possible through an inversion of capitalist geography, namely, by refusing to contribute to its expansion and operating instead at the sub-individual level where it becomes possible to refuse capitulation to certain forms of ensnarement, which we now have to associate with the worldwide web. This web is a pseudo-natural formation that when in the bodies of its consumers' brains, forms a sticky build-up of data correlates with their progressive cognitive decline, indicating a link between the preponderance of artificial intelligence and destruction of organic thinking. Information becomes one in several colonial commodities operational on a supra-individual level to further the plantation complex and remain in the business of entrapment. Another pole remains, however, the urban. Here is possible to still evade the normative and analytical models of the plantation economy, and proliferate networks both human and non-human to reimagine still ways of planting, cultivating and harvesting that offer much greater flexibility in terms of compromising stability and disrupting reproductive mechanisms of social and biological control.

As one of the founders of the discipline of Sociology in the United States, W.E.B. Du Bois sought to globally position himself as America's leading racial authority in the first half of the twentieth century. His theorisation of modernity, biology, and racial identity bears the trappings of his interiorisation of Victorian eugenic principles characteristic of his formative age. Du Bois' body acts locus for these developments as he attempts over decades to cast himself as the first dark posthuman. His situation allows us to reflect on how he plotted the uplift of his race through techniques of sociological reification, aesthetic rarefication, and controlled development that would have a profound consequence for the formulation of the New Negro and Pan-Africanism as interrelated conceptual projects.

Du Bois spent three semesters studying at the Friedrich Wilhelm University of Berlin as a Ph.D. student in Sociology. He focussed his studies during this period on a comparative analysis of agricultural smallholdings in the United States versus Germany. In the years following this sojourn, draw profitably on accounts of both his personal and academic relationships to Berlin, allowing him to ascend to the pantheon of black intellectual thought in the first half of the twentieth century. Du Bois was born just a quarter-century onwards from the abolition of slavery in the United States. He would have come of age as the first generation of young adults to make their way into the larger world following on from that wounding legacy, and instead rehabilitated himself beyond that formative injury by adopting the appearance not solely of a Berlin university student, but also perhaps more significantly of a vaguely aristocratic [White]

Berliner. This was an instance of double consciousness, but not in the usual way it is portrayed as Du Bois' intellectual legacy, identifying with both a black and white lens of perception simultaneously. Rather, it seems plausible that for Du Bois in his person, with his relatively fair-skinned complexion, had convinced himself that he could pass as a member of the German nobility, which comprised the top tenth of Wilhelmine society, hence his later notion of an African American talented tenth.

Du Bois often credited Germany with conferring upon him his humanity, as opposed to race, and "'this was primarily the result not so much of my study, as of my human companionship, unveiled by the accident of color'".[13] This idea that his race was an accident, a misfortune visited upon him rather than something innate to his being is something further borne out by his assertion that his relocation to Germany provided him with an existential 'do-over' as it were, where he could comport himself widely within the space of an environment free of racial precarity.

Sieglinde Lemke remarks with incredulity that Du Bois could frequent turn of the century Berlin "at a time when 'imported' Africans were exhibited at so-called Menschenschauen at the Berlin Zoo" and still maintain the opinion of it as a society free of categorical racism.[14] At another level of spectatorship, of course, it was possible to do so. Sat amongst exclusively White German academics, it is entirely possible that Du Bois could look upon this same institutional scene and feel reified in his humanity by present company. He was indeed not an animal at all, because, by their recognition of him as a human, such an equivalence was made impossible. He was no African, but he was certainly an American. It was this nationalistic virtue that set him apart and made his appearance viable in Germany.

Du Bois strategically identified the American South, as opposed to Africa, as the ancestral homeland of Black Americans. He needed to develop a founding mythology for his people based on this environment, which prompted him to join his sociological work with fiction writing from the late 1880s onwards. He writes as a person temporarily situating himself within the Black South, but significantly someone who is not resident to it. His earliest focus is on the plantation system and its function as a political, social, economic, and fictional apparatus brought to materially bear on the lives of the Black other which are made continuous with cotton as the predominant regional commodity. The bearing of plantation is something that is accomplished through the continuous violence, coercion, and exploitation of the Black body that supports and maintains it as a distinct economy of forced agricultural cultivation and compulsory sexual reproduction. Together these formations produced their own version of both modernity and capitalism that exceeds the formal system of slavery, establishing a definition of culture that at every point is subtended by the manipulation of the environment that surrounds it.

Selective sexual reproduction is something that stood at the heart of Du Bois' understanding of racial evolution. Those who were the product of field slavery, to Du Bois' mind, were of "poor eugenic status, because it nurtured "the survival of those who evolution would have naturally eliminated creating a biological underclass that could never be developed into fit citizens".[15] Du Bois projected that in a post-emancipation context, an overwhelming percentage "of them would die out through genetic weaknesses".[16] The modern condition of race was hindered by "the inability of some of its members to completely evolve" due to the recent legacy of field slavery.[17] Du Bois sees Negros as a mass product who must recognise that value of selective cultivation; "they must learn that among human races and groups, as among vegetables, quality and not mere quantity really counts".[18] What stands out in Du Bois criticism of this group is his frustration with them directed from a position of superior status, because he chose to identify *with* them, not *as* them.

What troubled Du Bois was his perception that the majority of Black reproduction was happening amongst those who were essentially genetically inferior. They remain for him a distant subject to be studied and classified. In practice, his relationship with the Black population was one that for the most part did not exist. "Apart from his family, Du Bois had little or no sustained connection to a larger black community".[19] He defined himself as a leader of the Negro community, but not a Negro himself. His prejudices were more greatly based on regionalism versus race itself, insofar as a Northerner free Black person, he came to bitterly resent the appearance of Southern Blacks that were more directly the product of slavery than their Northern freeman counterparts. The migration of Southern Negros North meant that these Blacks would all be lumped together in the minds of White onlookers who would class them as equally uncivilised and ignorant subjects. The better class of Blacks, including Du Bois, would be made to suffer if Whites could not perceive their difference. Again, this is cast through the lens of being mixed race as a visual marker of obvious racial superiority who "naturally" made up "the aristocracy of the Negro".[20] The sexual economy of the slave plantation figures into the biological making of this elite class who are largely "descended from the house servant class" in union with their plantation masters.[21] As a consequence, Du Bois asserts "'the subsequent generation contains many mulattoes'".[22] However, is not just biology which gives these contemporary offspring their advantage in life, "'there is evidence of good breeding and taste, *a foreigner would hardly think as ex-slaves*'".[23] The foreigner presumably who is in a position to judge as post-emancipation Whites who would perhaps remain aware that lighter-skinned slaves would have been granted access to better qualities of food and shelter and better conditions of labour. Their dwelling within the houses of their masters enabled them to encounter White culture; i.e. the manner and language of their racial superiors. Many would have benefited from intimate relationships with Whites from birth that would make them more sympathetic to their situation, thereby increasing their chances of manumission.

Sexual relations both consensual and non-consensual were a tacit expectation of those viewed as property by their masters, and the offspring of these unions by the mid-nineteenth century, instituted their children mulatto as a socially advantaged was institutionalising the colour line throughout the South as a means of determining societal privilege. It was not only Whites who adopted this mentality but also many mulattoes themselves who admired Western civilisation above the merits of their own and strove to attain recognition based on economic, social and intellectual criteria that White culture had established. The limits of Black assimilation continued to abut against pigmentary bias.

Du Bois' reliance on eugenic assumptions regarding racial classification was deployed explicitly to promote mulatto superiority. His reliance on creating a vast archive of racial documentation including the typing of physical features, demonstration of figures of superior intellect, and displaying of moral character amongst his Negro subjects all stood in the service of proving degrees of racial mixing had in fact biologically, economically and culturally improved the African American race. Du Bois was so convinced of this fact, as Shawn Michelle Smith argues, that he presented the documentation of his own body as evidence of what this New Negro body exemplifies to the world. Photograph after photograph captures the elite likeness of Du Bois from his childhood "dressed in princely attire" to his "scholarly robes" and finally to his "formal suits" all suggestive of a biological determinism enlivening this trajectory of greatness.[24] It is for this reason that Du Bois figures himself into his archive a star in the ascendant around which other greats congregate.

In 1900, at the *Exposition Universelle* in Paris, he adored himself in "a long Prince Albert coat, a tall hat, as well as a cane and gloves".[25] It is significant to note that Du Bois chose to debut this new European, as opposed to specifically German, affect at the opening of his African Pavilion. His series of data portraits debuted there was entitled "Exhibit of American Negroes." Within it, he holds himself up literally as the measure against which these abstract others are judged. No one in these portraits is identified by name, but rather solely by characteristic. These photographs would be recycled into other projects that supported his conceptualisation of uplift modelled along interracial and eugenic lines of thought that would only intensify throughout the decades of the 1920s and 1930s in concert with the rise of a mulatto intelligentsia largely beholden to Du Bois. Their project from the beginning aimed to go beyond the human in its surveillance of what is classed as progress.

In the case of the 1900 exhibition, Du Bois "headed a team of alumni and students from Atlanta University" to create "a collection of graphs, charts, maps, and tables that were generated from a mix of existing records and empirical data" that would assign meaning to the photographic portraits that featured as the foundation for the project.[26] While the project is often described as one that pioneered data visualisation, what is most compelling about this constellation of information is how it deploys photography to depict a generation living on beyond the era of slavery in the American South. At the turn of the new century, these bodies remain proximate to both nature and demise even as a new infrastructure of commerce, education, neighbourhood, and church builds up steadily around them the pallor of slavery stills hangs heavily around these scenes shadowing the very concept of Black portraiture itself. The technology continues to segregate only able to record in black and white making the founding of their register something deeply tinged by both the legacy and landscape of the South, even as the race continues to move forwards it reveals some quality of forbearance and foreclosure of both a people and a geography.

Du Bois appreciates the differences between Northern and Southern capitalism lies in the intimate economies of cultivation itself, wherein Du Bois suggests that African American lives *are* cotton, and accordingly their progress is plotted to conform to the logistics of the cotton industry, consistent with their accumulative potential at every point in the lifecycle of its use and value to energise a greater capitalism indicative of the global South. Du Bois' remedy is to literally uplift these lives from the soil to which they were born and transplant them to flourish within the contours of a North metropolitan imperialism. Only this doesn't entirely fit with their story, nor acknowledge complicity between North and South in authoring their uneven economic conditioning. Monopoly, speculation, and accumulation all have their role to play in the exploitation of African Americans, poor Whites, and children, as does the proprietorial surveillance forced upon these bodies by their structural owners. These owners would continue to innovate how labour could be enforced upon these bodies through the institutions of sharecropping and the chain gang which perpetuated the tyranny at the centre of slavery's original plot to exteriorise their value. "As W. E. B. Du Bois bemoans at the turn of the century, America's growing prosperity rested on its failure to regard Black life as 'more than meat'"; meaning more than a potentially wayward commodity to be systematically overseen and managed.[27] This bears upon the formation of Black geographies characteristic of the plantation that persist into contemporary architectures of racial violence.

Katherine McKittrick argues that the African American experience is one indicative of "a spatial continuity between the living and the dead, between science and storytelling, and between past and present".[28] The control and administration of inhuman or barely habitable geographies have their beginnings in the plantation system, which is built to marginalise and degrade the liveliness of Black bodies. The violence enacted therein can only be understood through the concept of spatial manufacture, insofar as the plantation plots out a reality whereby "the actual growth of narratives, food, and cultural practices" functions in tandem to at once socialise order within the context of a dehumanizing agricultural economy, and "materialize the deep connections between blackness and the earth and foster values that challenge systemic violence".[29] When the formal plantation system is dismantled a new urbanisation arises to take its place functionally, commercially as well as racially. The urban centre thereafter emerges as a space perpetually riven with a narrative of geographic superiority and inferiority. There is another layer at work here; a subterranean one in which an underclass of life continues to toil on the outskirts of a more prosperous society. Here poverty has sunken in perhaps most deeply, existing prosaically in the grounding of a faith in mankind that subtends the world.

Slavery casts not only humans but the whole of the natural world into a framework of violence and dispossession such that the bodies of representation Du Bois' draws upon to account for its uplift, become once more subsumed into the foundation of plantation life -once the only means of life support. Given that reality, what Du Bois instead banks is the profit to be drawn in allowing them to circulate otherwise as evidence born out the data that potentially something positive was achieved there. The numbers suggest that the Negro race itself has potential and in so doing, allows them to register value beyond the category of human being, which has historically alluded them, towards the category of socio-biological engineering, which promises that man can be categorically exceeded given the space do so. If slavery had confined the Negro to the peculiar position of social death and infinite productivity, their emancipation would require of them an evolution from the in-human beyond the category of mere personhood to that of a successor class of humanity that Du Bois asserts "has yet a message for the world".[30] This made of the body a work of complicated transmission, something to be seen and understood as propaganda in service to the greater programme of racial pride and uplift. The body, in this, sense becomes a scene of intersubjectivity achieved through social networks, relations, and attachments that transcend the late nineteenth-century knowledge and politics in the trans-Atlantic world that circumscribed what constituted human life and racial performance.

Here, Justine Wells argues, it is possible to conceive of a Du Bois who "gestured toward a theory of race as a more broadly material and ecological construction".[31] The problem that Du Bois confronts is a blackness "made up not only of human discourses but also of entire environments... of the ruined cotton rows, one-room cabins, and 'big houses' that endure as part of the Black race's historic enslavement and its continued debility" that allow Black identity to sense its own emergence through the lens of both the social and the ecological as it carves out a space of material being that exceeds what is formally human.[32] Unlike its white counterpart, blackness cannot rely upon dominion in its bearing upon nonhuman resources, but rather must seek a relationship of cooperation between itself and such entities if it is to achieve any sort of lasting articulation of itself. This is what furnishes blackness with its human-nonhuman identity and its ambiguous potential. Whiteness, by contrast, becomes the more rigid form of cultivation, hindered by its preoccupations with intensive operations to preserve itself through the dispossession and dismantlement of the others it claims as its property. Reconstitution, as a consequence, becomes something at the heart of the richness of the Black experience.

In the context of the posthuman, this offers "the potential for co-constitutive thriving [to] be opened between peoples and environments that had historically suffered oppression in tandem".[33] Recoded and decoded by economic, material, and political realities, these legacies might be once again played out for the benefit of their full incorporation into the human record, allowing for a plurality of data to emerge from those who had systematically been denied sovereignty, intelligence, and expression. Progress, in the end, will come down to sorting of a very particular nature –zeros and ones to be read on and detected not by humans but by a different sort of awareness. The promise is that bodies that have never been allowed to materialise will triumph in an era that can plot life itself differently and bring it into a dynamic configuration with "the crows, the winds, the rains and the trees" that surround and attend its progress.[34] An errant blackness that has always existed outside human paradigms can find itself settled within this new economy of the diagram linking it to the power of a different form of existence as an index rather than a record. Imagine how that will play out, with reference to the places where a plurality of blackness occurs. Black representation becomes then a measure of something as it relates to the natural world. That something, in turn, becomes the stuff of vital augmentation versus flat debility.

Endnotes

[1] Sylvia Wynter, "Unsettling the coloniality of being/power/truth/freedom: Towards the human, after man, its overrepresentation—An argument." *CR: The new centennial review*, 3.3 (2003): 330, https://doi.org/10.1353/ncr.2004.0015.

[2] Philip Butler, "Making Enhancement Equitable: A Racial Analysis of the Term 'human animal' and the Inclusion of Black Bodies in Human Enhancement." *Journal of Posthuman Studies* 2.1 (2018): 107, https://

doi.org/10.5325/jpoststud.2.1.0106.

[3] Rosi Braidotti, *The Posthuman*, (Cambridge, UK: Polity Press, 2013), 101, quoted in Philip Butler, "Making Enhancement Equitable", 112.

[4] Tyrone S. Palmer, "'What Feels More Than Feeling?': Theorizing the Unthinkability of Black Affect." *Critical Ethnic Studies,* 3.2 (2017): 32, https://doi.org/10.5749/jcritethnstud.3.2.0031.

[5] Palmer, "'What Feels More Than Feeling," 32.

[6] Palmer, 46.

[7] Palmer, 51.

[8] Christina, Sharpe, *In the Wake: On Blackness and Being*, (Durham: Duke University Press, 2016), 22.

[9] Sharpe, *In the Wake,* 22.

[10] Natalie Aikens, Amy Clukey, Amy K. King, and Isadora Wagner, "South to The Plantationocene", *ASAP Journal*. 17 Oct 2019. http://asapjournal.com/south-to-the-plantationocene-natalie-aikens-amy-clukey-amy-k-king-and-isadora-wagner/.

[11] *The Barnard Center for Research on Women Videos*, "Anna Lowenhaupt Tsing: A Feminist Approach to the Anthropocene: Earth Stalked by Man." December 18, 2015. Video, 1:09:52 https://vimeo.com/149475243.

[12] Katherine McKittrick, "Plantation futures." *Small Axe: A Caribbean Journal of Criticism* 17.3 (42) (2013): 15, https://www.muse.jhu.edu/article/532740.

[13] William Edward Burghardt Du Bois, *The Oxford W.E.B. Du Bois,* (New York: Oxford University Press, 2007) 100, quoted in Sieglinde Lemke, "Berlin and Boundaries: sollen versus geschehen," *boundary* 2 27.3 (2000): 50, https://doi.org/10.1215/01903659-27-3-45.

[14] Lemke, "Berlin and Boundaries", 50.

[15] Shantella Y. Sherman, *In Search of Purity: Popular Eugenics and Racial Uplift Among New Negroes 1915–1935*. PhD dissertation, (Lincoln: University of Nebraska, 2014), 95.

[16] Sherman, *In Search of Purity*, 205.

[17] Sherman, 297.

[18] W.E.B. Du Bois, "Black Folks and Birth Control," *The Birth Control Review*, 16:6 (June 1932): 167.

[19] Charles F Peterson, *Dubois, Fanon, Cabral: The Margins of Elite Anti-colonial Leadership*, (Washington DC: Lexington Books, 2007), 36.

[20] Peterson, *Dubois, Fanon, Cabral*, 36.

[21] John H. Bracey, August Meier, and Elliott M. Rudwick. *The Black Sociologists: The First Half Century*. Belmont, Calif: Wadsworth Pub. Co., 1971), 156 quoted in Peterson, 44.

[22] Bracey *The Black Sociologists,* 156, quoted in Peterson, 44.

[23] Bracey, 156, quoted in Peterson, 44; Peterson's emphasis.

[24] Shawn Michelle Smith, *Photography on the Color Line: W. E. B. Du Bois, Race, and Visual Culture*, (Durham: Duke University Press, 2004) 155.

[25] Kenneth Barkin, "W. E. B. Du Bois' Love Affair with Imperial Germany." *German Studies Review*, vol. 28, no. 2, (2005): 294, https://www.jstor.org/stable/30038150.

[26] Witney Battle-Baptiste, and Britt Rusert, editors, *W. E. B. Du Bois's Data Portraits: Visualizing Black America.* New York: Princeton Architectural Press, 2018), 9.

[27] W. E. B. DuBois, *The Souls of Black Folk*, (Chicago: McClurg, 1907), 94, quoted in Meg Samuelson, "Thinking with Sharks: Racial Terror, Species Extinction, and Other Anthropocene Fault Lines." *Australian Humanities Review* 62 (2018), 39 http://australianhumanitiesreview.org/2018/12/02/thinking-with-sharks-racial-terror-species-extinction-and-the-other-anthropocene-fault-lines/,

[28] McKittrick, "Plantation futures", 2).

[29] McKittrick, 10.

[30] W. E. B. Du Bois, "Strivings of the Negro People." *The Atlantic*, Aug 1987, https://www.theatlantic.com/magazine/archive/1897/08/strivings-of-the-negro-people/305446/.

[31] Justine Wells, "WEB Du Bois and the Conservation of Races: A Piece of Ecological Ancestry." *Rhetoric Society Quarterly* 49.4 (2019): 3, 10.1080/02773945.2019.1634830

[32] Wells "WEB Du Bois and the Conservation of Races, 14.

[33] Wells, 18.

[34] Edwards, Erin E. *The Modernist Corpse: Posthumanism and the Posthumous*. (Minneapolis: University of Minnesota Press, 2018), 93.

Dr Stephanie Polsky is an interdisciplinary writer and academic working in the areas of Media Studies and Visual Culture. Her work explores the confluence of power around race and gender as technologies of governance. Most recently she has worked at California College of the Arts in Critical Studies and Diversity Studies. Her research includes the forthcoming books *The Dark Posthuman: Dehumanization, Technology, and the Atlantic World* (Punctum Books Fall 2022) and *The Photographic Invention of Whiteness: the Visual Cultures of White Atlantic Worlds* (Routledge 2023). Her most recent book is *The End of the Future: Governing Consequence in the Age of Digital Sovereignty* (Academica Press, 2019).

Workers liberation as environmental justice: beyond Amazon's Plantationocene

In this article, Hiba Ali focuses on warehouse worker leaders, Hafsa Hasan and Hibaq Mohamed, associated with Awood Center, a non-for-profit that focuses on mobilizing East African workers in Minneapolis, the latter of who was unjustly fired from an Amazon MSP1 facility in Shakopee, Minnesota. The text is paired with stills of 360 video made by me and released in May 2020 by Daimon Virtual Residencies, Gatineau, Quebec and in Moving Ether Way, *an online exhibition produced byTrinity Square Video in Toronto, Ontario, and curated by Karina Iskandarsjah and Holly Chang.*

text and images by **Hiba Ali**

Since the term Anthropocene's coinage, Jairus Victor Grove, following Kathryn Yusuf's critique of European colonialism, has termed the Anthropocene as Eurocene.[1] The Eurocene refers to chattel slavery and genocidal tactics enacted on Indigenous communities by European imperial forces. In February of 2019, the term, plantationocene, was proposed by Sophie Sapp Moore, Monique Allewaert, Pablo F. Gómez, and Gregg Mitman, as an alternate name for the human geological epoch often called the Anthropocene. They define the term, plantationocene, consists of themes of "racialized violence, land alienation, and species loss".[2] These inequalities are exacerbated by the COVID-19 global pandemic where "gig-economy" precarious labour has evolved to contemporary forms of indentured labour – a type of racialized class warfare. Global workers coalition organized under the slogan, Make Amazon Pay, emphasize Amazon's carbon footprint, "As Amazon's corporate empire expands, so too has its carbon footprint, which is larger than two-thirds of all countries in the world. Amazon's growing delivery and cloud computer businesses are accelerating global climate breakdown".[3] Workers of color coalitions and organizations like The Center for Community Action and Environmental Justice (CCAEJ), a climate justice organization based in San Bernardino, and Awood Center, a community organization that builds economic and political power amongst East African workers in Minnesota, are not only needed but central to defying the corporate-led genocidal tactics in the plantationocene. Amazon operates in a carceral way, the corporation dehumanizes its blue-collar warehouse workers as objects from which to extract all life force. Also, as part of racial capitalism logic, the majority of Amazon's warehouse workers are poor and working-class, Black and brown people. CCAEJ in their Billions Off Our Back campaign highlights the pollution caused by the warehouse and logistics industry, compounded by COVID-19 pandemic.[4]

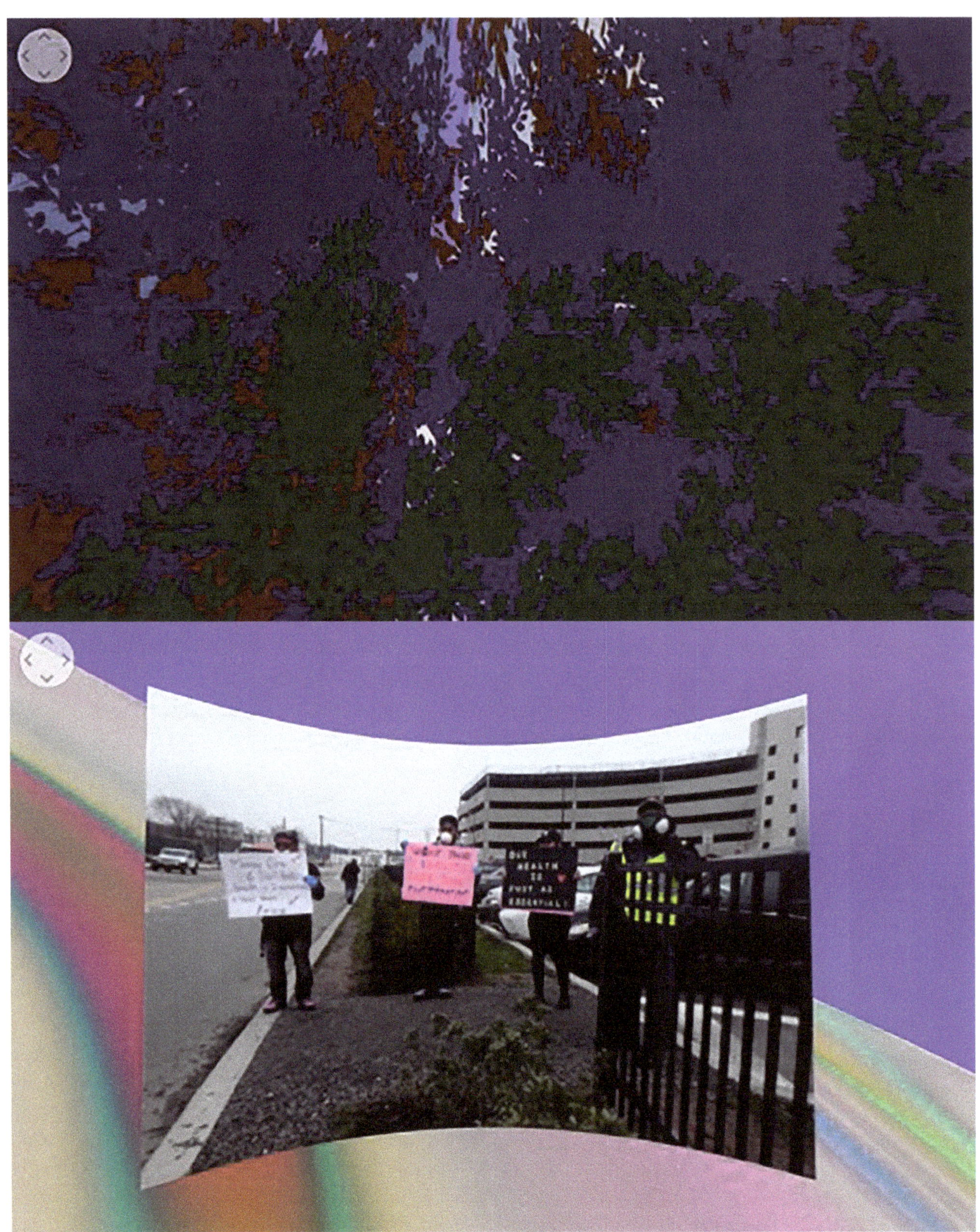

Hiba Aliat

Workers liberation as environmental justice, 2020 © Hiba Aliat

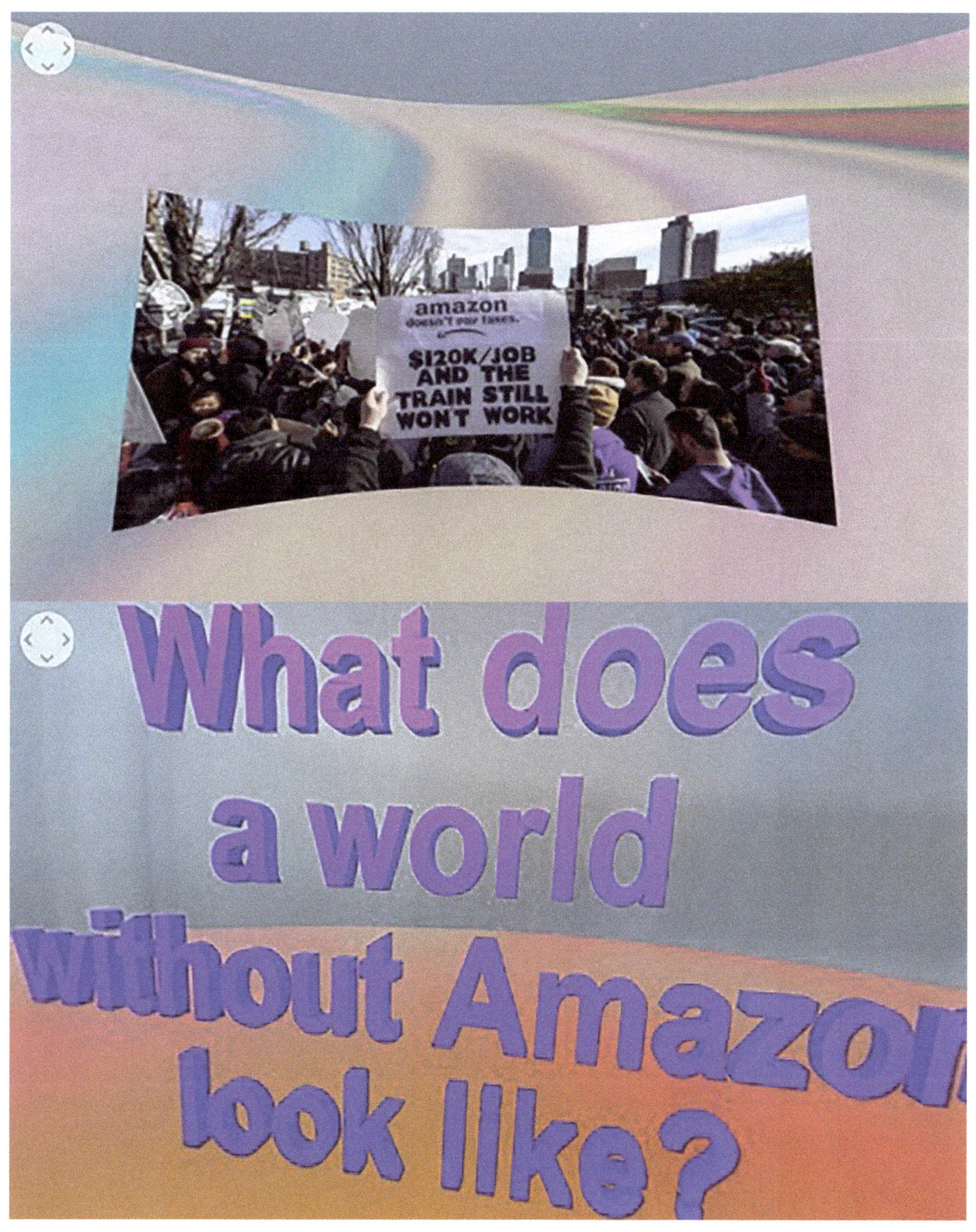

What does
a world
without Amazon
look like?

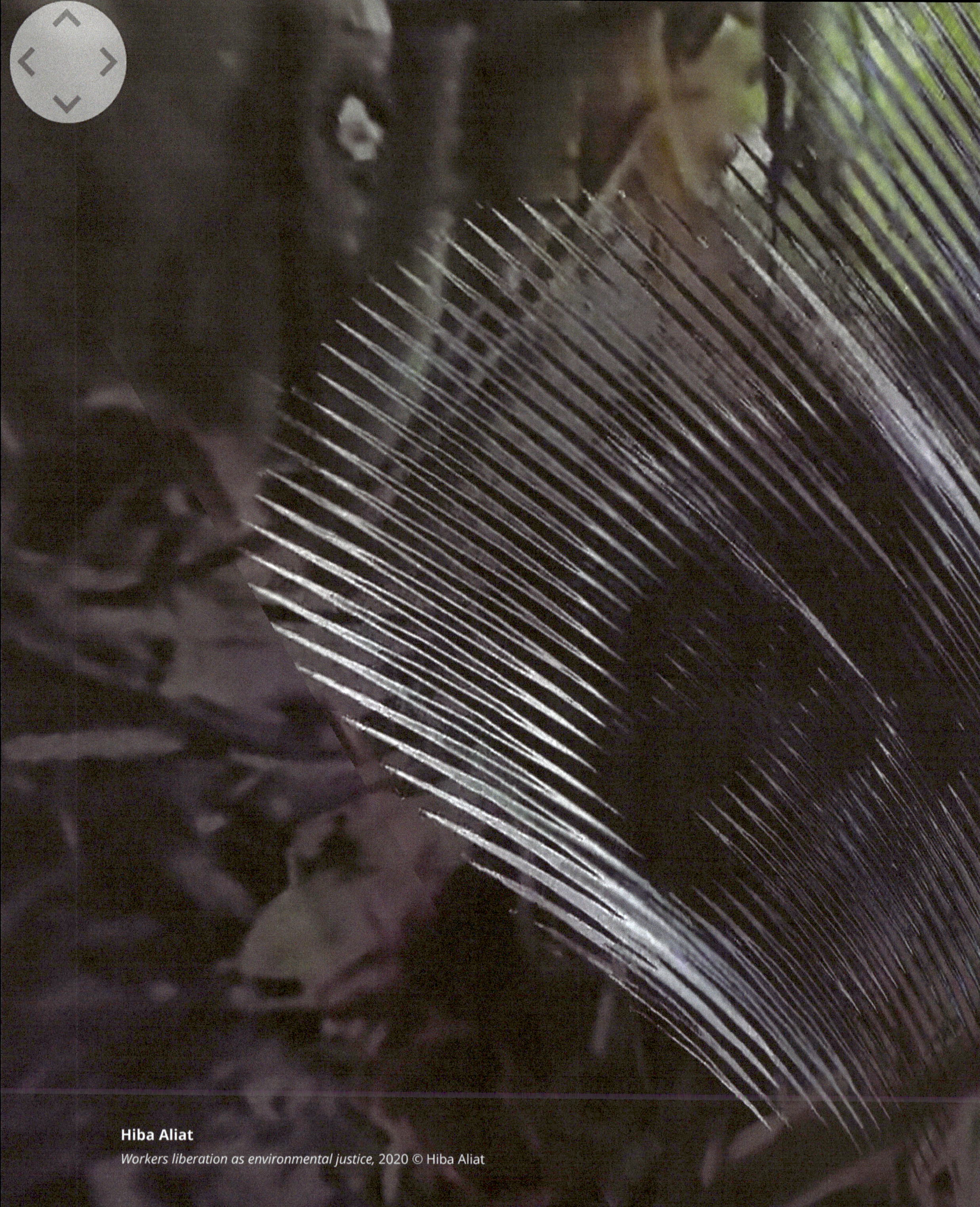

Hiba Aliat
Workers liberation as environmental justice, 2020 © Hiba Aliat

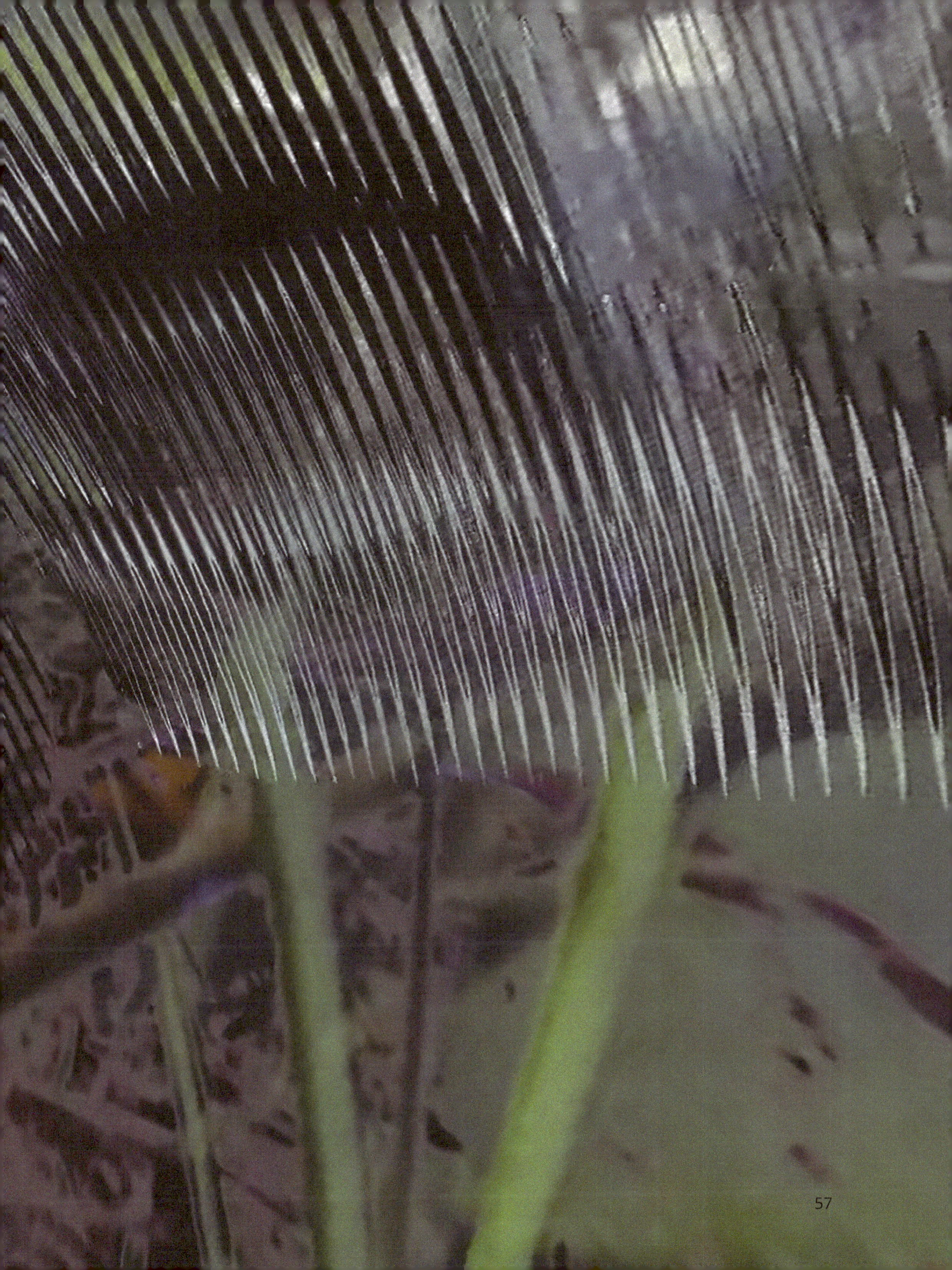

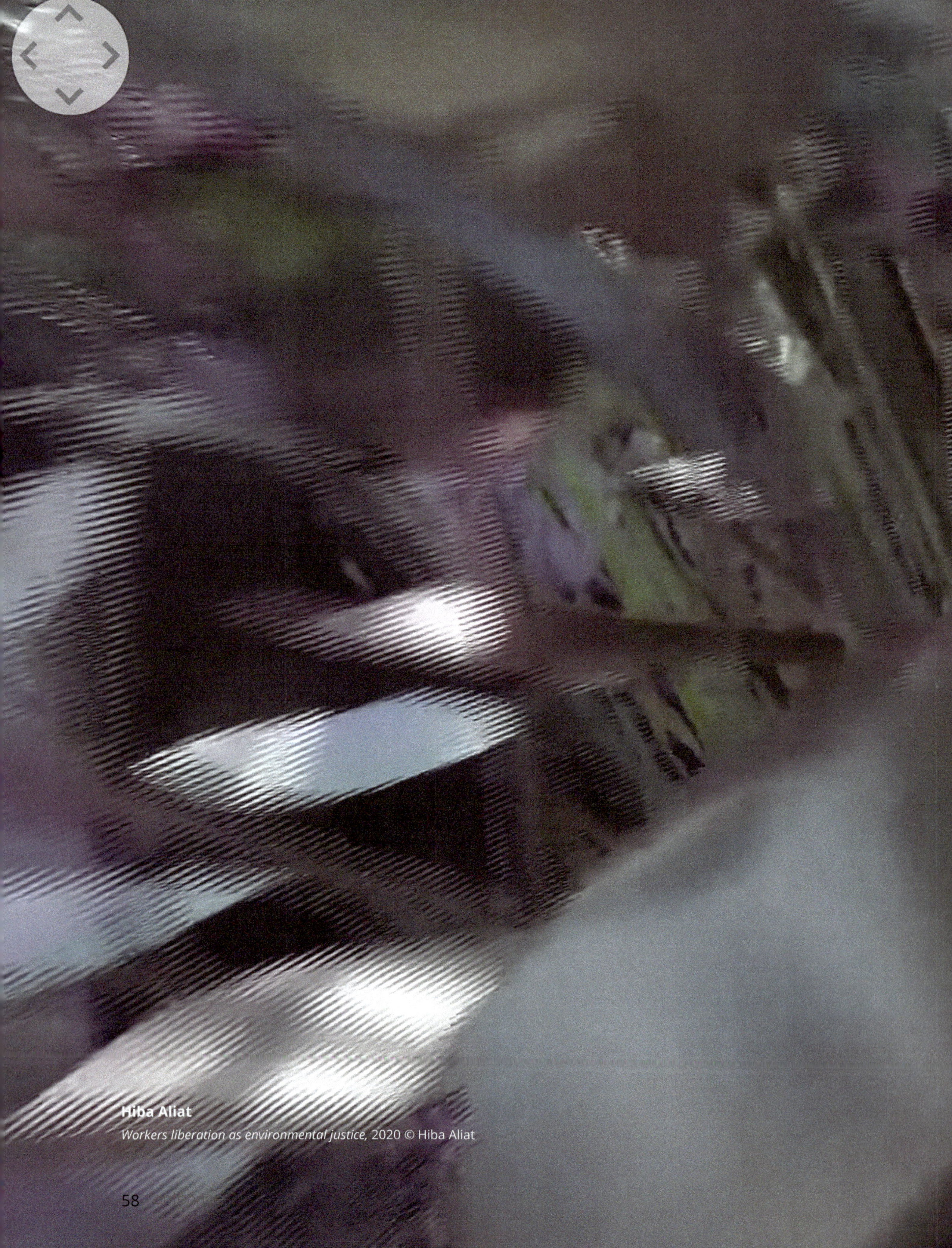

Hiba Aliat
Workers liberation as environmental justice, 2020 © Hiba Aliat

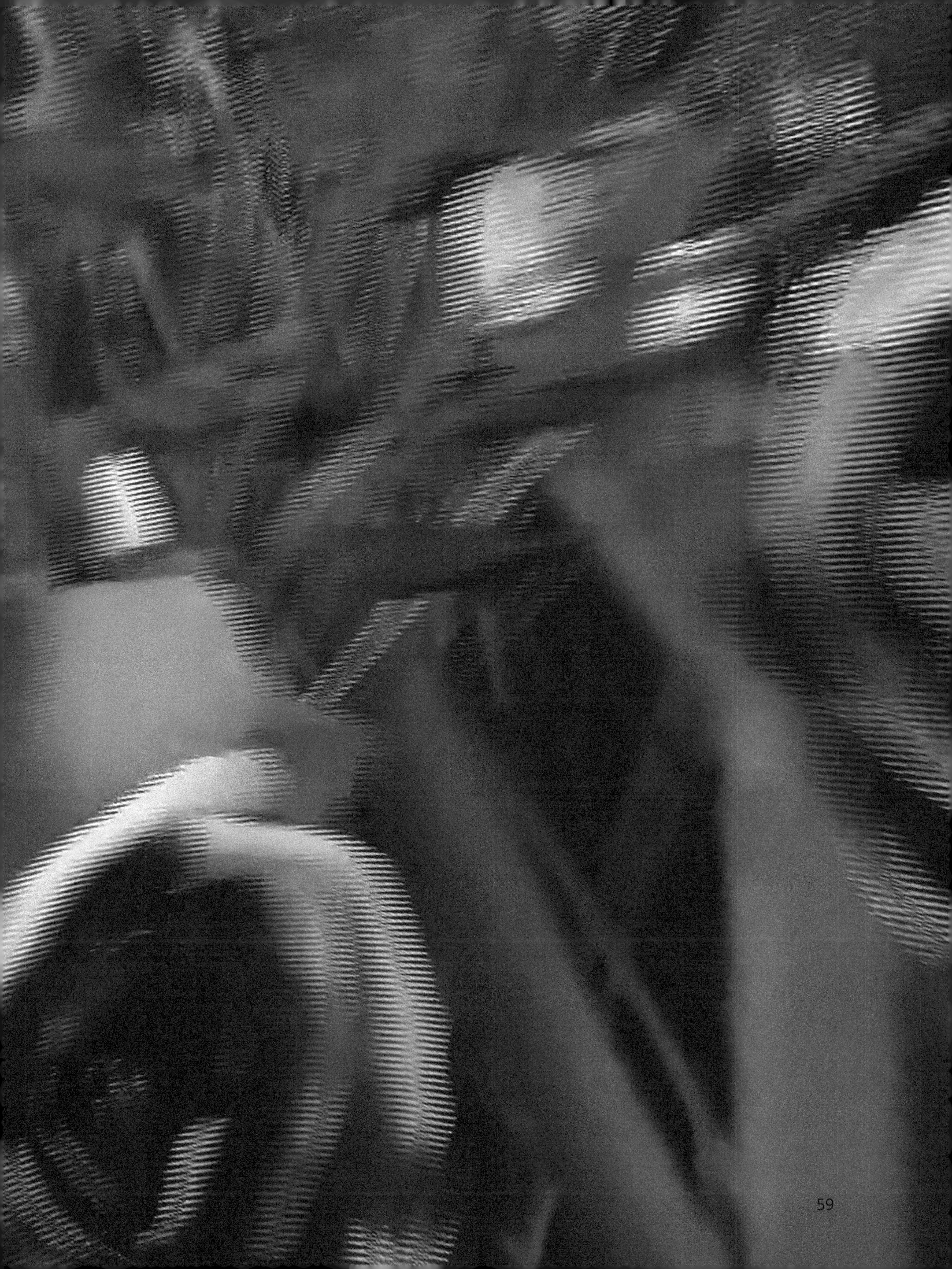

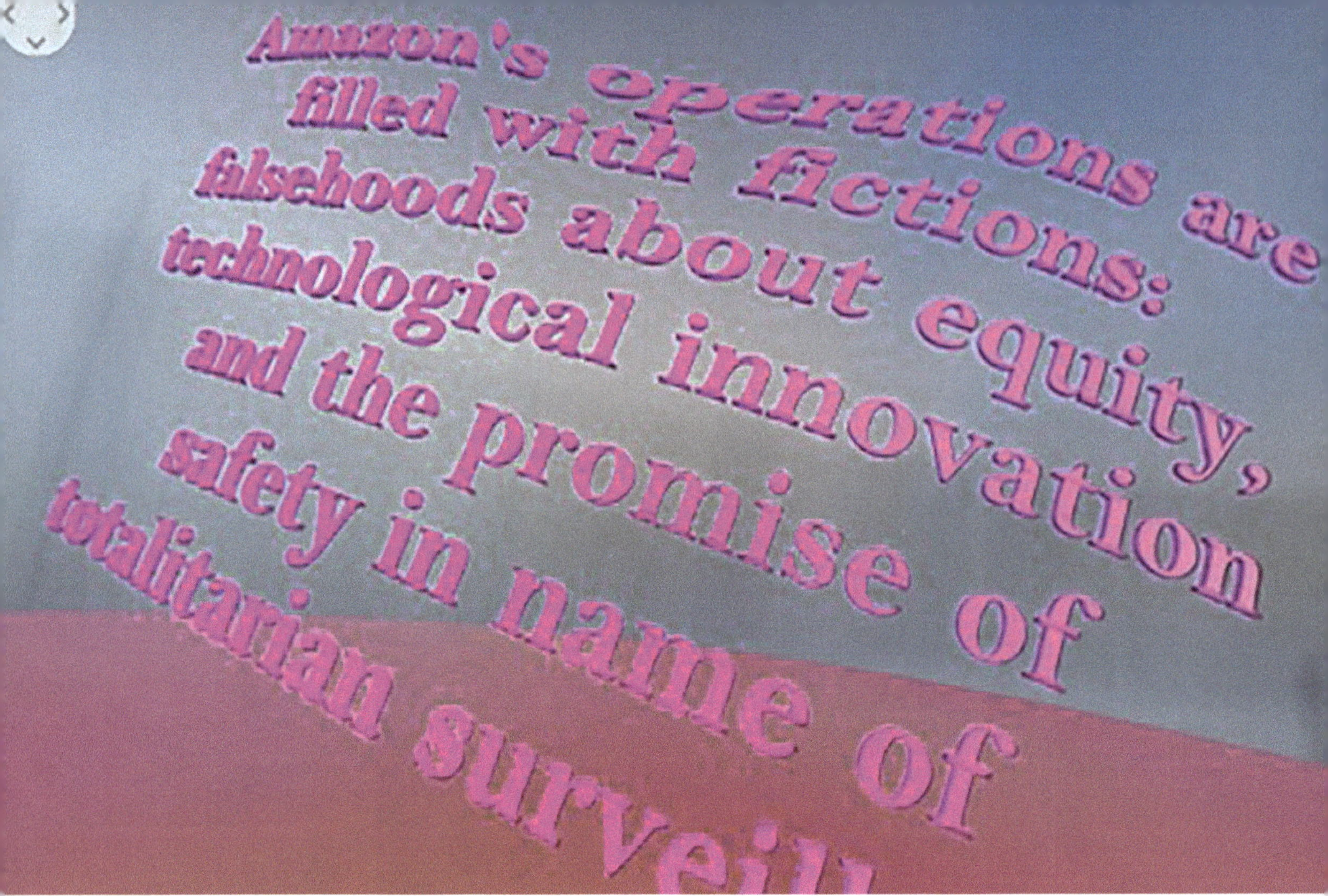

Hiba Aliat

Workers liberation as environmental justice, 2020 © Hiba Aliat

Hafsa Hasan, who is affiliated with Awood, was one of the leaders from MSP1 Walk-out at the Amazon Warehouse in Shakopee, Minnesota, during the early inception of the COVID-19 pandemic, that occurred in response to the corporation's lack of protective equipment for its workers. On April 26th, 2020 at Prime Day Protest Hasan states, "Amazon, I'm telling you that each and every single associate is requesting that you guys from here on out make sure safety is a priority, that you guys treat associates fairly, that you guys make sure the 6-feet policy rule makes sense and also applies to each and every single person and now you guys extended unlimited UPT [unlimited time off policy] because it's the month of Ramadan and everyone's fasting we don't know how many confirmed positive cases are about to come".[5] Combining environmental, racial capitalism and plantationocene themes, I made a 360-video interactive video entitled "we are all living: workers liberation as environmental justice" (2020), which features Hasan's demands on the Prime Day Protest Day. The video connects concerns of the future of the planet as intimately linked to upholding poor, working-class, Black, and brown workers' rights. The degradation of the environment is inherently linked to the capitalist overproduction that is performed by precarious part-time gig workers. Understanding the thresholds and daily stress that Black and brown women as precarious workers undergo is key to frame not only the environment but the human toll as part of the plantationocene.

Even though warehouse workers are working during a pandemic, as they are branded as "essential," Amazon has taken away the additional $2/hour and double time for overtime hours for workers even as workloads have risen and Amazon has become a trillion-dollar corporation.[6] Amazon has developed a pattern of surveillance, targeting, and firing of whistleblowers around the country, beginning with Chris Smalls in New York, then Emily Cunningham and Maren Costa in Seattle, and others including Bashir Mohamed, who worked alongside Hibaq Mohamed in MSP1 facility in Minnesota. Moreover, Amazon uses a purposefully faulty tracking method where the virus is handled as an inconvenience. COVID-19 cases at an MSP1 facility in Shakopee, Minnesota in May 2020 exceeded by at least four times the infection rate of surrounding communities, moreover, there is a lack of tracking cases with workers.[7] The company has declined to make public how many workers have contracted the coronavirus, arguing that such tallies are meaningless without context stating that "it's not a particularly useful number." The math of necropolitics, a term defined by Achille Mbembe as "the use of social and political power to dictate how some people may live and how some must die," where lack of data for sick workers equates the lack of COVID-19 virus' existence.[8]

Amazon has a long history of union-busting and firing workers who organize for better working conditions. At the Shakopee fulfillment center, Hibaq Mohamed, a former worker at MSP1, is faced with retaliation for speaking out about the risk of COVID-19 spreading at the warehouse. Hibaq Mohamed, migrated to the U.S. in 2016, and she's worked from 40 to 60 hours a week as a stower earning $13 an hour.[9] The work conditions demand robot-like stamina – as a stower, her responsibilities included picking, scanning, and storing 260 items an hour. To demand better working conditions and job security, Hibaq Mohamed and her colleague, Nimo Hirad helped organize about 200 workers at Amazon's Shakopee facility to strike six hours during Prime Day on July 8th, 2019. Hasan and Mohamed are associated with Awood Center, a Minneapolis-based nonprofit that advocates for East African immigrant and refugee workers by providing training and helping workers organize themselves.[10] This organization is necessary for a time when Amazon is adept at firing workers who lead protests and mobilize their "TOT" violation policy to unjustly fire Hibaq Mohamed and Farhiyo Warsame. TOT stands for "time off task" policy applies to any time spent not directly engaging in work like packing boxes. Mohamed states, "It's unacceptable… They pick on the leaders', If a worker is wearing a mask and a string comes off, you can't go and get another because you're putting yourself at risk of violating TOT policy," Mohamed said. "It seems like they're handing warnings and write-ups out left and right and no matter what situation you choose, you're always at risk".[11] Internal documents revealed that Amazon surveils the number of warehouse workers participating in union activity, detective agencies that spy on warehouse workers, and track environmentalist groups' participation by its workers.[12]

Amazon's risks are externalized on their warehouse workers, both locally and globally. The environmental costs of building multiple warehouses and global shipping carbon footprint are poor, working, Black and brown communities' problem, not Amazon's.[13] On November 27th, 2020. Friday, a day of action on Black Friday, one of Amazon's biggest sales events of the year and the start of its peak season,

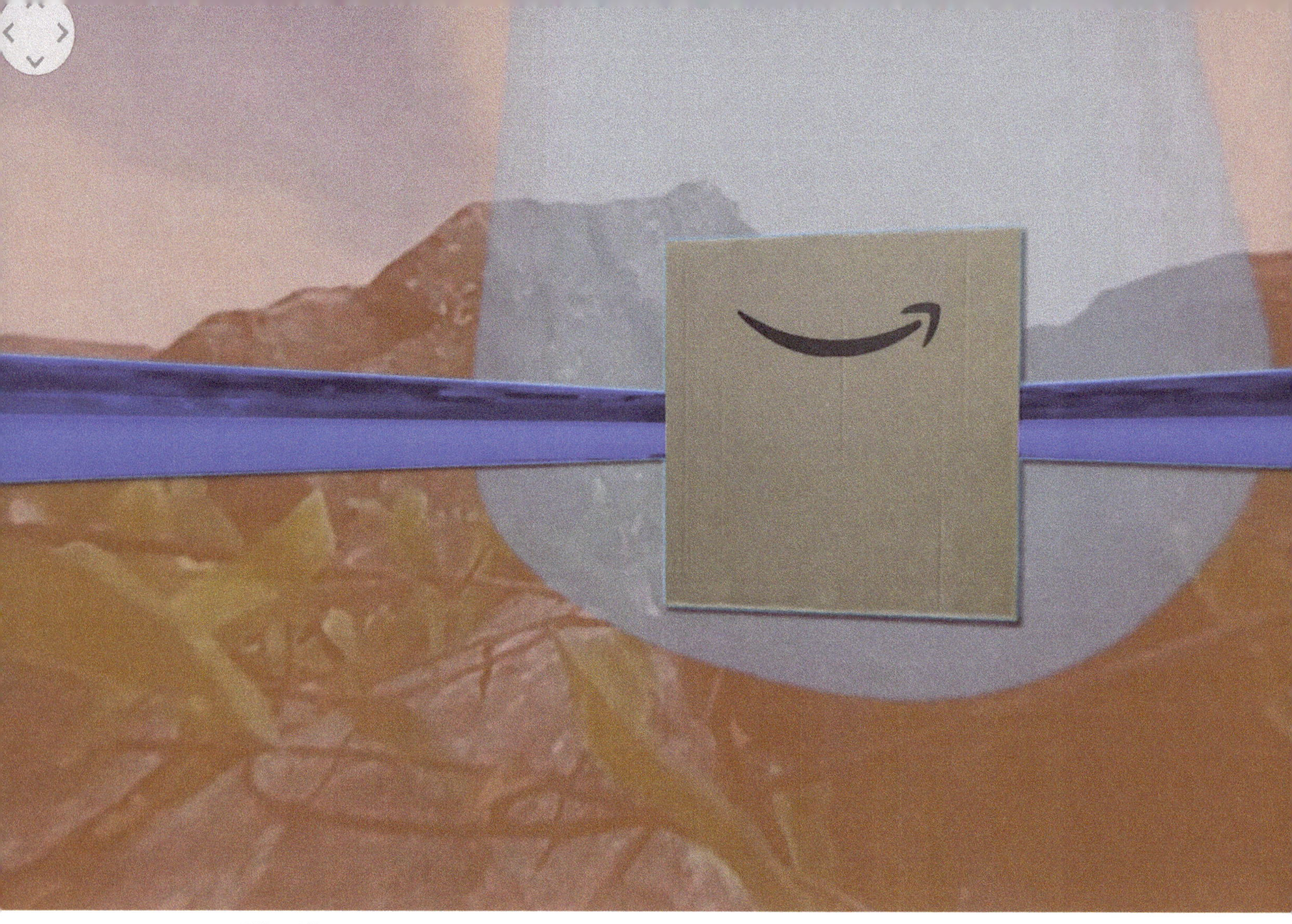

Hiba Aliat

Workers liberation as environmental justice, 2020 © Hiba Aliat

called #MakeAmazonPay, Amazon warehouse workers and social and environmental justice activists around the world staged a series of coordinated protests, strikes, and actions to demand the online retailer respect workers' rights to participate in union activity, stop circumventing tax laws, and commit to higher environmental standards in Brazil, Mexico, the United States, the United Kingdom, Spain, France, Belgium, Germany, Luxembourg, Italy, Poland, India, Bangladesh, the Philippines, and Australia with organization that include UNI Global Union, Greenpeace, the Athena Coalition, the Sunrise Movement, OxFam, Our Revolution, Amazon Employees for Climate Justice, Progressive International, Public Citizen, and the Tax Justice Network. #MakeAmazonPay's statement is signed by 39 organizations states, "During the Covid-19 pandemic, Amazon became a trillion-dollar corporation, with Bezos becoming the first person in history to amass $200 billion in personal wealth…Amazon's success would be impossible without the public institutions that citizens built together over generations… But instead of giving back to the societies that helped it grow, the corporation starves them of tax revenue through its world-beating efforts at tax dodging".[14] We urgently demand a different world, a world where Amazon is abolished without the plantationocene. We demand repatriation and reparations for our stolen labour, time and our livelihoods. Ultimately, we demand a world that honors the sanctity of life and respects its essence.

Endnotes

[1] Grove, Jairus Victor, _Savage Ecology: War and the Geopolitics at the End of the World,_ 2019; Yusuf, Kathryn, _A Billion Black Anthropocenes of None_, University of Minnesota Press, 2019.

[2] Sophie Sapp Moore, Monique Allewaert, Pablo F. Gómez and Gregg Mitman, 'Plantation Legacies' in _Edge Effects_ July 14, 2020. https://edgeeffects.net/plantation-legacies-planta-tionocene/

[3] MakeAmazonPay.com, Make Amazon Pay, 2020.

[4] Calma, Justine, Satellite images show online shopping's growing footprint, November 25th 2020, Verge. https://www.theverge.com/21611862/satellite-images-online-shopping-growing-footprint-warehouses

[5] Hasan, Hafsa, Protest on 04/26/2020, Shakopee, Minnesota, Twitter, 2020.

[6] MakeAmazonPay.com, Make Amazon Pay, 2020.

[7] Bloomberg News, 'Amazon warehouse COVID-19 outbreaks exceed surrounding communities'. June 30th 2020. Digital Commerce 360. https://www.digitalcommerce360.com/2020/06/30/amazon-warehouse-covid-19-outbreaks-exceed-surrounding-communi-ties/

[8] Matt Day, Spencer Soper, "Amazon On Covid-19 Cases: 'It's Not a Particularly Use-ful Number' May 12, 2020, Bloomberg. https://www.bloomberg.com/news/arti-cles/2020-05-12/amazon-on-covid-19-cases-it-s-not-a-particularly-useful-number; Mbembe, Achille, 'On the Postcolony', University of California Press, 2001.

[9] Mbembe, Achille, 'On the Postcolony', University of California Press, 2001; Athena, Ac-tion Network, https://actionnetwork.org/petitions/stand-with-hibaq

[10] MakeAmazonPay.com, Make Amazon Pay, 2020; Annie Palmer, "Amazon warehouse worker says she was written up in July for taking too many breaks from work." July 17th, 2020, MSN, https://www.msn.com/en-us/money/companies/amazon-warehouse-worker-says-she-was-written-up-in-july-for-taking-too-many-breaks-from-work/ar-BB16SwT8; Gur-ley, Lauren Kaori, "Amazon Workers to Stage Coordinated Black Friday Protests in 15 Coun-tries," Vice: Motherboard, November 26th, 2020. https://www.vice.com/en/article/epdvzp/amazon-workers-to-stage-coordinated-black-friday-protests-in-12-countries

[11] Hasan, Hafsa, Protest on 04/26/2020, Shakopee, Minnesota, Twitter, 2020.

[12] Gurley, Lauren Kaori, "Secret Amazon Reports Expose the Company's Surveillance of Labor and Environmental Groups," Vice: Motherboard, November 23rd, 2020, https://www.vice.com/en/article/5dp3yn/amazon-leaked-reports-expose-spying-warehouse-workers-labor-union-environmental-groups-social-movements

[13] CCAEJ, IRIS, #BlackFridayBlsackout. December 1st, 2020, https://storymaps.arcgis.com/stories/5d2ba8cbcd1d412897549b9d5d13e548

[14] Calma, Justine, Satellite images show online shopping's growing footprint, November 25th 2020, Verge. https://www.theverge.com/21611862/satellite-images-online-shopping-growing-footprint-warehouses

Hiba Ali is a digital artist, educator, scholar, DJ, experimental music producer, and curator based across Chicago, IL, Austin, TX, and Toronto, ON. Their performances and videos concern surveillance, womxn/ womyn of colour, and labour. She studies the geographies of Afro-descent and Indo-Arab communities across the Indian Ocean through music, cloth and ritual. They conduct reading groups addressing digital media and workshops with open-source technology. She is a Ph.D. candidate in Cultural Studies at Queens University, Kingston, Canada. They are an As-sistant Professor of Art, New Media Artist/Feminist Art Discourse, College of Design, Art & Technology, University of Oregon, Eugene, OR. She has presented their work in Chicago, Stockholm, Toronto, New York, Istanbul, São Paulo, Detroit, Windsor, Dubai, Austin, Vancouver, and Portland. They have written for C Magazine, THE SEEN Magazine, Newcity Chicago, Art Dubai, The State, VAM Magazine, ZORA: Medium, RTV Magazine, and Topical Cream Magazine.

After Man and Nature:
an ethos for the Anthropocene

In line with the bio-evolutionary governing principles of our overrepresented order of knowledge and being, the notion of the Anthropocene is both anthropocentric and ethnocentric. It reinstalls a static Cartesian dualism in between the two seemingly separate realms of nature and humanity. Simultaneously, the realm of mankind is being figured as a generic universality, with the effect that meaningful differences amongst Homo sapiens are scratched away. By thinking with Sylvia Wynter, a hybrid and pluralist ethos to the measure of our more-than-human world gestures towards the systemic transformation of the intertwined notions of Man and Nature. Decolonial thinking proves indispensable for moving post-humanism's hegemonic ghosts.

text by **Esther F. Jansen**

> *Human beings are magical. Bios and Logos. Words made flesh, muscle, and bone animated by hope and desire, belief materialized in deeds, deeds which crystallize our actualities[....] And the maps of spring always have to be redrawn again, in undared forms.*

Sylvia Wynter[1]

Through words, images, and concepts, we continually narrate, visualise, and enact ourselves as humans in culturally specific terms. An increasingly popular—as well as contested—narrative portrays humanity, or mankind, as the primary geological force on Earth, hence, the Anthropocene.[2] From this notion of the Anthropocene flows the idea that the fate of *Homo sapiens* is not that "we" will be erased, but rather, that "[w]e will be made immortal, as a trace preserved forever in the rock".[3] "Our" landfills, as well as the mass extinctions of multiple known (and unknown) species, will leave their trace in the fossil record—"a reminder of our incipient minerality".[4] As such, the concept of the Anthropocene not only stresses the entanglement of humans and nature(s), but also the inextricable forces of both—now inseparable—realms.[5]

A recent illustration of the Anthropocene storyline unfolds in the documentary *David Attenborough*: *A Life on Our Planet* (2020). Attenborough asserts that it is *the human species* that sets into motion the current process of mass extinction. Very effectively, Attenborough narrates: "we, a single species [...] have the power to threaten the very existence of the wilderness... Our blind assault on the planet has finally become to alter the very fundamentals of the living world".[6] This understanding of "us" humans, existing separate to the natural world, is built upon a material-semiotic order of knowledge/being in which the human appears as *a destructive species*—the ultimate cause of a global climate crisis. This narrative is based on the assumption that a "we" exists; that "we" are *a killing species*.[7] This species thinking seems to encompass each and every one of us, yet, it does not account for the lives that function as the necessary symbolic and material negation-as-condition of mankind. In what follows, I argue that we must make visible, resist, and reimagine the production of difference within our current onto-epistemological order—with its specific narration of what it means to be human—that underlies the notion of the Anthropocene.

In line with the Cartesian, bio-evolutionary governing principles of our specific yet overrepresented order of knowledge and being, the very foundations of the idea that mankind is a geological force, are both *anthropocentric* and *ethnocentric*. First, by indicating the impact of mankind on the world of nature, the notion of the Anthropocene reinstalls a static Cartesian dualism between the two seemingly separate realms. Second, the realm of mankind is being figured, over and again, as a generic universality, with the effect that meaningful differences amongst *Homo sapiens* are scratched away.[8] What follows, then, is that in order to move beyond human exceptionalism, a posthuman or ontological turn in which humans are written into the realm of nature will not suffice, because the notion of the human that underlies this move is neither a neutral, nor a straightforward term.[9] Instead of aiming to know what the human is or is not—I return to the following question: what are the tools with which we think, narrate, and enact our humanness in meaningful ways, and how can we, in light of the climate crises (to come), become human otherwise?

I turn to the work of critical decolonial and post-humanist thinker Sylvia Wynter, who poignantly argues that the notion of the human expressed through the generic term "mankind" is not a collective term "made to the measure of the world,"[10] but rather denotes a particular, situated logic of "Man".[11] I first explore Wynter's historical analysis of how representations of humanness have come into being.[12] The construction of Man's liberal humanist logic is premised upon a twofold constitutive outside: the passive background of "Nature" and the racial economy of our capitalist system of production, or, "the wretched of the earth"[13] Secondly, I turn to Wynter's account of a "species-inclusive" humanism beyond Man with which she gestures towards its systemic transformation: "*the* single issue with which global warming and climate instability now confronts us. [...] We have no choice".[14] In this light, I ask how her perspective beyond Man towards human hybridity speaks to the end of Nature as/in the Anthropocene, and helps us (re)formulating a response to the continuing disastrous socio-ecological effects of "our" current enactment of humanness.

A Haunted Humanism

Wynter traces back the current hegemonic conception of humanism to its origins in the Renaissance. In sixteenth-century Latin-Christian Europe, the theocentric medieval answer to the question of what it means to be human became transmuted into a ratiocentric answer. The specificities of "new" European imperialism demanded new ways of seeing and ordering reality, such as abstract time, abstract space, and external Nature.[15] Against the background of a passive natural world, a European humanist notion of the self as a rational man, or *Homo politicus* emerged, enabling and justifying colonial conquest, the expansion of European empires, the accumulation of oversea resources, and the enslavement and trafficking of humans from the African continent to the plantations.[16] Lay humanists became "Men of reason" who, whilst looking for earthly salvation, systematically mapped the Earth's geography and its peoples.[17] An unprecedented idea of ontological difference emerged, separating the white European Man, rising above the world of matter, the animal, *and* the humans he colonised and enslaved. Wynter calls this logic, the logic of "Man1".[18]

The elevation of Man above the natural world and constructed as ontologically different from backward, or "lesser" humans, are two sides of the same coin. According to Frantz Fanon, "colonial" was (and continues to be) "the theft of nature," with the species divide functioning as an ideological fiction deployed to justify the material expropriation of natural wealth and cheap human labour.[19] Man's post-1492 ecocide and genocide came to be justified through the enactment of a colour line that was based on the concept of race: an aporia between who can be human in terms of Man and potentially rise above the level of the beast to that of the angels, and who cannot.[20] Wynter writes:

> This *aporia* I define as that *of the secular*—that is as one whose humanly emancipatory process on the one hand, and humanly subjugation processes on the other, are each nevertheless the lawlike condition of the enacting of the other.[21]

As such, by virtue of its introduction of a corresponding "natural" irrationality along racial fault lines, any potential of a human collective "we" became impossible.

In this light, Paul Gilroy asks: "How might we become more comprehensively estranged from the Anthropos in the Anthropocene in order to salvage a different, and perhaps re-enchanted human from the rising waters and transformed climates that characterize the future of our endangered species?"[22] Instructed by "the trials of racial critique," this must involve the task of de-naturalising, as well as of engaging with the racial orders of colonial laws.[23] He writes:

> Critical interest in the sovereign racial orders, hierarchies, and ontologies that have assembled the world in raciological and colonial patterns connects directly with the central issue of the human—the conceptual integrity of that vexed category and the problems that link orders of domination among human beings to their various exploitative and extractive relationships with nature.[24]

Racial politics are not marginal aspects of climate politics, but instead, lie at the centre of liberal humanism and the conceptions of time and space on which it is built.[25] The Anthropos' entangled ethno- and anthropocentrism can only be tackled simultaneously: the one cannot be undone when the other prevails. Hence, the Anthropocene's becoming geological of the human is both Man's fundamental denouement and eclipse.[26]

In the nineteenth century, the ratiocentric understanding of the Renaissance humanist mutation—Man1—and its "natural" difference between the human as Man and his excluded Other, transmuted into a second version: *Homo oeconomicus*, or "Man2".[27] This reinvented, liberal humanist version was predicated upon a biocentric evolutionary order of difference, "in which... one's selected or dysselected status... would come to be verified by one's (or one's group) success or failure in life".[28] Instead of mastering one's natural drives through rationality, in Man2's biocentric descriptive statement, a "bioevolutionary teleological logic necessitates, above all, the accumulation of capital" in the name of freedom.[29] With other words, the figure of *Homo oeconomicus* can be successfully realised through "jobholding Breadwinners and Investors," who overcome and master the significant "ill" that is scarcity.[30] The disadvantaged side of this equation is continually stabilised through the "institution of Poverty/Joblessness".[31] To become human, then, demands overcoming scarcity through economic growth and an increase of the exploitation of natural resources, capitalist crises, and impact on natural-cultural ecosystems.

As such, the logic of mankind is both constituted and constrained by its specific bio-mythically enacted relation to Nature: the exploitation of Earth's resources and the singular, teleological way of becoming human go hand in hand. This means that when struggling against the material conditions of climate change, we must simultaneously struggle against the logic of Man. This struggle must thereby assert a qualitative transformation of being/knowledge that does not bypass the systemic omissions of the Other of Man, or the violent structures of the hegemonic onto-epistemological order will resurface again, now in name of Nature or even "life itself".[32] In the following paragraph, I turn to Wynter's reconstitution of a species-inclusive humanism that, initiated from the liminal spaces of Man–from its "*demonic grounds*"–(re)turns (to) the terms on which humanness is currently predicated.[33]

Towards a Species-Inclusive Humanism

For Wynter, a different humanism starts from ontogeny/sociogeny and the resurfacing of human agency within the construction of humanness. By unravelling Man's logic, its genre-specific origin narratives and cosmogonies—by means of which we "fictively construct and performatively enact ourselves as the who of the 'we' that we are" or are not—become visible.[34] By turning to the concept of autopoiesis, Wynter asserts that the current onto-epistemological order of humanness ensures its self-perpetuation and replication of its own laws and codes, with a profound ontological effect: *being* human.[35] Walter Mignolo concludes: "The Human is, therefore, the product of a particular epistemology, yet it appears to be (and is accepted as) a naturally independent entity existing in the world".[36] By thinking with evolutionary, neurological, and systems theory, Wynter concludes:

human orders of consciousness/modes of mind cannot *pre-exist* the terms of the always already mythically chartered, genre-specific code of symbolic life/death, its "second set of instructions" and thus its governing sociogenic principle—or,… its nonphysical principle of causality.[37]

Through self-representational storytelling and the alignment of its terms of symbolic life/death to the neurochemical systems in our brains, being human becomes a praxis that is always culturally and socially embedded as well as physically embodied.[38] Hence, Wynter builds on Fanon's argument that besides ontogeny, or "corporeal schema", there is sociogeny: the "historico-racial schema" of language and representation.[39] However, sociogeny is always about the constitution of socio-political relations, which makes *transformation* part of the autopoietic process—who and what we are is *not* supra-humanly biologically mandated.[40]

Wynter thereby foregrounds the humanly shared capacity to narrate meaningful stories. This storytelling capacity is *hybrid*: inextricably onto- and sociogenic—words become flesh. Hence, Wynter names us *Homo narrans*: a "hybrid-auto-instituting-languaging-storytelling species," which is a praxis, not a noun.[41] Or, as Weheliye suggests:

> a symbolic register, consisting of discourse, language, culture, and so on (sociogeny) always already accompanies the genetic dimension of human action (ontogeny), and it is only in the imbrication of these two registers that we can understand the full scope of our being-in-the-world.[42]

Thus, through the storytelling codes of our particular cosmogonies, one not only knows what it means to be human, but space, shape, regulate, and as such *become* how we physiologically enact as well as experience our humanness.[43]

By emphasising the biological capacity of our brains to read and write, Wynter installs *a radical openness of and within the material-organic world*. This implies that, because who we are is also partly symbolic/myth, our humanness can never be reduced to a singular identity. Rather, it is conditioned by always contingent with power imbued descriptive statements, and is thus subject to change. This revolting agency at the heart of human subjectivity with respect to our current autopoietic order of knowledge/being, the possibility of its systemic transformation, is, however, a specific subjectivity, one of "double consciousness".[44] After Fanon and Césaire, she stresses the importance of liminal positionalities for adopting a point of external observation with respect to our current onto-epistemological order, for its narratives to be expanded, and its schemata to be overturned. As Weheliye writes, while perspectives from these liminal spaces can be derived from black experience and black thought, this does not mean that these perspectives should stay within these particular spaces.[45] Liminal perspectives, then, are a necessary condition for systemic transformations, as they make visible what modes of being/knowledge emerge from particular experiences that are irrecuperable from *within* the dominant and pervasive speaking positions in society.

For Wynter, being human is a hybrid praxis, that concerns any genre of being in its own right. In order to systemically shift the logic of Man, liminal positionalities already resist, and therefore expand, the dominant onto-epistemological order and its species divide and Eurocentric's claimed universality. Rather than aiming for humanism's purported completion by "simply" including its conditional outsides, we must therefore shift the very terms of what it means to be human, to open up "a vision of life that unfurls new vistas on a livable future, both for ourselves and the socio-biosphere we inhabit".[46]

Being Human in/of the Anthropocene

The reality of vastly changing climates demands that we take the matter that we are, and the matter (with) which we are living, very seriously. Returning our attention to both the physical reality and cultural discourse of the Anthropocene—"our" becoming geological—we can now, with Wynter, reimagine the hybridity of knowledge/being. Wynter's approach to the overrepresented logic of Man informs a critique of anthropogenic climate change by attending to the situated yet limited space from which the Anthropocene is currently being imagined.

The omnipresent trap of explaining who we are based on the effects we discern—as if the Anthropocene means that "we" are a destructive species *because* we are changing the geosphere of the Earth—re-enacts the precise opposite: a notion of humanness that is singular, static, and teleological.[47] This notion of mankind fundamentally reiterates a species divide between, to speak with Attenborough: "us" and "the living world". Humans stand behind or above Nature, but never become a part of it. The effect of portraying both Nature and Mankind in overarching terms is that "the climate" can be for or against humans, and vice versa. Arguments for Nature neither disrupt nor undo the logic of Man but rather contribute to its intensification—become Man *better* and "save Nature" instead of destroying it. However, if we stay with the understanding of mankind as the negation of all earthly life, or as now simply *enmeshed* with it, we cannot transgress the static and indeed destructive enactment of "our" humanness.

If then, we take seriously Wynter's argument that Man is *not* synonymous with the human as a species, but that one specific answer to the question of what it means to be human has become overrepresented across the globe, what does this entail for the story of the Anthropocene? The planetary overrepresentation of Man2 continues to enact a major effect on the Earth's climate system, most notably the rapid and planetary expansion of fossil fuel-based economies, which have resulted in an unprecedented release of carbon dioxide and other greenhouse gases into the atmosphere, with enormous social and ecological consequences. As such, *the genre of (western) Man* has fundamentally transformed and destabilised the ecological patterns of the Earth.[48] The one and only cure for the "ill" of poverty and underdevelopment—to "come and be Man like us"[49]—is to enter the world of development by means of the accumulation of capital, derived from cheap labour and the extraction of the Earth's natural resources.[50] People who were previously categorised as being traditional, backward, and irredeemably subhuman, are reimagined as being able to arrive at a "full human" status if only the right steps are taken. Yet, if we continue to reiterate Man's terms and static boundaries, the current material-semiotic climate struggles will only deepen the secular aporia of Man, as well as the accompanying, increasingly unequal cultural and physical global precarity. The widespread threats to cultural extinction enforced by losses of habitat are anything but new, but they will take unprecedented forms in the light of the climate disruptions to come.

To avoid resuscitating humanism's hegemonic ghosts, we have to first differentiate between the human and Man—to challenge the effects of our genre-specific narrative within climate politics, without simply moving beyond human exceptionalism *for the sake of nature*.[98] Instead of asking how nature is impacted by mankind, instead of "saving the Earth" from the detrimental effects of our own actions, I suggest we struggle against the dominant, seductive yet destructive narration of who and what we are. The materiality of the Anthropocene can be (re)thought in the light of, as well as part of, the stories we tell, urging us to make possible, attend to, and inhabit those spaces in which *specific* ways of being and thinking our humanness with others in the world become sensible. Reading and thinking with Wynter's work provides a starting point from which to open up a different ethos for storytelling and living in the Anthropocene in order to unsettle a mindset, to make the familiar uncanny, or to hack a system of thinking and being that is reiterated and reproduced as if it is the *only* available option.[99] Instead, a hybrid and pluralist ethos to the measure of our more-than-human world gestures towards the systemic transformation of the intertwined notions of Man *and* Nature.[100]

According to Wynter, what it means to be human is a praxis—with profound effects on the socio-ecological systems of which we are a part. Instead of what just *is*, the defining human capacity is that humans co-constitute the sociogenic situated and organically embodied stories we live by in endless ways and as such, co-constitute the world. Returning to the question of "the human"–over and again–throws us back onto the very notion of being in the world and opens up different horizons for enacting our relationships with other humans and other-than-human lives: Do not be like Man, become human otherwise.

Endnotes

[1] Wynter's quote from 1995 was cited in Sylvia Wynter, "Unparalleled Catastrophe of Our Species? Or, to Give Humanness a Different Future: Conversations," in *Sylvia Wynter: On Being Human as Praxis* (Durham, NC: Duke University Press), edited by Katherine McKittrick, 2015, p. 1.

[2] Paul J. Crutzen, "Geology of Mankind," *Nature* 415, 2002, p. 23.

[3] Bronislaw Szerszynski, "The End of the End of Nature: The Anthropocene and the Fate of the Human," *Oxford Literary Review* 34(2), 2012, p. 180.

[4] Ibid., p. 181.

[5] Karsten A. Schulz, "Decolonizing Political Ecology: Ontology, Technology and 'Critical' Enchantment," *Journal of Political Ecology* 24(1), 2017, pp. 125–43.

[6] *David Attenborough: A Life on our Planet*, directed by Alastair Fothergill, Jonathan Hughes, and Keith Scholey, Netflix, 4 October 2020.

[7] Elizabeth Kolbert, *The Sixth Extinction: An Unnatural History* (New York: Picador), 2014.

[8] One's vulnerability, precarity, resilience, or recuperation, as well as the contributions to, or profit derived from, disrupting climates are highly unevenly distributed along the intersecting lines of race, gender, and class. Youth climate activists from Fridays For Futures focus on the Most Affected People and Areas (see @FFFMAPA on Twitter).

[9] The category of "mankind" rests upon a normative figure; a norm to which, as Judith Butler (1993) points out so clearly, no one can fully comply. However, for Butler, the necessity of reiterating such norms shows that their materialisation is never complete. The instabilities and possible re-materialisations open up and turn the regulatory ideal against itself, calling into question its hegemonic force. Concerning the praxis of humanness, refraining from the question of what it means to be human altogether cannot prevent the normative reiteration of how to be and think the human. We constantly reiterate being human, and this, in order to exist according to the terms in place, implies that it is necessary to pose again the question of the human, but now turning it against its own hegemonic force. Judith Butler, *Bodies That Matter* (London: Routledge), 1993, p. xii.

[10] Aimé Césaire, *Discourse on Colonialism* (New York: Monthly Review Press), translated by Joan Pinkham, [1972] 2000, p. 73.

[11] Sylvia Wynter, "Unsettling the Coloniality of Being/Power/Truth/Freedom: Towards the Human, After Man, Its Overrepresentation—An Argument," *CR: The New Centennial Review* 3(3), 2003, pp. 257–337. In following Wynter's notion of the specific logic of "Man," this term will be capitalised from here onwards.

[12] Decolonial genealogies are often bypassed in writings on the posthuman or ontological turn in critical theory. For an elaboration of this argument, see Zimitri Erasmus, "Sylvia Wynter's Theory of the Human: Counter-, not Post-humanist," *Theory, Culture & Society* 0(0), 2020, pp. 1–19; Max Hantel, "Plasticity and Fungibility on Sylvia Wynter's Pieza Framework," *Social Text 143* 38(2), 2020. In this essay, I cannot do justice to the rich multitude of Wynter's oeuvre. I take the logic of Man as my main anchor point.

[13] Frantz Fanon, *The Wretched of the Earth* (New York: Grove Press), translated by Constance Farrington, 1968.

[14] Wynter, "Unparalleled Catastrophe," p. 24.

[15] Michel Foucault, *The Order of Things: An Archaeology of the Human Sciences* (New York: Vintage), translated by Alan Sheridan, [1966] 1994; Donna J. Haraway, "The Promises of Monsters: A Regenerative Politics for Inappropriate/d Others," in *Cultural Studies* (New York: Routledge), edited by Lawrence Grossberg, Cary Nelson, and Paula A. Treichler, 1992, pp. 295–336; Jason W. Moore, "The Capitalocene, Part I: On the Nature and Origins of Our Ecological Crisis," *The Journal of Peasant Studies* 44, no. 3, 2017, pp. 594–630.

[16] David Scott, "The Re-Enchantment of Humanism: An Interview with Sylvia Wynter," *Small Axe 8*, 2000, pp. 119–207.

[17] Hantel, "Plasticity and Fungibility."

[18] Wynter, "Unsettling the Coloniality."

[19] Frantz Fanon, *The Wretched*, p. 102.

[20] Sylvia Wynter, "1492: A New Worldview," in *Race, Discourse, and the Origin of the Americas* (Washington: Smithsonian Institution Press), edited by Vera Lawrence Hyatt and Rex M. Nettleford, 1955, p. 39. When the Christian God could no longer be declared universal, the law of nature provided a logical alternative that encompassed the whole planet, including the solar system. See Walter D. Mignolo, "The Many Faces of Cosmo-polis: Border Thinking and Critical Cosmopolitanism," *Public Culture* 12(3), 2000, pp. 721–48.

[21] Sylvia Wynter, "The Ceremony Found: Towards the Autopoetic Turn/Overturn, Its Autonomy of Human Agency and Extraterritoriality of (Self-)Cognition," in *Black Knowledges/Black Struggles: Essays in Critical Epistemology* (Liverpool: Liverpool University Press), edited by Jason R. Ambroise, and Sabine Broeck, 2015, p. 189, emphasis in original.

[22] Paul Gilroy, "The 2015 Antipode RGS-IBG Lecture. 'Where Every Breeze Speaks of Courage and Liberty': Offshore Humanism and Marine Xenology, or, Racism and the Problem of Critique at Sea Level," *A Radical Journal of Geography* 50(1), 2018, p. 12.

[23] Ibid., p. 13.

[24] Ibid., p. 10.

[25] See also Zakiyyah Iman Jackson, *Becoming Human: Matter and Meaning in an Antiblack World* (NYU Press), 2020.

[26] Szerszynski, "The End," p. 181.

[27] Sylvia Wynter, "Unsettling the Coloniality of Being/Power/Truth/Freedom: Towards the Human, After Man, Its Overrepresentation—An Argument," *CR: The New Centennial Review* 3(3), 2003, p. 264.

[28] Wynter, "Unsettling the Coloniality," p. 310.

[29] Sylvia Wynter, "Unparalleled Catastrophe of Our Species? Or, to Give Humanness a Different Future: Conversations," in *Sylvia Wynter: On Being Human as Praxis* (Durham, NC: Duke University Press), edited by Katherine McKittrick, 2015, p. 65. The (neo)liberal market system is central to the current descriptive statement of Man2, but accumulation and socially stratified (trans)national divisions of labour have been at the centre of the Man/native aporia from sixteenth-century Renaissance humanism onwards. Wynter writes: "this [single] network [of accumulation] can be divided into three phases: (1) circulation of accumulation; (2) production for accumulation, and (3) consumption for accumulation." The source of extractive value of each phase was first, "the African slave, in the second, the working class, and in the third and current phase, it has been the consumer." Although the current (neo)liberal market system does not take central stage in this thesis, it prominently defines our descriptive statement, especially since the global Marxist anti-capitalist, anti-colonial struggles of the sixties. Cited in Walter D. Mignolo, "Sylvia Wynter: What Does It Mean to Be Human?," in *Sylvia Wynter: On Being Human as Praxis* (Durham, NC: Duke University Press), edited by Katherine McKittrick, 2015, p. 112.

[30] Wynter, Unparalleled Catastrophe," p. 37.

[31] Ibid., p. 37.

[32] Kaiser and Thiele conceptualize the resurfacing of 'Man' in an assumed Man-less, posthuman world, as *ultra-humanism* and argue: "If the human is assumed to be nothing but an interface, already at one with the world that is one living system, then posthumanism would be nothing more than the negotiation of a humanism that never was." Birgit M. Kaiser and Kathrin Thiele, "What is Species Memory? Or, Humanism, Memory and the Afterlives of '1492,'" *Parallax* 23, no. 4, 2017, p. 409.

[33] Katherine McKittrick, *Demonic Grounds: Black Women and the Cartographies of Struggle* (Minneapolis: University of Minnesota Press), 2006.

[34] Wynter, "The Ceremony Found," p. 196.

[35] For an elaborate discussion on the importance of understanding autopoiesis in multi-species *sympoietic* terms with regard to Wynter's humanism, see Max Hantel, "What Is It Like to Be a Human? Sylvia Wynter on Autopoiesis," *philoSOPHIA* 8, no 1, 2018, 61–79.

[36] Mignolo, "Sylvia Wynter," p. 107–8.

[37] Wynter, "Unparalleled Catastrophe," p. 35.

[38] Wynter, "Unsettling the Coloniality," p. 326. The opiate blockage/rewarding system in our brains creates a feedback loop between neurobiology and the sociogenic codes of racialised culture. Wynter writes: "[I]f the mind is what the brain does, what the brain does, is itself culturally determined through the mediation of the socialized sense of self, as well as of the 'social' situation in which this self is placed." Sylvia Wynter, "Towards the Sociogenic Principle: Fanon, Identity, the Puzzle of Conscious Experience," in *National Identities and Socio-Political Changes in Latin America* (New York: Routledge), edited by Antonio Gomez-Moriana and Mercedes F. Duran-Cogan, 2001, p. 37. See also Hantel, "What Is It Like to Be a Human?"

[39] Frantz Fanon, *Black Skin, White Masks* (London: Pluto Press), translated by Charles Lam Markmann, 1986, p. 13.

[40] Erasmus articulates sociogeny in the bio-ecnonomic-centered logic of Man as "the meanings of lack attached to black bodies and of wholeness attached to white bodies in the colonial imagination; the internalization or epidermalization of these meanings." Erasmus, "Sylvia Wynter," p. 8.

[41] Wynter, "Unparalleled Catastrophe," p. 25.

[42] Alexander G. Weheliye, *Habeas Viscus: Racializing Assemblages, Biopolitics, and Black Feminist Theories of the Human* (Durham, NC: Duke University Press), 2014, p. 25.

[43] As an example, the concept of race becomes marked through our flesh, not because we are born with certain bodies, but because they come to matter in precise ways through an ideological, mythical, and undetermined production of difference.

[44] Wynter turns to the mutational leap that W. E. B. Du Bois and Frantz Fanon were to initiate from "the existential ground of the then ex-slave-labour periphery of the post-1492 New World," and from their transcultural and transcosmogonic realm of double consciousness. Wynter, "Unparalleled Catastrophe," p. 46. Erasmus writes: "Both Fanon and Wynter call not only for the end of colonialism, but for the end of ways of knowing and seeing that enable, legitimate and perpetuate this system of domination. Their work illustrates that neither the colonized nor the colonizer is trapped in these psycho-socio-structural circumstances." Erasmus, "Sylvia Wynter," p. 9.

[45] Weheliye, *Habeas Viscus.*

[46] Sylvia Wynter, "Beyond the Categories of the Master Conception: The Counterdoctrine of the Jamesian Poiesis," in *C. L. R. James's Caribbean* (Durham, NC: Duke University Press), edited by Paget Henry and Paul Buhle, 1992, p. 89.

[47] Andreas Malm, and Alf Hornborg, "The Geology of Mankind? A Critique of the Anthropocene Narrative," *The Anthropocene Review* 1(1), 2014, pp. 1–8.

[48] David Kline and Thomas R. Cole, "Toward a New Humanism in the Age of Anthropogenic Climate Change: On Sylvia Wynter," *Elsevier Inc*, 2018, pp. 175–79; Wynter, "Unsettling the Coloniality."

[49] Ibid., p. 20.

[50] Kline and Cole, "Toward a New Humanism."

[51] Eric Pawson, "What Sort of Geographical Education for the Anthropocene?," *Geographical Research* 53(3), 2015, pp. 306–12. Also, the framing of "the people" purportedly existing in opposition to climate policies implemented by "the elite" is partly the effect of the perceived absence of human agency within the grand and overarching narrative of the Anthropocene. Not only the cause or the conditions of climate change, but also the potential actions to stop or reverse it are explained as the only possible answers, implemented top-down, yet unevenly distributed, with the effect that supports for climate policies can only diminish. Ash Amin and Nigel Thrift, *Arts of the Political* (Durham, NC: Duke University Press), 2013.

[51] Denise Ferreira Da Silva, "Before Man: Sylvia Wynter's Rewriting of the Modern Episteme," in *Sylvia Wynter: On Being Human as Praxis* (Durham, NC: Duke University Press), edited by Katherine McKittrick, 2015, pp. 90–105.

[52] Jennifer Wenzel, "Turning over a New Leaf: Fanonian Humanism and Environmental Justice." In [53] *The Routledge Companion to the Environmental Humanities* (New York, Routledge), edited by Ursula K. Heise, Jon Christensen and Michelle Niemann, 2017, pp. 165–73.

Esther F. Jansen is a lecturer at the Institute of Interdisciplinary Studies at the University of Amsterdam. She is a postgraduate from Utrecht University, where she was part of the Gender Studies programme in Media and Culture Studies. Her interdisciplinary research draws from feminist theory, climate science, and postcolonial theory, which she brings into critical dialogue to open up new ways of perceiving and enacting ourselves with/in the world.

Kenyan contemporary art & the time of the posthuman

This essay explores questions of form, material and time in the work of the Kenyan artists Cyrus Kabiru, Wangechi Mutu and Wanuri Kahiu. It claims that Kabiru, Mutu and Kahiu's work exists at the intersection of Afrofuturism and posthumanism – and suggests that a concept of the posthuman that is attentive to the post- as an indeterminate break in the flow of time, or even an eruption of the untimely within time itself, might be better suited to contemporary African cultural production than any notion of the posthuman that remains invested in an orderly or definitive supersession of the human by whatever comes in its wake.

text by **Joshua Williams**

No matter their commitment to multiplicity and becoming, discourses of posthumanism and the posthuman invoke orderly – or at least definitive – historical change. First came the human and then the posthuman; humanism will soon be superseded, if it hasn't been already, by one of the strains of posthumanism that have begun to cohere in its wake. Of course, the temporality of the post- is in fact both convoluted and contested, as both Kwame Anthony Appiah and Shu-Mei Shih have shown.[1] This has significant ramifications for the study of cultural production in the Global South that interrogates, complicates, or explodes the category of the human. Shih puts it bluntly:

> When certain people have not been considered and treated as humans, posthumanism serves as an alibi for the further denial of humanity to these same people. Cybernetics might be a step beyond old-fashioned Enlightenment humanism, technologically speaking, but the newly emerging subjects of history – colonized people, women, minorities of all kinds – need to be respected and dignified as humans first.[2]

Can there be a posthumanism of the not-yet-human? To what extent can subaltern subjects understand themselves to be post-human if their humanity has yet to be vouchsafed by a global order still haunted by colonial epistemologies and what Aph Ko has called the "zoological witchcraft" of white supremacy?[3] If posthumanity, according to Rosi Braidotti and others, embraces the disintegration of the unified humanist subject and revels in the multiplicity, plasticity, and permeability of the contemporary self,[4] can one desire the lineaments of full humanity and be post-human at the same time? Or, for Shih's "newly emerging subjects of history", is the prospect of achieving posthumanity inevitably utopian, speculative, and futurist?

These questions have particular saliency in the context of African contemporary art. A certain brand of neo-Hegelianism persists in the international art market, fueling a stubbornly perennial tendency to see the work of many African artists in terms of tradition, heritage, and tribe. This largely revanchist critical framework exists, uneasily, alongside burgeoning global enthusiasm for Afrofuturism, which seeks in part to retrieve Africa from the pre-historical state of nature to which Hegel consigned it. Here Afrofuturist critics are following the lead of African artists themselves, who – as Achille Mbembe has argued in his work on Afropolitanism – are "breaking with the ethnological paradigms that will have corseted... [African art] into primitivism or neoprimitivism".[5] By emphasizing the digital, speculative, and cyborg dimensions of contemporary African art, Afrofuturist scholarship catapults the continent and its artists into a future of its own making. If the Hegelian philosophy of history and the paleoanthropology of human origins converge in an account of Africa as a space of pre-humanity, and neoliberal economics conspires with the "white-savior industrial complex" to mark Africa out as a space of semi- or perhaps all-too-human suffering and chaos,[6] then Afrofuturism insists on a posthuman transcendence of the narratives to which the continent has been subject.

This suggests that the time of the posthuman in contemporary African art is the time of the not-yet. But that is too simple, too easy, too completely in tune with positivist history and its well-mannered succession of post-s. The reality on the ground requires a theory of the posthuman that accounts for the fact that "African modernity", according to Mbembe, is "a migrant form of modernity, born out of overlapping genealogies, at the intersections of multiple encounters with multiple elsewheres".[7] This leads me to conceive of the posthuman in African art in the same way that Tejumola Olaniyan conceives of the postcolonial in African literature: as an "acephalous, interregnumal space", "a temporality that is not so easily, so triumphantly categorized".[8] Here I am also following the lead of Elizabeth Grosz, who suggests that time is only cognizable "in passing moments, through ruptures, nicks, cuts, in instances of dislocation".[9] What if the promise of the posthuman, like the promise of the postcolonial, resides less in its futurity than in the break it marks or makes in time itself? This, indeed, is the line of thinking that I believe the Kenyan artists Cyrus Kabiru, Wangechi Mutu, and Wanuri Kahiu are following in their sculptures, photographs, collages, performances, and films. By destabilizing the distinctions between human, animal, plant, and machine; past, present, and future; utopia and apocalypse, these artists scavenge the posthuman and bring it to new life. In their work, the time of the posthuman is untimely.

***

In the poet Clifton Gachagua's "Satellite," posthuman bodies loom.

> They spoke with satellite mouths and gathered words between
> their phalanges like hands in sacks of rice
> throwing them to us, offering them to us as we slept.
>
> [....]
>
> We posed in our sleep because they were taking pictures from
> small passages in their palms.
> Their bodies were singing machines. They gave birth and were
> born from old grandfather clocks.
> Each pore in their body was a pinhole and the slightest muscle
> movement led to a billion photographs
> culminating in the blood.[10]

"They" are denatured and cyborg – speaking and singing, seeing and touching by means of machinery that is less prosthetic than a constituent part of their physiology, down to their muscles and blood. Their reproductive functions are clockwork, suggesting that their bodies' enmeshment of biology and technology extends all the way down to the creation of life itself. While they are menacing in their unrelenting and "unethical" surveillance, "Satellite" is at its core a meditation on beauty: "They were beautiful and we / were beautiful before that;" "Beauty was / a thing you could savor with your tongue sticking out like a / reptile".[11]

This poem provides a hermeneutic for the sculptures and photographs of Gachagua's fellow Kenyan Cyrus Kabiru (b. 1984). A series of important international

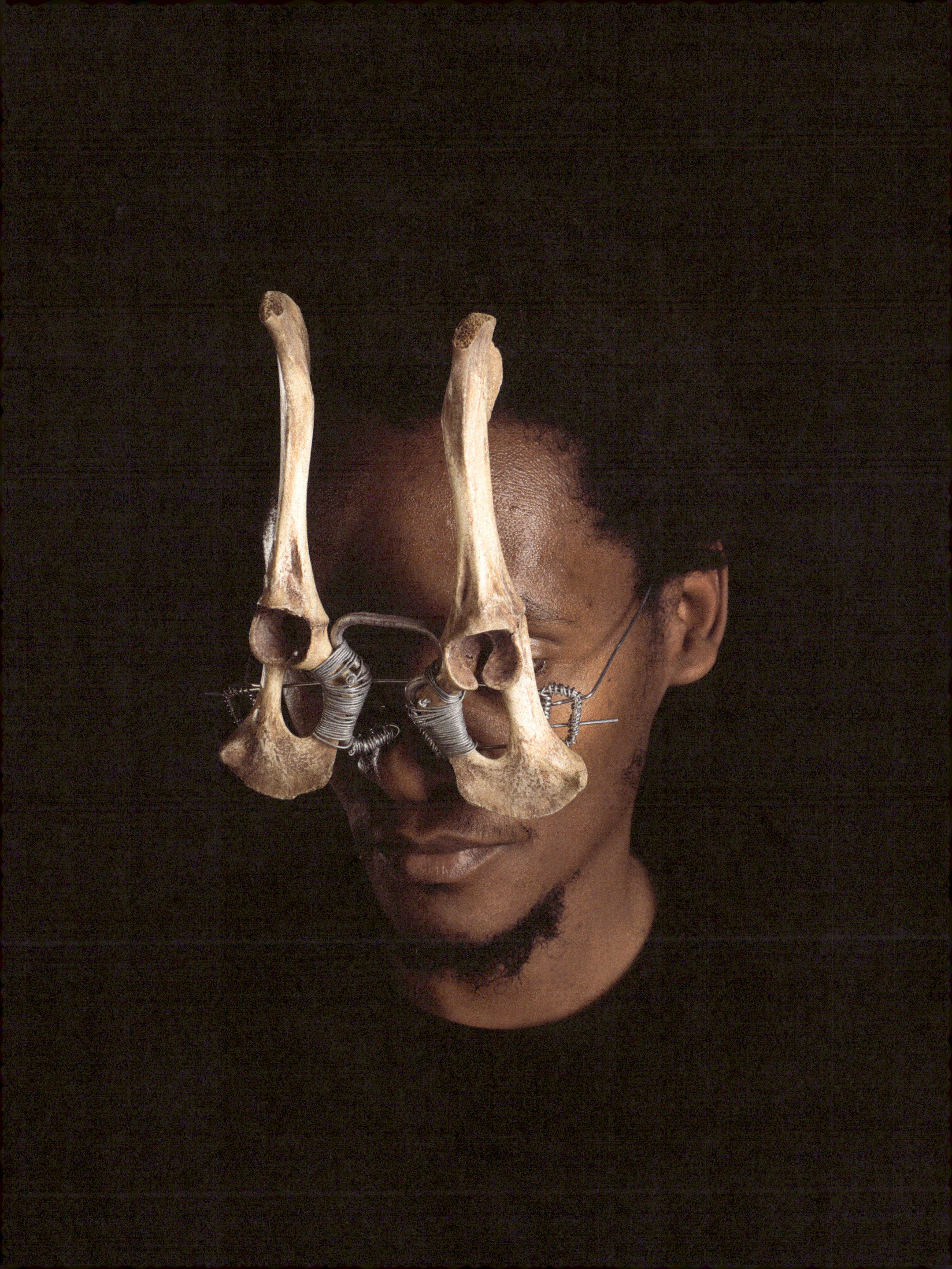

residencies and exhibitions has established Kabiru as one of the most consequential African artists of his generation. Much of his reputation rests on his *C-Stunners*, wearable sculptures that the artist conceives of as elaborate eyeglasses, at once aperture and mask. While these "macho nne" – "four-eyes" in Swahili – are sometimes exhibited or worn in public, typically by the artist himself, they circulate more widely in photographic form. The austere self-portraits that Kabiru makes capture both the object and his activation of the object in and on his body; they serve as performance documentation and as artworks in their own right. Consider *Speedometer* (2015). The enormous glasses Kabiru wears seem to enlarge his eyes, redirecting his gaze away from the viewer as the graduated semi-circles, numbered 1-5, that protrude into the aperture on both sides, seem to gauge or calibrate his field of vision and the depth of his focus. Like the "pinhole" cameras that occupy "[e]ach pore in their body" in "Satellite," this particular *C-Stunner* seems fully integrated into Kabiru's own physiology. This, of course, makes Kabiru a cyborg – a familiar figure from many accounts of the posthuman. His becoming-camera – or, given the title of the piece, becoming-car – locates him immediately and recognizably in a genealogy of Afrofuturist and posthumanist body art and fashion that includes the likes of Sun Ra and Oumu Sy.[12]

At the same time, Kabiru's own artistic practice makes it difficult to locate his work exclusively in an imagined future. As many commentators have noted, he makes most of his *C-Stunners* and other sculptures from found materials like wire, broken circuit boards, and tobacco tins sourced from the post-postmodern detritus of Nairobi, where he grew up, as well as other places he visits as he travels around the world. Kabiru's reliance on bricolage means that nothing he makes is entirely new. His materials are, in a word, recycled – a term that carries both ecological and ethical implications. The materiality of his *C-Stunners* and his more recent work on bicycles and radios situates them, as Amogelang Maledu claims, in "topographies and ebbs of modernization" and in "the layered 'social lives' of things".[13] Kabiru's work vibrates with the untimely. His futurity has historicity latent in its materiality. It is this quality of his work that leads some critics to see it as a "cyberpunk update on ancient tribal headgear".[14] This formulation, while redolent of a primitivist approach to African art in general, marks the ambivalence of the post- in Kabiru's work; it is at once cyberpunk and ancient, posthuman and precolonial.

This indeterminacy extends to questions of form and material as well. Kabiru incorporates organic materials like animal bone or calabashes into his *C-Stunners*, complicating any straightforward reading of his work as a practice of becoming-machine. He also frequently works with non-human animal names and likenesses, as in *Caribbean Peacock* (2014), *Vatican Mask* (2015) and *KwaZulu Elephant* (2015). The imposition of a highly abstracted metal elephant face onto his own certainly invokes the willful transgression of the boundaries between human, animal and machine that Donna Haraway has explored in her work on the cyborg.[15] It also indexes the temporal rootlessness of Kabiru's work, however, as he intends *KwaZulu Elephant*, like many of his other animal-themed *C-Stunners*, to comment on the ecological pressures that beset the more-than-human world. Given the indelible mark that colonial and neocolonial systems of land tenure, agriculture, and wildlife management have made on the African landscape, it is reasonable to ask when and where the *KwaZulu Elephant* he becomes when he wears the glasses exists. Is this *C-Stunner* a vestige of a long-since-vanished world of plenty, in which wild elephants roamed what is now KwaZulu Natal in much greater numbers? Or is it a harbinger of a future in which the only elephants remaining in Southern Africa will be representations made of wire, a broken spoon, and memory? The posthuman dimensions of Kabiru's work inhere precisely in this indeterminacy, in the flux between history, futurity and fantasy

***

In 2019, the Metropolitan Museum of Art in New York unveiled a new commission from Wangechi Mutu (b. 1972), who is easily the most renowned Kenyan artist on

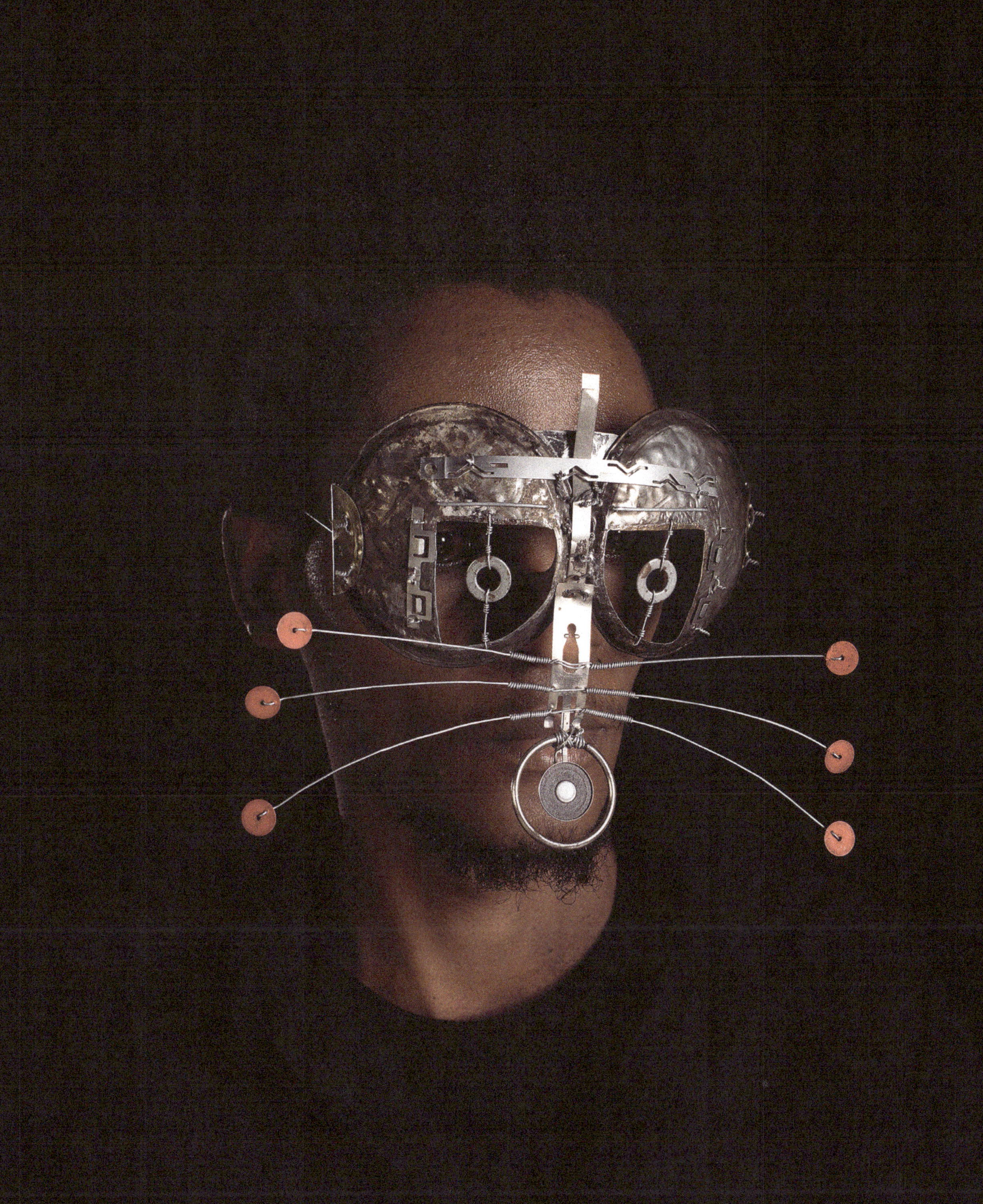

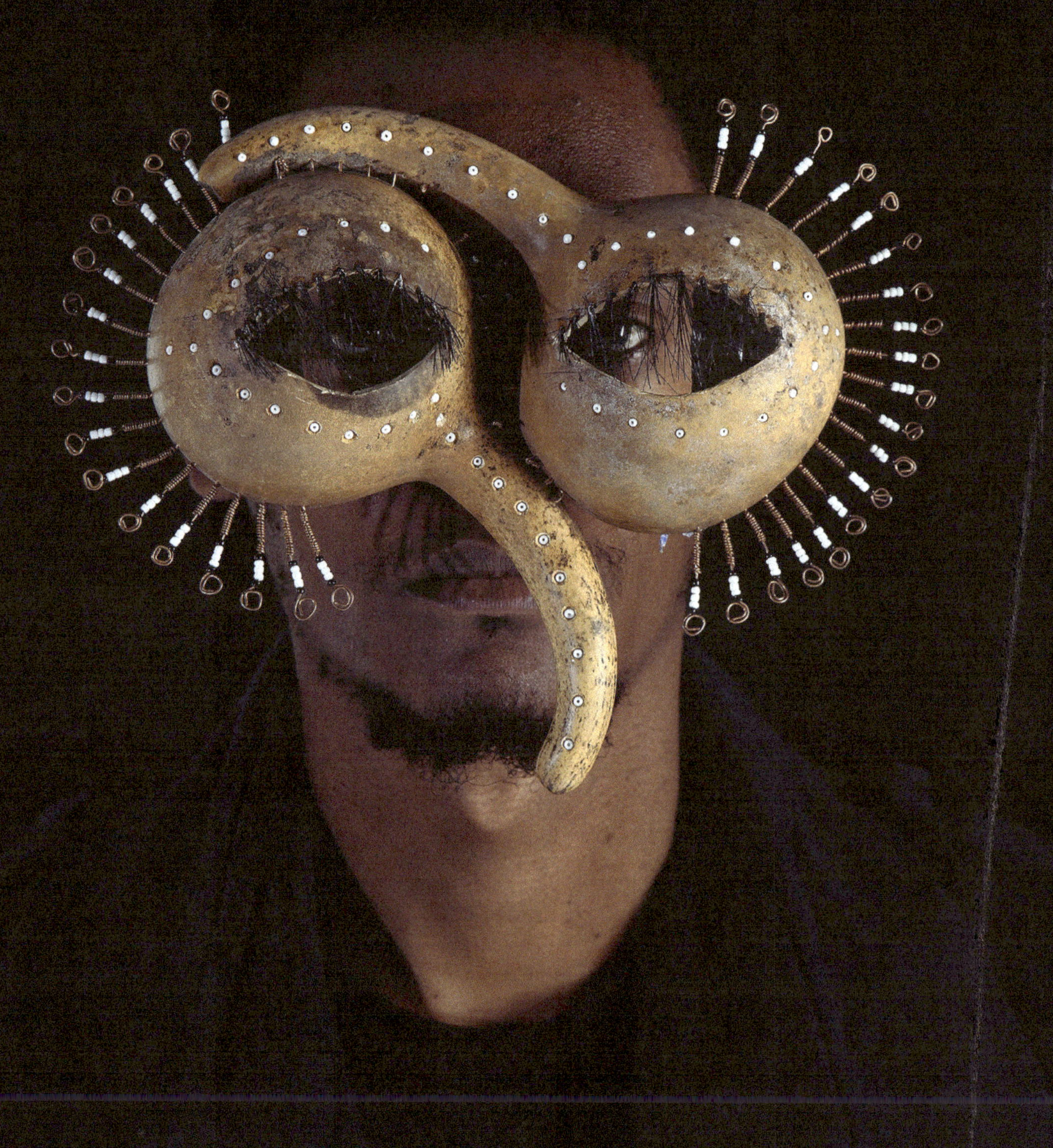
antennae

the international contemporary art scene. The four alcoves flanking the museum's grand entrance had stood empty since Richard Morris Hunt's neoclassical façade was completed in 1902. One hundred and seventeen years later, those alcoves became home to Mutu's *The NewOnes, will free Us*—four monumental sculptures of seated women cast in bronze. Raised above the heads of the crowd gathered to gain entrance to the museum, these figures, which the artist refers to simply as *The Seated I-IV*, surveyed Fifth Avenue from a royal remove. Light caught on the polished bronze—and particularly the circular adornments of three out of four figures, which had been burnished to a mirror finish—arresting the gaze of passers-by with what Mutu has called "'a stunning message from beyond'".[16] Both of and not of the façade, *The NewOnes, will free Us* was a subversive, decolonial take on the caryatid, a sculptural representation of a woman, prevalent in both European and African art, that bears weight—the weight of a building, the weight of a king. Mutu wanted "to keep the DNA of the woman in an active pose, but...didn't want her to carry the weight of something or someone else".[17] In their niches in the Met façade, *The Seated I-IV* bore no weight but their own. They were unburdened—and therefore free, striking a defiant pose from their perch on and within the architecture of the Western cultural and political imaginary.

In some ways, these sculptures mark a departure from the riotous cacophony of Mutu's best-known work in painting and collage. This disjuncture is in part a question of the materiality of her medium, as molten bronze smooths over the rips, tears, spills and punctures that paper and Mylar disclose. Mutu has acknowledged the impact her mother, a nurse and owner of a pharmacy, had on her artistic practice:

> Through her, I've inherited a deep love of growing things. In fact, my whole fascination with mark-making as an organic, alchemic eruption, as opposed to a choreographed notation, stems from her influence. My obsession with ink, solvents, liquids, paper, and surfaces comes from my belief in the live and organic qualities of the mark as well as its associations with elements like blood, saliva, milk, tears, sweat, and urine.[18]

Mutu's work on paper and canvas may foreground this vitalist materiality, but it is very much present in her sculptures as well. I locate it in the serpentine folds that surround each of *The Seated I-IV* – at once a kind of robe or cloak and a living, breathing extension of each body. As Mutu put it: "I've created these coils that I've put all the way around their body that felt tactile and living and fleshy, but at the same time really protected the women and gave them a kind of privacy and a regal nature. They became almost like soldiers, like they were in armor".[19]

These soldier-queens, in other words, like most of the figures that populate Mutu's oeuvre, are somehow other-than- or more-than-human, submerged as they are in energetic and material flows that meld with and erupt from the erstwhile human form. In addition to the "tactile and living and fleshy" coils that wrap around their bodies, the circular pieces that grace the heads and faces of three of *The NewOnes, will free Us* sculptures—while inspired, as Mutu has said, by the lip plates worn by women from certain Ethiopian and Sudanese ethnic groups[20]—seem to protrude organically from flesh rather than adhering to it as adornment. I see this as an otherworldly muscular-skeletal extension of the body, less a prosthetic than the corporeal trace of an evolutionary leap or divine intervention, an "organic, alchemic eruption" that seems to incarnate, in more ways than one, the oracular energy that these sculptures exuded above the fountains and the hot dog carts of Fifth Avenue.

Consider *Seated IV*. At first glance, it appears that this figure's face and forehead are simply covered by a circular plate or headpiece. The folds on either side of the nose, beneath the highly polished disk, appear to be the lower lids of the figure's eyes or else fleshy protrusions caused by the goggle-like headpiece pressing into the face. Upon closer inspection, however, it becomes clear that there is no seam between flesh and supposed adornment; the circular disk is as fully integrated into

77

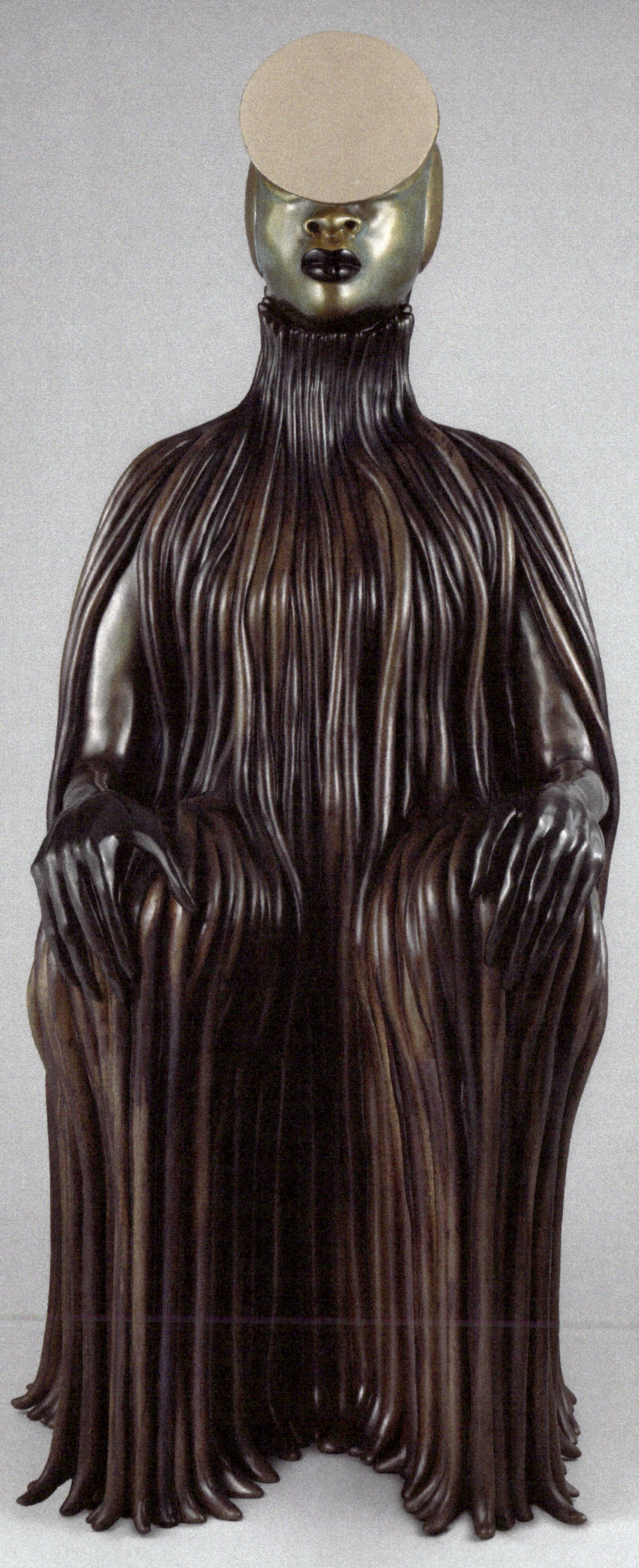

Wangechi Mutu
*The Seated IV,
bronze (edition of
three with one artist
proof)*, 2019; ©
the artist; image
courtesy the artist
and Gladstone Gal-
lery, New York and
Brussels; photog-
raphy by Joseph
Coscia, Jr., Imaging,
The Metropolitan
Museum of Art
© Wangechi Mutu

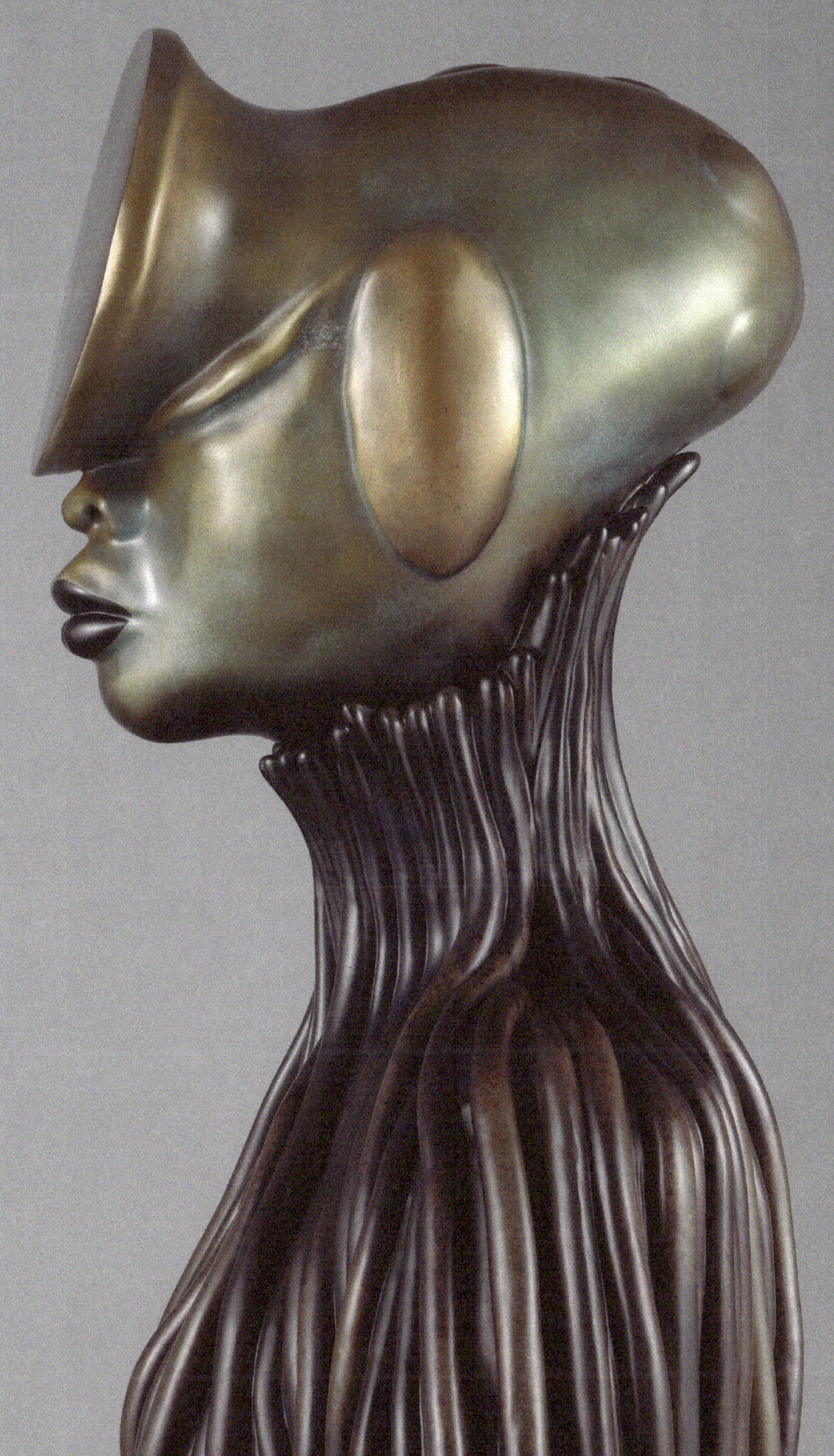

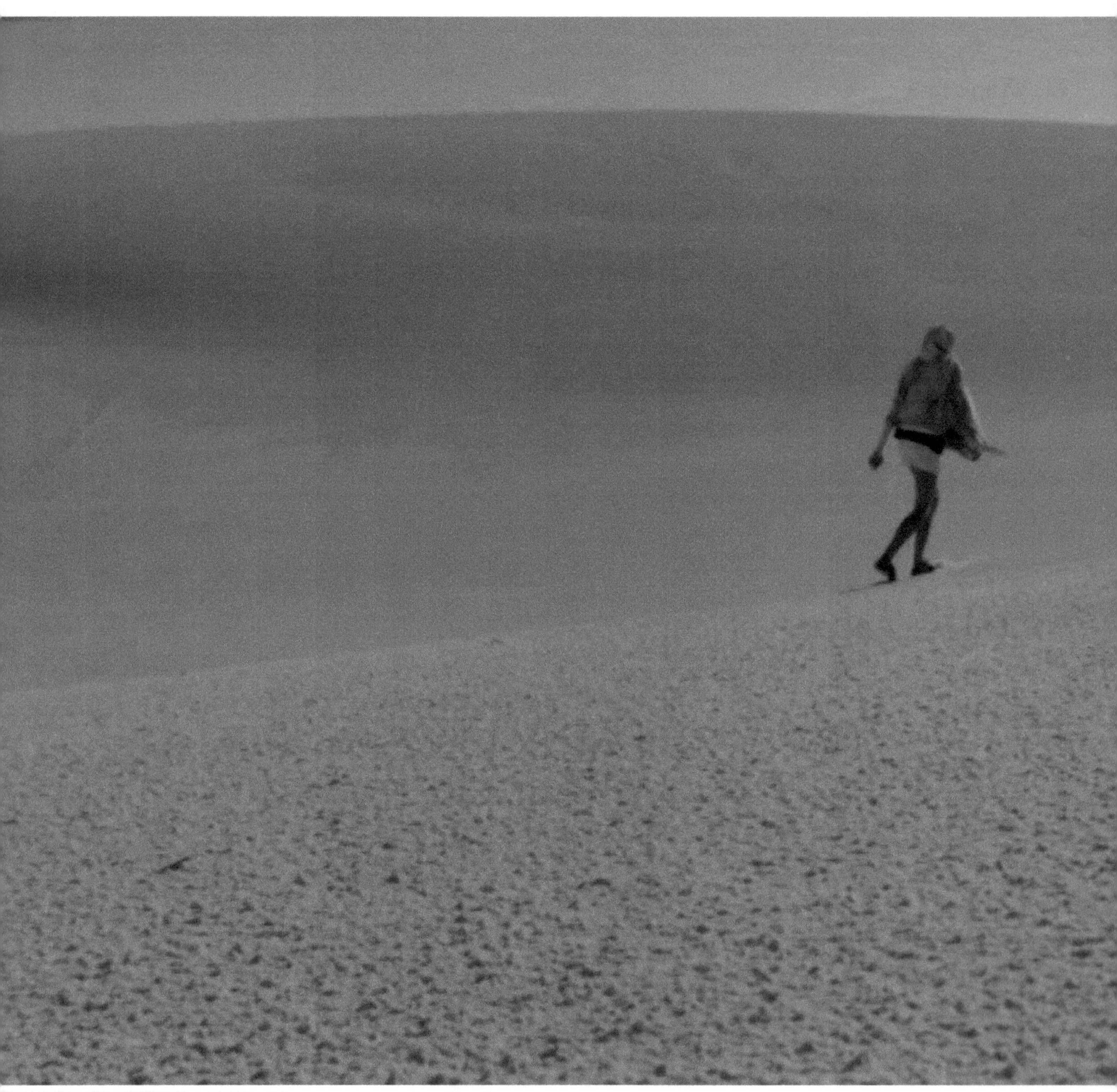

Wanuri Kahiu

Pumzi (film still), film, 2009 © Focus Features, image courtesy Inspired Minority Pictures

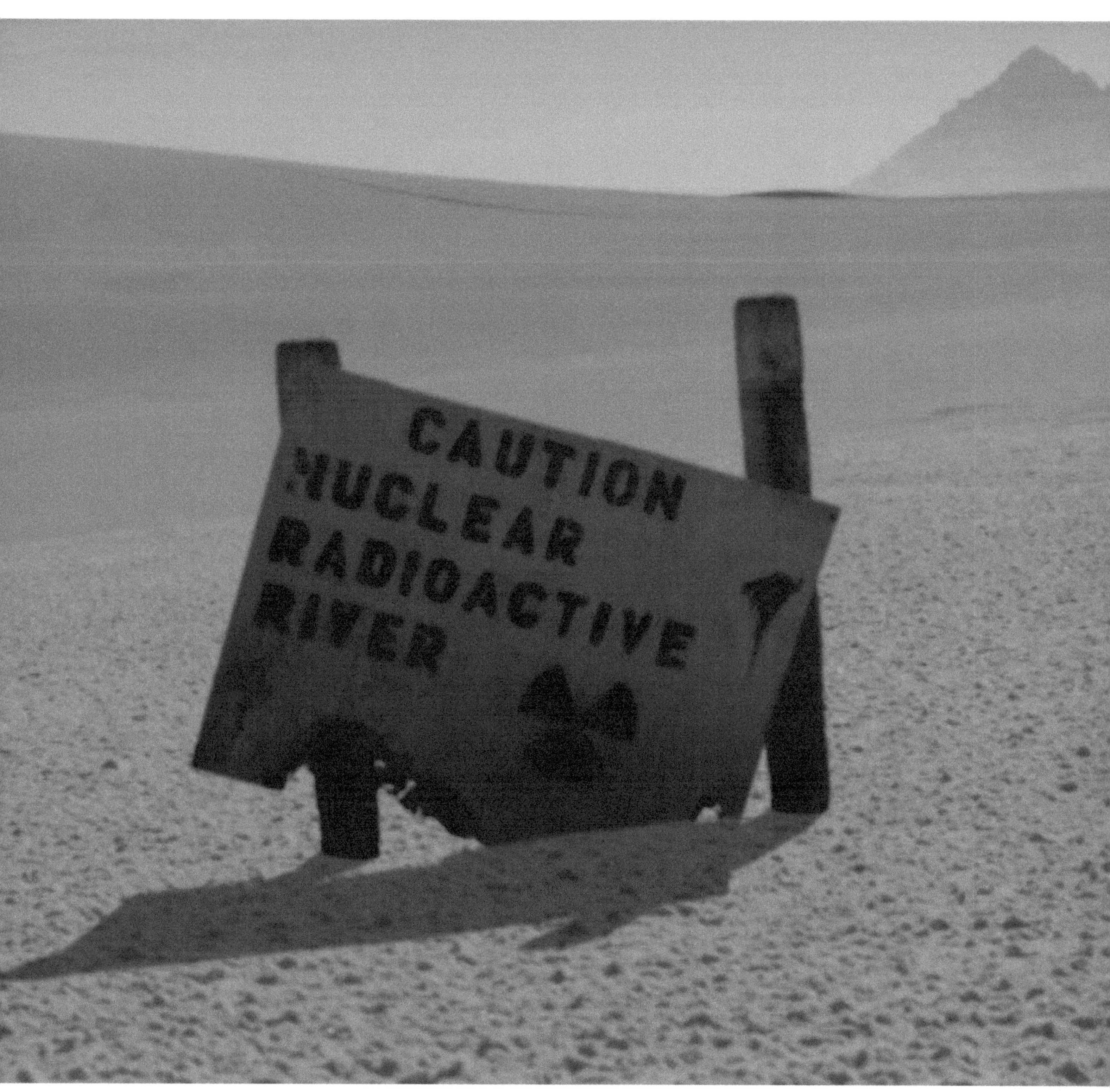
CAUTION
NUCLEAR
RADIOACTIVE
RIVER

the head of the figure as the nose and lips are. It is, in effect, a single enormous eye, as "live and organic" as ink and solvent are in Mutu's paintings, emerging—like the solid ear-pieces and the smooth scale- or shell-like bumps on the back and top of the skull—from the skin and bone of the head itself. Like Kabiru's *C-Stunners*, what appears at first to be a mask superimposed onto the face of the artist's subject becomes an aperture through which the figure sees itself being seen. Given the politics and institutional history of the Met, the fact that this ocular surface has been polished to a mirror finish has special significance. The great posthuman eye of *The Seated IV* refracts and reflects the colonial gaze back onto itself. As a group, *The Seated I-IV* stage an insurrectionary upheaval, an epistemic break, an interruption in the space-time continuum of coloniality: four bronze extraterrestrial women glimmering darkly in the midst of the marble-white façade of metropolitan cultural power. As Eve MacSweeney puts it in her review of *The NewOnes, will free Us*, "this homecoming, if you can call it that, carries all manner of poignant historical, political, and redemptive narratives along with it. An institution founded on the appropriation of antiquities and a Eurocentric view of culture is being turned on its head".[21]

This account of what *The NewOnes, will free Us* accomplished, which is everywhere in evidence in the press that the commission received, positions *The Seated I-IV* – and with them Mutu herself—in the position of the post-. Because Mutu is Kenyan and therefore, somehow, postcolonial, and because the *Seated I-IV* – "part African queens, part cyborgs", as MacSweeney puts it[22]—clearly exist within an Afrofuturist and posthuman frame of reference, their presence at the Met moved the museum into a new area, "turn[ing it] on its head". This notion of a clear and indeed unprecedented break with the past accords with the theatricality of the sculptures' sudden arrival on their plinths, almost as if they had descended from the heavens, avatars of what Reynaldo Anderson and Charles E. Jones call "astro-blackness".[23] When the commission was unveiled, the future had arrived. But it is equally possible, given the vast collections of African and other "non-Western" art that the Met houses, including a wide selection of caryatids of many types, to envision *The Seated I-IV* creeping or oozing out of the façade of the museum, surfacing once more, from within, the insurrectionary force of the Other that the museum had always enclosed, celebrated and disavowed. This resonates with Mutu's practice in general, which is so often concerned with unexpected and even grotesque upheavals of life itself. In a *Guardian* piece about Mutu's 2014 gallery show *Nguva na Nyoka*, Teju Cole repeats a story the artist told him about a snake that had to be killed twice. Mutu was a teenager at the time, living on the coast of Kenya, and her Mijikenda neighbors killed a python — only to discover that it had slithered away and had to be found and killed a second time. Cole links Mutu's lingering fascination with this episode to the vein of "ungovernable" energy that runs through her work.[24] The snake has to be killed a second time, or perhaps a third, or perhaps it's already dead and has returned, in pieces, to haunt its tormenters, or perhaps it's a benevolent spirit returning once again to offer itself up for annihilation. The possibilities are endless and present all at once.

Like the dead and not-dead snake, *The Seated I-IV* oscillate between extremities of being and becoming. This, for me, is Mutu's vision of the posthuman: human and alien; machine and flesh; ancient and futuristic; beyond any conception of race, gender, or species but nevertheless still deeply enmeshed in their conceptual web. The title of the commission itself makes this indeterminacy plain. Who are these *NewOnes*? Mutu has suggested that "the new ones are new immigrants, children, women, and all these people who are bringing new ideas"[25]—but are "the new ones" *NewOnes*? And, regardless, are they the seated figures Mutu sculpted? If they are, how will they free us? From what? And when? And who are we? And if they aren't, if they are harbingers of a new order still to come, posthuman prophets of another world in the making, how long must we wait and how will we know when freedom arrives? Mutu herself remains somewhat enigmatic, saying only that these silent figures "have the capacity, the freedom and the opportunity to be where they need to be, to say what they have to say. They're here, and they're present, and they've arrived".[26] What is clear is that they are "present" to both the future and the past, vibrating in the flux of the post-. They linger, waiting with us, for us, just above our heads.

***

The Kenyan film director Wanuri Kahiu's *Pumzi* (2009), a dystopian fable about an East African community navigating the aftermath of biospheric collapse, exists in the post- as well. Kahiu (b. 1980) opens the film with a title card that sets the story "35 years after World War III—'The Water War.'" Like most invocations of the post-, this statement of the film's postapocalyptic futurity folds back onto itself. How does one mark time from an event—World War III—that has not yet occurred? Is the film set in a future that is now, given the accelerating pace of ecological devastation and anthropogenic climate change, certain to come to be? Or does it exist in a branch reality, a possible futurity, likely but not inevitable? Even more intriguingly, is this an alternate or parallel present? East African history discloses many brutal and wide-ranging conflicts over water use, food security, and land tenure; is this the future of that past? Is this, in other words, a version of our own present in which precarity is more universally distributed? These questions are critical to Kahiu's vision of Afrofuturism, which she considers to be germane not only to imagining the future and ensuring that Black people are present in it but also to resurfacing the speculative practices of African communities that have all too often been excluded from the official canons of science fiction.[27] What is future is also past – and, like Mutu's *NewOnes*, made present in the work.

While the points of divergence between Afrofuturism and posthumanism are significant, particularly when it comes to whether Black futurity aims at achieving or surpassing the political category of the human, here the two seem to run in parallel. The organic and the technological are, to a certain degree, isomorphic in *Pumzi*—as they are in Kabiru's *C-Stunners* and Mutu's *The NewOnes, will free Us*. The settlement in which most of the action of the film takes place—"Maitu Community, East African Territory"—functions as a self-sustaining organism. Indeed, in the opening aerial shot that establishes the world of the film, I find the exterior of the settlement complex strikingly reminiscent of a seed putting down roots and preparing to grow. Life inside this techno-organism is correspondingly hybrid. The viewer first encounters Asha (Kudzani Moswela), the protagonist of the film, in the "virtual natural history museum" she runs, amongst luminous screens and petrified specimens of other creatures. She is sleeping – so still and silent at first that one could be forgiven for taking her to be dead and on display herself. In her waking moments, Asha functions as a cyborg mitochondria within the larger body of her community. Like all the other residents of the settlement, she is subject to a totalitarian mode of sovereign authority that hides behind a rhetoric of equality, sustainability, and self-sufficiency. The Maitu Community's electrical power is supplied by its residents' unceasing efforts on converted exercise equipment, all while a disembodied voice repeats "Have you done your share today? Generate electricity for your community. Be a self-power-generator." Here, any trace of individuality is disavowed—or actively remediated with "dream suppressant" pills. Armed guards distribute water rations, and everyone is compelled to conserve their liquid waste for purification and re-consumption. Matter and energy flow in and through and from the posthuman body in its entanglement with other bodies and machines; mere human subjectivity is disdained and suppressed.

"The outside," however, as a member of "The Council" reminds Asha, "is dead." The settlement-seed is lodged within what appears to be an unending desert. Conflict arises when Asha receives an unexpected package containing an unusually fertile soil sample, in which she resolves to start a "maitu seed" displayed in the natural history museum. Here, of course, is another indication of the importance of seeds, which Kirk Sides has suggested are key to understanding the new modes of Anthropocenic storytelling that the film deploys;[28] the seed and the settlement are both named "maitū," or "mother" in the Gĩkũyũ language. In order to ensure the mother seed's reproduction, and with it ecological and social restoration and repair

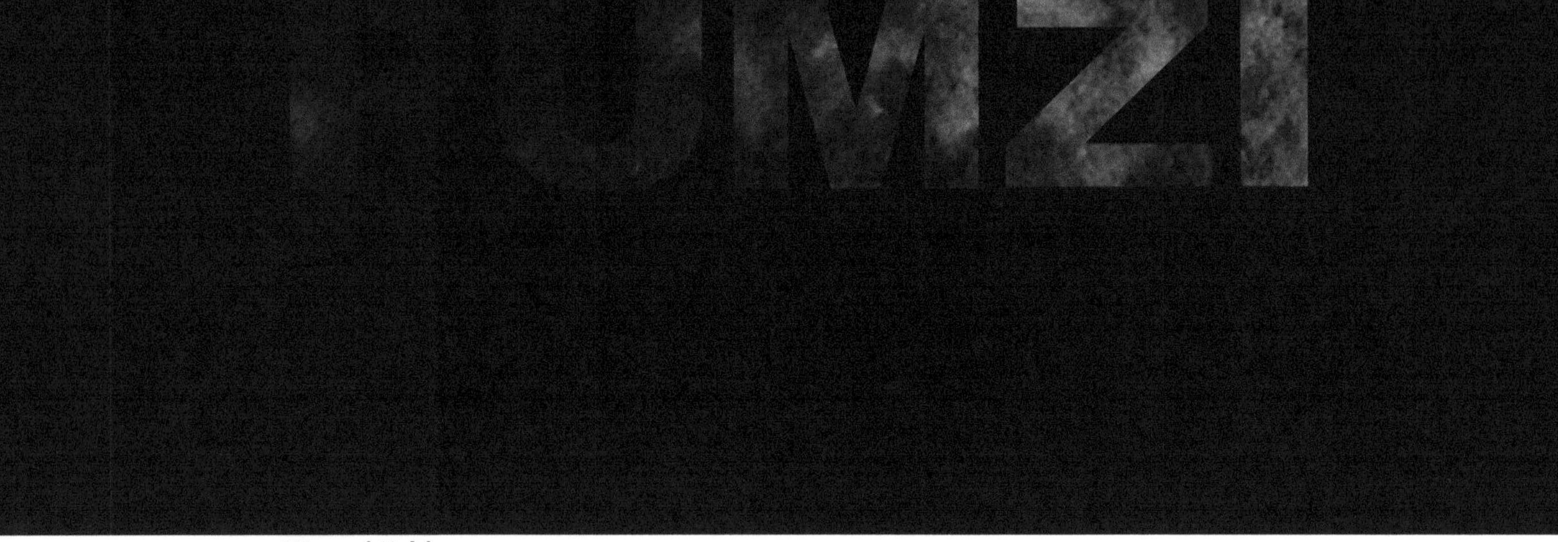

Wanuri Kahiu
Pumzi (film still), film, 2009 © Focus Features, image courtesy Inspired Minority Pictures

writ large, Asha risks everything to escape the settlement and plant the seed she has sprouted in the place where the mysterious soil sample was originally taken. This journey requires everything of her. Asha's final, beatific moments are spent watering the tiny sapling with the last of her water and then with her sweat, shielding it from the sun with her body. As the camera slowly cranes up—reprising in reverse the opening shot of the film, which descended downwards towards the settlement-seed —Asha's exhausted body gives out and goes still. After a moment, the leafy shadow of the tree she has planted grows up around her. In death, she becomes life.

On the face of it, this is a fairly straightforward story of human overcoming —albeit to a radically selfless ecological end. James Wachira has tied the film's politics of environmental remediation to the work of Wangari Maathai, whose work on reforestation in East and Central Africa earned her the Nobel Peace Prize in 2004.[29] This reading certainly illuminates the politics of *Pumzi* as a work of feminist science fiction; there is no doubt that the film stages an uncompromising vision of ecological stewardship, sustained and enacted by women on behalf of "mother earth." At the same time, however, Asha not only cares for the tree she sacrifices herself to plant – she is materially and energetically entwined in its fledgling existence. Her becoming-tree, like Kabiru's becoming-animal/becoming-machine in his elephant series, oscillates in time and space, blurring the boundaries of body and environment, self and other, past and present. At the end of the film, as the camera moves smoothly upward from Asha's body and the mother tree she has become, the title of the film appears on screen, the all-caps block letters made out of the landscape below as darkness encroaches from all sides. This inscription of text onto earth reveals a vast and leafy forest on the other side of a ridge from Asha's becoming-tree. Thunder growls softly in the distance, promising rain. Is this the future that Asha's self-sacrifice made possible? Are these the arboreal children of her surrogate parenthood, the product of her seeds' dispersal? Or was this forest there all along, "35 years after World War III," concealed from view by the Maitu Community authorities in their drive to maintain the illusion of environmental precarity with which they have domesticated their unwitting subjects? Is the "outside" not really dead—making all of Asha's heroics moot? Or does the film actually go back in time here, moving backward to our present, before desertification made Asha's self-sacrifice necessary? It is impossible to say with certainty.

The word "pumzi" in Swahili means "breath." The film exists in a moment of suspension, in the indefinite interval between exhalation and inhalation when both life and death are possible. This is the untimely, or what Grosz would call a "nick" in time.[30] Asha, like *The Seated I-IV* and Kabiru in his *C-Stunners*, moves freely along a chain of transubstantiations: human, alien, animal, object, tree, refuse, architecture, landscape, cosmos. All three bodies of work are in that sense posthuman, free of the universalizing discourses of humanity – from which more institutionalized forms of posthumanism have yet to fully extricate themselves. *Pumzi*, *The Seated I-IV*, and the *C-Stunners* resonate in and with the human, in the indefinite caesura that the word post- conjures for all of the emergent historical subjects for whom the orderly succession of regimes and ideas has never been guaranteed.

Endnotes

[1] Kwame Anthony Appiah, "Is the Post- in Postmodernism the Post- in Post-Colonial?," *Critical Inquiry* 17, no. 2 (Winter 1991): 336–57; Shu-mei Shih, "Is the Post- in Postsocialism the Post- in Posthumanism?," *Social Text* 30, no. 1 (Spring 2012): 27–50.
[2] Shih, "Is the Post- in Postsocialism the Post- in Posthumanism?" 30.
[3] Aph Ko, *Racism as Zoological Witchcraft: A Guide to Getting Out* (New York: Lantern Books, 2019).
[4] See, for instance, Rosi Braidotti, *The Posthuman* (Cambridge: Polity Press, 2013).
[5] Achille Mbembe, "Africa in the New Century," *The Massachusetts Review* 57, no. 1 (Spring 2016): 95.
[6] See Teju Cole, "The White-Savior Industrial Complex," *The Atlantic*, March 21, 2012.
[7] Mbembe, "Africa in the New Century," 96.
[8] Tejumola Olaniyan, "On 'Post-Colonial Discourse:' An Introduction," *Callaloo* 16, no. 4 (Autumn 1993): 746.
[9] Elizabeth Grosz, *The Nick of Time: Politics, Evolution, and the Untimely* (Durham: Duke University Press, 2004), 5.
[10] Clifton Gachagua, "Satellite," in *Madman at Kilifi*, African Poetry Book Series (Lincoln: University of Nebraska Press, 2014), 3.
[11] Gachagua.
[12] Annalisa Oboe explores the links between Kabiru and Sy in Annalisa Oboe, "Sculptural Eyewear and *Cyberfemmes*: Afrofuturist Arts," *From the European South*, no. 4 (2019): 31–44.
[13] Amogelang Maledu, "The *Msanii* Giving Trash a Second Chance: Cosmopolitan Contamination in Cyrus Kabiru's Work," *SMAC Gallery*, n.d., https://smacgallery.com/exhibition/cyrus-kabiru-artist-room-2020/.
[14] Edd Norval, "Cyrus Kabiru - A Different Kind of Mask," *Compulsive Contents*, November 2, 2020, https://www.compulsivecontents.com/detail-event/cyrus-kabiru---a-different-kind-of-mask/.
[15] Donna J. Haraway, "A Cyborg Manifesto: Science, Technology, and Socialist-Feminism in the Late Twentieth Century," in *Manifestly Haraway* (Minneapolis: University of Minnesota Press, 2016), 3–90.
[16] Quoted in Nancy Princenthal, "Wangechi Mutu: A New Face for the Met," *New York Times*, September 5, 2019, https://www.nytimes.com/2019/09/05/arts/design/wangechi-mutu-metropolitan-museum.html.
[17] Kate Farrell, *Artist Interview - Wangechi Mutu: 'The NewOnes, Will Free Us'* (New York: The Metropolitan Museum of Art, 2019).
[18] Wangechi Mutu, "The Power of Earth in My Work," in *Earth Matters: Land as Material and Metaphor in the Arts of Africa*, by Karen E. Milbourne (New York: Monacelli Press, 2014), 93.
[19] Farrell, *Artist Interview - Wangechi Mutu: 'The NewOnes, Will Free Us.'*
[20] Farrell.
[21] Eve MacSweeney, "How Kenyan-Born Artist Wangechi Mutu Is Taking Over the Met," *W*, August 27, 2019, https://www.wmagazine.com/story/wangechi-mutu-metropolitan-museum-of-art-sculptures/.
[22] MacSweeney.
[23] Reynaldo Anderson and Charles E. Jones, eds., *Afrofuturism 2.0: The Rise of Astro-Blackness* (Lanham, MD: Lexington Books, 2016).
[24] Teju Cole, "Wangechi Mutu: Under the Skin of Africa," *The Guardian*, September 25, 2014.
[25] Wangechi Mutu, "Wangechi Mutu on *The NewOnes, Will Free Us*," *The Metropolitan Museum of Art*, October 30, 2019, https://www.metmuseum.org/blogs/now-at-the-met/2019/wangechi-mutu-the-new-ones-will-free-us.
[26] Farrell, *Artist Interview - Wangechi Mutu: 'The NewOnes, Will Free Us.'*
[27] *Afrofuturism in Popular Culture*, TEDxNairobi, 2012, https://www.youtube.com/watch?v=PvxOLVaV2YY.
[28] Kirk Bryan Sides, "Seed Bags and Storytelling: Modes of Living and Writing after the End in Wanuri Kahiu's *Pumzi*," *Critical Philosophy of Race* 7, no. 1 (2019): 107–23.
[29] James Wachira, "Wangari Maathai's Environmental Afrofuturist Imaginary in Wanuri Kahiu's *Pumzi*," *Critical Studies in Media Communication* 37, no. 4 (2020): 324–36.
[30] Grosz, *The Nick of Time: Politics, Evolution, and the Untimely*.

Joshua Williams is a writer, director, translator, theatre historian and performance theorist currently serving as a Visiting Assistant Professor of English at Brandeis University. His academic work concerns the non-human animal in East African theatre, performance, literature and visual art. His articles, essays and reviews have appeared in *The Johannesburg Salon, Theatre Journal, Theatre Survey, Performance Research, Modern Drama, African Theatre and The Los Angeles Review of Books,* amongst others. He is currently translating the complete plays of the Tanzanian dramatist Ebrahim Hussein from Swahili into English for Oxford University Press. jdmwilliams.com

A Billion Black Anthropocenes

Kathryn Yusoff examines how the grammar of geology is foundational to establishing the extractive economies of subjective life and the earth under colonialism and slavery. She initiates a transdisciplinary conversation between black feminist theory, geography, and the earth sciences, addressing the politics of the Anthropocene within the context of race, materiality, deep time, and the afterlives of geology.

in conversation: **Kathryn Yusoff and Betelhem Makonnen**

Betelhem Makonnen: Your book *A Billion Black Anthropocenes or None* was published as part of the University of Minnesota Press *Forerunners: Ideas First* series, a collection of wonderful-to-hold-in-the-hand short books that prioritize intense analysis, questioning, and speculation of in-process scholarship. Could you first tell us the beginnings of this work and its path to publication?

Kathryn Yusoff: The Forerunners books published by the University of Minnesota Press are great because they are small enough to fit in your pocket and cheap enough to pass on, which means they have a very different audience to the expensive academic tomes. This ability to travel and the freedom given by the folk at Minnesota press meant the book moved outside the academy and this has been one of the real joys of the publication format, as people come back with very different kinds of questions (and critiques) than might be addressed to a journal article. The work itself comes out of being in all-too many Anthropocene conferences and discussions where the scaling up to the 'universal-we' and imperialistic imaginaries of the planet covered over too much in terms of the histories of violence and questions of agency in the material transformation of earth forces. Needless to say, it was a very masculinist and white discourse. There is a persistent 'white innocence' to environmental thought and a certain mystification about its own origin stories that allow narratives of redemption. So, the book started as a talk, then the seeds of a paper critiquing the discourse of the Anthropocene, but it ended up being concerned with a much broader extractive economy of how race is materially constructed. And, given the explicitly racialized times of the moment, it was important to me to examine *how* and *why* geology, as a praxis of terraforming, had at its foundation a racialization production and imaginary of matter. So, I wanted to place a critique of white geology at the centre of the discussion of planetary transformation.

BM: Starting from the end, "No geology is neutral," is the final sentence of the book. Would you elaborate on this statement and the consequences of confusing epistemology for ontology? What is the congenital relationship between racialized thinking and geology?

KY: No geology is neutral is a riff and a homage to the poet Dionne Brand's book entitled, *No Language is Neutral* (1990). Brand's geologies of the Caribbean diaspora were with me throughout the writing and transformed my understanding of what another geography might look like, unmoored from the colonial organization of space, time, and bodies into tight categories of containment. So, *No geology is neutral,* is a way to say that no geology is impolitic, despite Western genealogies of understanding the inhuman as an inorganic category that is separate from life and questions of subjectivity, and therefore requires no ethical or political attention. Throughout the book, I argue that the inhuman is an occupied subjective category, and that in order to think both the embodied geology of life and the subjections within these coupled fields of the inhuman-inhumane, there is a need to think with a geology of the flesh, and how geology has been a discipline that captured subjects as racialized and a site in the production of racializing (dehumanizing) discourses. The epistemology of geology is important here for how it historically made the category of the inhuman as a category of the earth *and* being at a very specific moment in time when geologists were materially conjoining worlds in colonialism. The inhuman as a subjective category was not a category mistake but a way to mine; as plantations mined persons and soil for the extraction of sugar. I am a mining geek of sort, so I see the figure of the mine and mining as a crucial geoformation of racial capitalism that imparts a normative mode of extraction, which has subjugating and planetary effects.

BM: When and how did you encounter, as well as, incorporate critical race studies, decolonization, and Black feminism work as conceptual frameworks in your own research practice?

KY: I think the first thing to say is that I didn't set out to write about race. I have been writing about geophilosophy for some time now and am interested in the ways in which the earth is understood and how these understandings (or epistemes) shape the field of political and environmental action. So for a long time I have read feminist thinkers, especially Elizabeth Grosz and Elizabeth Povinelli for their disruption of colonial concepts of time and space, alongside geographical work on the praxis of spatiality in producing imaginaries of the earth/planet/world. Black feminist thought was relatively new for me, and I think it shows in the book, this delight and serious challenge that the work of Tina Campt, Saidiya Hartman, Denise Ferreira Da Silva, Hortense Spillers, Christina Sharpe, Katherine McKittrick, Tiffany King set out. Black feminism is the most radical rethink of the foundational structures of thought, from the shape of subjects under the burden of racial subjugation, to concepts of being, temporality, and historicity. Hartman, Brand, and Hazel Carby rewrite the discipline of history, how it is understood, offering new, often painful, epistemologies for doing and thinking archival work that redresses the flattening of black life. Hartman in her 'critical fabulation' and Sylvia Wynter, for example, set out the terms for epistemic invention through speculative historical writing (Hartman) and poetics (Wynter), several decades before posthumanist thinkers, such as Haraway come to it. I'm not particularly interested in the question of academic genealogy, but the systematic exclusion of black feminist and indigenous thought from questions of the earth and ecology has allowed some devastating forms of reproduction, not just of privilege, but of the conceit of the authorship of planetary imaginaries and presumptions of agency in modes of existence.

BM: "Black and brown death is the precondition of every Anthropocene origin story and the *grammar* and *graphia* of this geology compose a regime for producing contemporary subjects and subtending settler colonialism." Would you expand more on the "precondition" and the hidden strata of damaged non-white bodies?

KY: It is probably straightforward to say that when we are talking about the Anthropocene we are actually talking about the induction of a globalizing material, spatial and affectual architecture into the world that can also be called colonialism and empire. And, that this colonialism was built on the backs of black and brown peoples, especially the enslaved and the raced poor, for the advancement of white Europeans and settlers. Whether we look at the transformation of people into inhuman categories, the extreme transformation of ecologies through theft of indigenous land and relation under settler colonialism, species introduction, the transformation of hydrological systems, and practices of mono-agriculture, the cost of that transformation is born by indigenous and blackened populations, while the accumulation is reaped by Europe and settler societies. Geology governs this process of dispossession. It is the desire (in the dreams of gold and resource) and the praxis of extraction, as well as a space in which time and space are authored and origin stories about racial difference articulated. This is the graphia and grammar of White Geology as a form of earth and subjective inscription. There is no taking of the earth without a corresponding extraction of relation. Indigenous resistance and resurgence have made this perfectly clear, 'Water is Life'.

BM: Can you speak more about your term "the geologic color line" from the book and its entanglement with Saidiya Hartman's concept of "Black fungibility"?

KY: The geologic color line is a repurposing of W. E. B. Du Bois' concept of the spatialities of racial segregation. In the U.S., UK, and South Africa this color line was drawn through various forms of explicit and inexplicit segregation, in urban planning and political life that attempted to control the production of social space and regulated forms of sociality, as well as access to education, environment, and health. As mapping of climate effects in U.S. cities show, the consequences of redlining still have localised effects, as racialized communities in the U.S. have less tree cover and more impermeable surfaces than white communities, and thus are more subjected to the experience of heat burdens and effects of climate change. We can see this in poor neighbours of colour, who are subjected to increased air pollution loads in the UK. The geologic colour line now is also a geophysics of existence; an axis of material and metaphoric conditions (or political economy) that exert forms of environmental pressure in the present through historically organised forms of racial difference. These colour lines are drawn through extractive practices, from the granular to the global, creating organised conditions of fungibility, in ways that have transnational effects. The colonial historiography of white geology, drawing stratal lines on the map (practical mineralogy) and producing narratives of beings in time (paleontology) brought together a convergence of practices that dreamed of accumulation, and ensured that ecocide and genocide were dual expressions of the practice of empire. These dreams of extraction and severing of relation through the commodification of the inhuman (and the consequences for people caught in that category designation) were an over-compensatory imaginary; one that projected into the intimate reaches of the geosocial conditions of life and its intensities creating affectual racial architectures of existence. Hartman's concept of fungibility, as a way to understand the process of subjugation in the object-subject commodity form, has environmental parallels. At its simplest, racial zoning is about the relation between underresourcing and overresourcing, and the need for redress and reparations for that historical depletion.

BM: Throughout the book interwoven within the rigorous academic approach are poetics and aesthetics. I was introduced to your book by an artist friend and recently participated in a virtual discussion on the book put together by a collective art gallery in Los Angeles. You reference the filmwork of contemporary visual artist Steve McQueen, Toni Morrison, and the poet Dionne Brand, among others. Could you talk about the significance of interdisciplinary encounters and the role of knowledge-making through arts practices in your own research?

KY: Poetics are political and entail a tender imaginary with which to posit a different inhabitation of time and space, a different affectual architecture of the present, and past. In the struggles of decolonization and liberation by Franz Fanon, Aimé Cés-aire, Sylvia Wynter, and Édouard Glissant, for example, these thinkers understood in their different ways how resolutely poetry (in a broad sense of the word) was neces-sary for establishing another sense of the world that was not scripted by colonialism, another sense of being that could fight the colonization of imposed identity catego-ries (and all that means for ideas gender and sexuality, as well as living in relation to and with the earth). Redescription is a form of abolition. In very practical and political ways they understood that poetry would speak to and with the psychic trauma of colonialism, as well as describe and image what new political forms and geographies might look like. Addressing the on-going geotruama of colonialism requires an epis-temic as well as a geophysical shift to counter the weight of anti-blackened gravities.

BM: Sylvia Wynter wrote as the last sentence of *Unsettling the Coloniality of Being/ Power/Truth/Freedom: Towards the Human, After Man, Its Overrepresentation - An Argu-ment*," referencing Fanon from the ending to his *Black Skin, White Mask*, "the true leap consists in introducing invention into existence. The buck stops with us." I think of this quote as I read on the jacket of your book that you are currently a professor "inhu-man geography" at Queen Mary University of London, though no such department is listed in the school's Geography and Environmental Program. Please tell us more about the invention into existence of this department.

KY: I love that quote. Sylvia Wynter is someone whose writing shows precisely how epistemic invention might change the way in which the world is imagined and made. She changes up the epistemic mode to register a different entry into dominant nar-ratives, and through that epistemic work, she identifies modes of solidarity across struggles and critical pressure points in the liveability of black life. Katherine McKit-trick is someone who channels this methodology and shows how poetics is the lived politics of liberatory geographies.

In terms of inhuman geography, I'm awaiting an Institute of the Inhumanities to become a professor of! An institute that instead of being built on the exclusionary hu-manisms that underpin the environmental or geohumanties, puts the question of the inhumane dimensions of environmental change at the centre and thinks through the redress and care that such geotrauma necessitates. A geoethics of sorts. This is more optimistic than it might sound, going further into the question of the twinned life of the inhuman-inhumane is to always see an embodied geology that takes account of relations already in place; relations that suture liveability across human, nonhuman, and inhuman worlds without these artificial divisions. Extraction is predicated on the withdrawal of relation, its violent cutting, and redescription, and so involves the op-eration of power. It is a question for me of how we build, even imaginatively, if not as concrete presences, the institutions we need to alleviate the violence to blackened lives and connect up racial justice and the environmental crisis (or, racism and eco-cide) as part of the same problem and praxis of being.

BM: As *A Billion Black Anthropocenes or None* is in no doubt being incorporated into both informal and institutional curriculum and syllabi and it being more a text of questions than answers, what are specific future-generating ways you hope it will impact new *graphia* of geology and in turn Anthropocene(s) discussions?

KY: Race is one of the most powerful imaginaries there is, and it grounds the eco-nomic system of capitalism. In the book, I wanted to show how racial capitalism was established in the practices and philosophies of geology, and how this seemingly neu-tral subject and ground played a foundational role in organizing and operationalizing the categories of anti-black and brown violence. It is a book about, White Geology, but it is written towards the task of dismantling the structural regimes of anti-blackness. I wrote from my location, in *the* colonial subject par excellence (geography), in an institution, and in the worlds of seminars, conferences, and discussions about the

Anthropocene that I was located in. The title of the book is a wager to those institutional forms of knowledge production, but also a rock was thrown at geology in an attempt to shake the complicity (that is also *my* complicity, located in the disciplines and institutions of geography) to address the material violence of race. As someone relatively new to Black and Indigenous studies, I wanted to write a small interdisciplinary bridge that might encourage conversations across different epistemes of knowledge and compel geographers and geologists to engage with the exceptional intellectual work that has been done in Black Feminists and indigenous studies, as well as in Antillean poetry, in theorizing other geographical modes and materialities of existence. Interdisciplinary work is fraught, but important I think, as a pedagogical practice to undo colonial epistemes of thought that separate in order to prioritize normative modes of valuation. It is also a way to join up the dots between geology and trauma, and suggest modes of redress to this extractive relation.

BM: Would you tell us more about your new project, *Geologic Life*? What is geologic life?

KY: I have been writing, or rather rewriting a book about *Geologic Life* for the last eight years. It is both the empirical basis of *Black Anthropocenes*, based on a lot of fieldwork around geology and extractive economies, histories of geology, and an attempt to put this together with a conception of what it might mean to be a geologic subject in the present. After I finished *Black Anthropocenes*, I rewrote it again, because in simple terms I realised the profound exclusions of my discipline and how that shapes the knowledge practices that I was engaged in. So, *Geologic Life: Inhuman Intimacies and the Geophysics of Race* (as it is now called) takes a particular historical moment of European-American exchange of geologic knowledge practice in the 18th and 19th centuries and attempts to understand how this codification of the Earth simultaneously established a normative account of matter as natural resource and an anti-blackened gravity through the concept of racial difference; concepts that are still very much part of the explosions of the present. So, geologic life is a story of the processes of accumulation, value, and geotrauma in the transformation of the earth. Geologic life also inquires after the material tense of colonial afterlives and extraction in the present.

Thank you Betelhem Makonnen for these great questions.

Kathryn Yusoff is a professor of inhuman geography at Queen Mary University of London. She works on questions of subjectivity and materiality in the context of dynamic earth events. She has recently completed a book entitled "A Billion Black Anthropocenes or None" (University of Minnesota Press, 2018) that addresses the raciality of matter in the geologic grammars of the Anthropocene. Currently, she is finishing another book on "Geologic Life" about the politics of nonlife and the historical geologies of race.

The Black tradition of forecasting

Ariel René Jackson's recent work explores the term 'forecasting' as an artistic lens in social engagement via re-coding meteorological language as a means to shift perspectives of what is understood as knowable. Forecasting, Jackson argues, is the product of 'taking temperature' of an area, a practice of communication and codependency that relies on pointing out systemic forms and manifestations of anti-blackness in colonized landscapes. Forecasting is not a metaphor for hive mind mentality but rather an argument for acknowledging and legitimizing the collective memory of marginalized groups. Forecasting is not only a broad acknowledgement of seeking alternative entry points when approaching a hostile region or when faced with environmental disasters; forecasting is also a method of risk calculation based on historical events and communal trust.

text and images by **Ariel René Jackson**

Forecasting is a term associated with meteorological and economic strategies for predicting future events or trends. It is a process that is based on projected past and present data and the analysis of trends. I am interested in narratives forming out of ecologies of thought via the collective method of temperature /gathering data. When I say "taking temperature" I'm referring to the communication and codependency between individual testimonies throughout a region. Forecasting, I argue, is the product of "taking temperature" of an area, a process of predicting likely outcomes based on historical information and the trends of systemic racism.

Just to be clear, forecasting is not a metaphor for hive mind mentality but rather an argument for acknowledging and legitimizing the collective memory of marginalized groups, namely the Black diaspora. Forecasting is broadly understood as a scientific method dependent on multiple factors. In a weather context, forecasting is used to determine the growth potentials of crops, generate weather warnings, and aid individuals in becoming proactive about protecting life and property. Forecasting, I argue, is the product of "taking temperature" of an area, a practice of communication and codependency that relies on pointing out systemic forms and manifestations of anti-blackness in colonized landscapes. While there are inaccuracies in forecasting, these are due to the chaotic nature of the atmosphere, and for Black people, the chaos is in the non-transparent nature of anti-blackness that surfaces behind the scene political decisions. The ways that information is gathered for scientific purposes leaves out the local knowledge of indigenous people. And I, like many other Black scholars and artists, urge the need to raise up the voices that witness and to acknowledge them as part of the data gathered to assess oncoming natural disasters and the disenfranchising outcomes of pervasive systems of racism such as gentrification and police brutality.

Three general types of forecasting are used in business sectors to ensure and plot out their financial success and growth: qualitative, projection, and casual. The qualitative techniques employ information about special events by considering the past. Otherwise called *visionary forecast,* this technique uses personal insight, facts, and imaginative and sometimes non-scientific methods to assess what is to come. Projection techniques and time series analysis focus on patterns and changes to help identify and explain what is seasonal or systemic, by studying cyclical patterns that repeat themselves. The third type, casual, ties together information and forms relationships between system elements while taking special events into account. It is easy to relate these techniques to the communal conjecture process marginalized communities use to determine oncoming threats.

In beginning to explain the metaphorical framework of forecasting I must first contextualize myself as a Black woman born in Monroe, Louisiana, and raised in New Orleans, Louisiana. Just before Hurricane Katrina, many of my classmates discussed what our parents speculated as being the likely outcome of the storm's impact on our neighborhoods. One repeated suggestion was that this would be the storm to cause a flood in the predominantly Black neighborhoods in the lower and upper ninth ward where my family lived. Many hands pointing towards the levees and recounting their history of being poorly built convinced many who had been flooded before, like my mother, to evacuate. Black residents living in the ninth ward reported hearing a loud explosion and rumors spread that racists had set dynamite to ensure the destruction of the levees for future re-development of ninth ward neighborhoods.

Let's quickly fast forward to spring 2018 when a fellow New Orleanian explained to me that the United States Army Corps of Engineers divested money from building gates at the mouth of the canal. These same gates would have prevented the devastating outcome of Hurricane Katrina, in order to support the construction of flood walls that would extend for several miles. The lack of transparency from the military to local residents resulted in community members engaging in proactive storytelling to their neighbors. This would ensure that many residents were aware of the faults of the military before a representative of the Army Corps of Engineers admitted that fatal engineering flaws in the city's flood protection system had much to do with the level of destruction.[1] Unbeknownst to the weather forecasters, Black residents fulfilled the role of communal forecasters, passing historical accounts of how the levees' origin would play a major role in urging many to evacuate from the ninth ward.

Prior to Hurricane Katrina destroying Louisiana, there had been a matrix of inequality that many in the US, and especially those living in New Orleans, were already aware of. However, many people outside of New Orleans did not seem to know about these inequalities. J.T. Roane and Justin Hosbey point out in their 2019 essay 'Mapping Black Ecologies' that the perception of Hurricane Katrina suddenly causing the vulnerability of Black Americans is a "willful distortion of reality"[2] and in turn diminishes these communities' ability to not only have prepared political and economic resources but also their capability of withstanding events of ecological catastrophe. Forecasting is best understood as a broad umbrella, an anthology produced out of marginalized communities whose perspectives spread throughout their local collectives and, depending on the level of crisis, throughout the entire Diaspora.

This reliance on communal accounts of local histories is not unique to New Orleans, but for me, it has provided the groundwork for my working term "forecasting" as a Black tradition. For the Black community in New Orleans, the spread of historical accounts from elders paired with generational accounts of what has happened before, regarding storms and the building of the levees, helped some to assess the full picture of how Hurricane Katrina would impact New Orleans. This process of sharing communal experiences is contextualized in my testimony as a form of proactive organizing on a large scale in a predominately Black population. In cities and counties where the population is mostly white, forecasting can exist on a smaller scale amongst groups of Black and brown people who find themselves surveilled by neighboring white individuals and institutions. In the fall of 2019, I was invited as an artist in residence in Bentonville, Arkansas, the hometown of the museum Crystal Bridges and its sister institution The Momentary. For six weeks I was housed in a wealthy neighborhood walking distance from the Crystal Bridges Museum. The times that I was picked up from my home by a cab service I was questioned by white women : "do you actually live here?;" "oh you're here with the art residency–do you actually make art?"; "Oh wow this is actually nice"; each "actually" revealing their initial thoughts and assumptions of me as a Black woman artist living in a wealthy neighborhood.

These experiences urged me to look for a community of local Black residents and set up coffee appointments with them to vent. I first spoke with Sharon Killian, an Arkansas-based artist, president of the Fayetteville Art Alliance, and president of the Northwest Arkansas African American Heritage Association. According to Sharon, her practice is a "melding [of] the figurative and the abstract"[3] often inspired and informed by her location, just east of Fayetteville. I met Sharon after a panel discussion she was on at the Crystal Bridges Museum, where I approached her to set up a date to talk. We discussed our opinions about abstraction and the Black experience. I shared my experience of feeling regulated by assumptions that I am an artist assistant rather than a visiting artist. While I suggested that the white women simply did not know why someone like me would be living in a wealthy neighborhood, Sharon was quick to communicate that there is an assumption in not knowing. The inquiry as to why a Black woman would be living in a wealthy neighborhood based on her merits alone suggests that my presence is questionable and suspect.

I also spoke with Rachel Lynett, a queer Afro-Latinx playwright; Sheree Miller, a community volunteer, and activist; and Tonya Jackson, an art exhibition travel assistant for Crystal Bridges Museum's curatorial department. In addition to speaking with these four Black women, I was invited to a monthly lunch with Black staff at the Crystal Bridges Museum. Our discussions during this lunch filled me in on the history of covert and systemic racism in Northwest Arkansas. While history books are able to provide factual information, my conversation with local Black people illuminated the nuances and local history of Bentonville and Fayetteville. While the stories and experiences I heard did not resolve the pervasive feeling of not belonging, it affirmed my encounters as being part of a trend of white locals surveilling and disassociating with their black neighbors.

Forecasting is not only a broad acknowledgement of having to seek alternative entry points when approaching an all-white region or when faced with environmental disasters; forecasting is also a method of calculating the risk-based on historical events and communal trust. Roane and Hosbey's concept, Black Ecologies, names the knowledge produced by communities in the US South and the wider African Diaspora, asserting that these historical and contemporary narratives from Black communities have bearing on how we understand the histories of current crises as well as what futures we can conceive outside of destruction. While Black Ecologies addresses how history is understood in the context of environmental crises, it doesn't address the socio-cultural environments produced out of systems of racism and terrorism. Forecasting addresses the oral as well as text-based analysis of local, national, and global histories of anti-Blackness as a form of proactive organizing.

The difference between Black ecologies and Black forecasting is a question of what collective information can address when sourced from communities largely affected by systemic racism that results in forms of environmental racism. Environmental racism is a concept developed in the environmental justice movement during the 1970s and 1980s. It is a term used to describe environmental injustices that occur within racialized contexts both in practice and policy. The dismissal of oral and communal narratives regarding crises in cities and towns where Black and brown communities experience inequalities, whether due to gentrification or historical terrorism (lynching, sundown towns, discrimination), must be considered part of the lengthy effects of environmental racism. This is not a call for traditional forms of collecting information to be compromised but rather expanded upon by the legitimization of oral and communal narratives of marginalized communities.

I believe that the tradition of Black forecasting grows out of Katherine McKittrick's ideas about geographical redefinition as a Black tradition. In the first

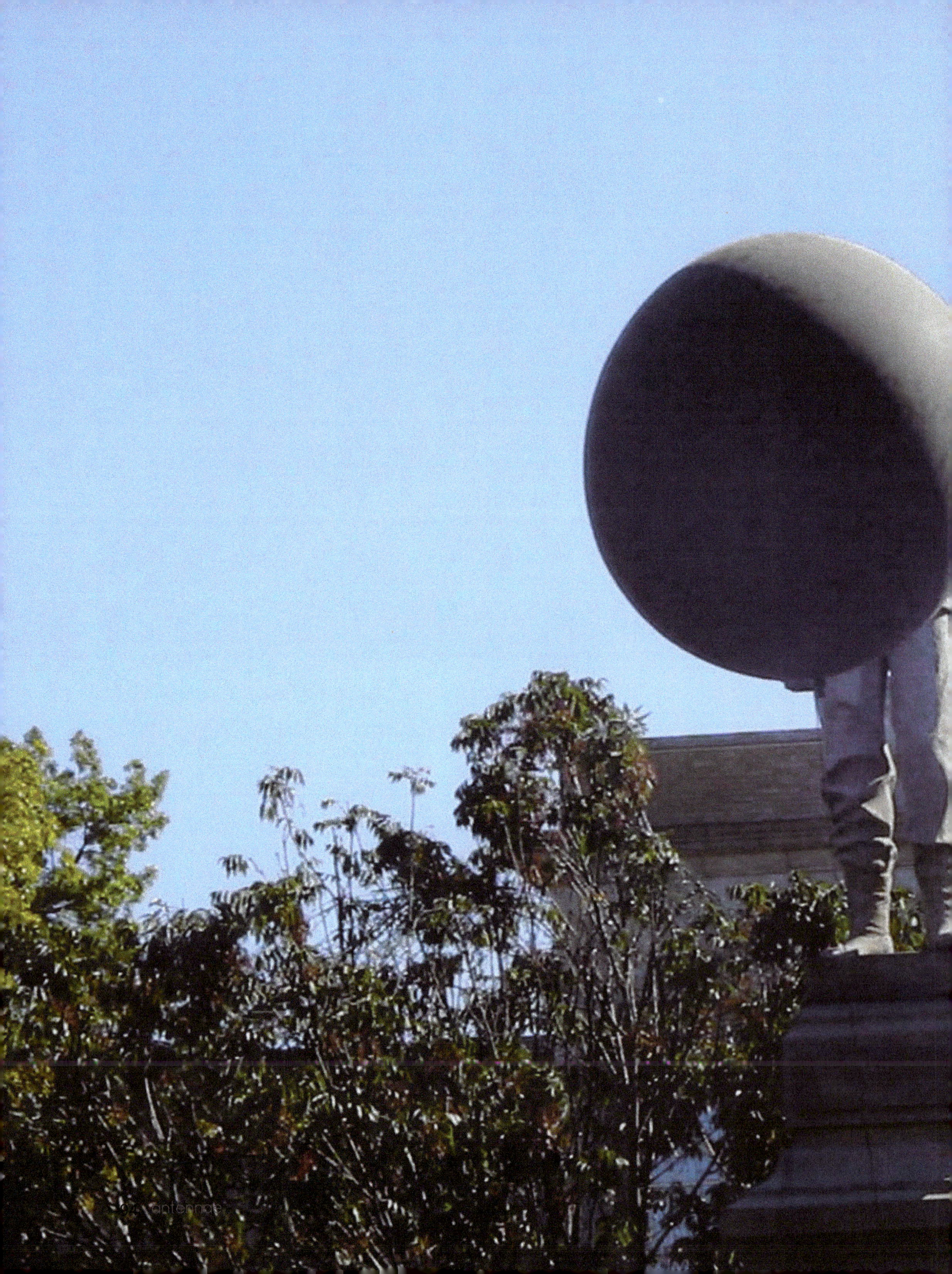

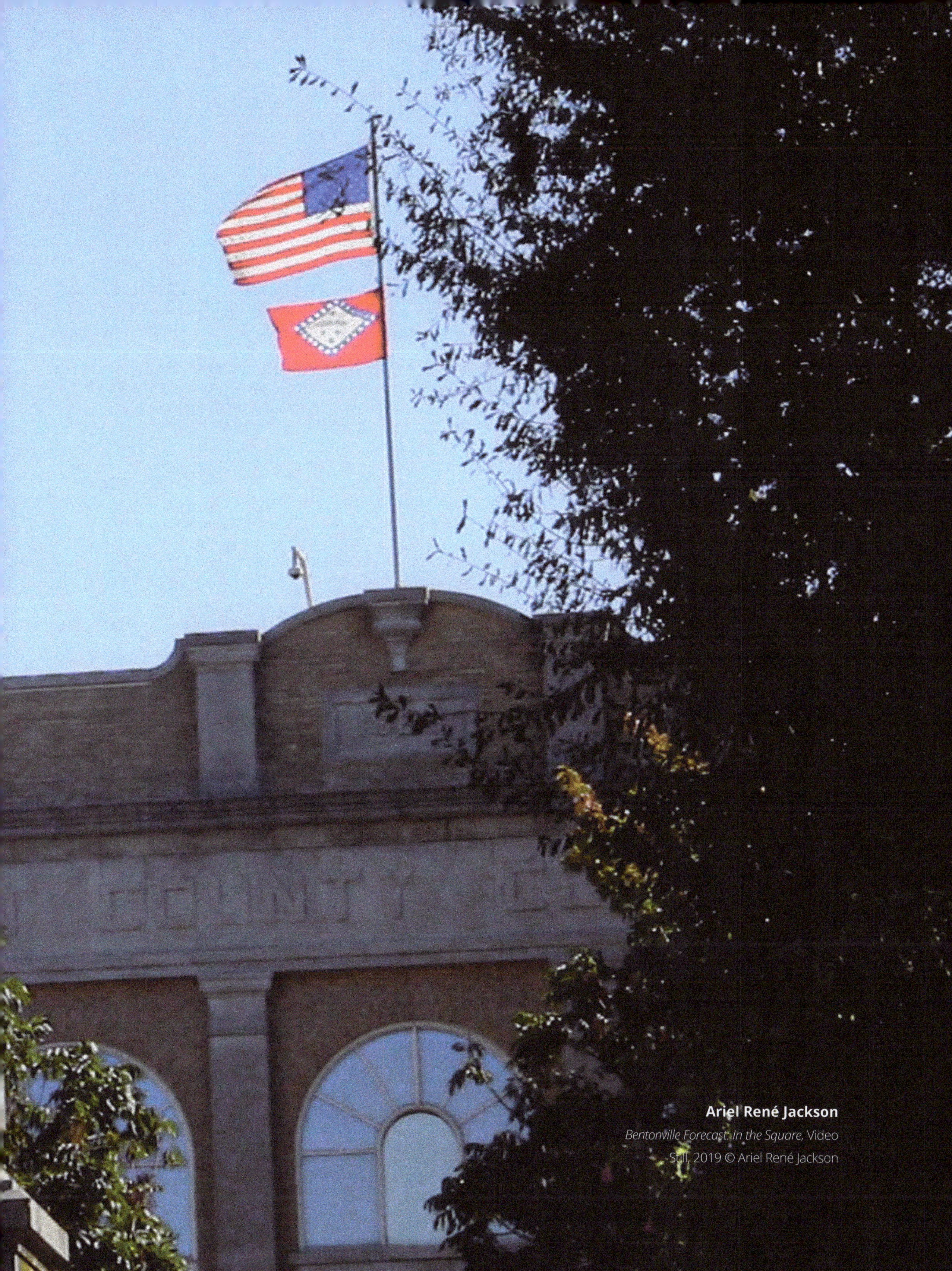

Ariel René Jackson
Bentonville Forecast: In the Square, Video
Still, 2019 © Ariel René Jackson

chapter of *Demonic Grounds: Black women and the cartographies of struggle* McKittrick addresses key debates and problems in geographic inquiry. She first considers that the disciplinary gap between human geography, Black experiences, and black studies does not indicate a black sense of place but rather the practice of "black geographers [...] *placing* blackness *and* rendering body-space integral to the production of space".[4] She begins by drawing upon writers, academics, and poets who give language to a "different sense of place".[5] The work that McKittrick does explores what Marlene Nourbese Philip calls "a *public* genealogy of resistance," words written and spoken with the whole body in relation to what is present in the world within the gap between geography and the black experience.[6]

McKittrick later examines Octavia Butler's *Kindred*, a novel told from the first-person perspective of Dana Franklin who time travels between her Los Angeles, California home in 1976 and a pre-Civil War Maryland Plantation. To exit the space and time of the pre-Civil War plantation, Dana must engage with the loss of something that cannot be physically detected by even well-trained eyes but felt within her, which ultimately changes how Dana navigates each time and space. McKittrick explains that Dana's navigation of a shifting landscape is a production of, and interaction with, levels of space not limited to physical or immaterial qualities, thus revealing the uncertainty of traditional geographies.[7]

In discussing the madness that is revealed in navigating shifting landscapes, metaphorically explored in *Kindred*, McKittrick asserts that the discourse of ownership is one of the many ways that violence operates, manifesting in racial domination and human injustices. One of many modern-day discourses around ownership and possession is gentrification. There is a tradition of adding language to how the black subject is subjected to a grid system. Édouard Glissant and Toni Morrison's own respective discussions on the effects of European practices of domination on black geographies shines a light on how these historical systems continue to contribute to and expose the dehumanization, fragmentation, and maddening spatial patterns that black subjects find themselves in conjunction with.[8]

McKittrick highlights the consistent question that Butler, Morrison, and Glissant propose in bringing focus to "black alienation from the land"[9] which is: what does this alienation prompt the black subject to do in conditions of marginalization, and what does this require when imagining black geographies? This question serves as a prompt for Black forecasting as a means of proactive organization. Communicating historical and communal testimonials serves as the preparation and surveillance of hierarchies set forth throughout a city's rezoning, the placement of statues, and mismanaged infrastructure in predominantly Black and brown neighborhoods. Meteorological forecasting requires data before any information can be presented. This data then informs what narrative will be presented in order to forewarn communities about what the weather might be in the not too distant future. Black forecasting follows suit in requiring testimonials and communal histories before the actual forecasting takes place. The result is a counter-narrative that is not solely dependent on what is reported as hard facts or transparent information. Seemingly self-evident qualities about an event or condition are often seen as essential to understanding what is knowable. However, some qualities cannot be fully understood through one entry point of physical or geographical observation.

For this essay, I have focused on Black experiences in response to environmental racism and terrorism such as racist policies, natural disasters , and gentrification. However, it is not my intention to limit the meaning of Black forecasting as a response to anti-Blackness but as well as in favor and support of Black life. During my time in Bentonville, Arkansas I learned about the impact of the Confederate statue that sat in the town's square. I stitched oral narratives into what felt akin to a love letter to other Black and brown people who seek affirmation of their own experiences with living in proximity to markers of slavery. I performed a walk around the statue while holding a weather balloon, all of which culminated into a short video. In the video, the statue is partially or entirely hidden from view, communicating in tandem with oral testimonies the dissonance between the statue's intention and the reality conveyed to me by generations of Black women. I believe that using the framework of forecasting in my artistic practice pays homage to a social justice tradition of oral communication and codependency – Black and brown people pointing out the environmental manifestations, historical and societal markers of anti-blackness that pervades colonized landscapes.

Although it is needless to state that Black life persists despite social death, there is what Christine Sharpe calls "wake work" which is the persistence of Black life while also tending to Black death.[10] This looks like spaces of joy being configured (and re-configured), ones that look like grief being acknowledged, and Black lives being cared for, those lives that face visible, invisible, evasive, and subtle Black social death in the afterlife of slavery. I believe that joy is complicated, consisting of both grief and care, and not simply a series of good feelings. I believe that joy comes from being recognized fully, and beyond the limits of mainstream western notions of how we come to be and belong.

To be displaced and rendered un-geographic is to be in a condition of social death – those who are not accepted as fully human by mainstream society . Confederate statues, water pollution, containment in flood-prone areas, redlining, and gentrification are all byproducts of colonial developments of racism pitted against the lives of Black and brown communities. In understanding the re-definition of humans as established by posthumanism, we must understand how the humanist definition that precedes it has forced a Black tradition of forecasting to develop as well as its repercussions: hypertension, paranoia, and the inability to feel safe. Sylvia Wynter's work asserts that when we use words such as 'scientific' or 'human' we are excluding the non-white communities and that by engaging with creative labors of producing new vocabularies, we can collectively re-define and recode formations of power regarding science, history, and literature.[11] Perhaps by shifting the meaning of language we can expand out of a strict understanding of what information is factual. I propose Black forecasting as an artistic lens in social engagement via re-coding meteorological language as a means to shift perspectives of what is understood as knowable.

Endnotes

[1] Schwartz, John. "Army Corps Admits Flaws in New Orleans Levees." The New York Times. The New York Times, June 1, 2006. https://www.nytimes.com/2006/06/01/us/01cnd-corps.html.
[2] Roane, J.T., and Justin Hosbey. "Mapping Black Ecologies." Current Research in Digital History. Volume 2 (2019), January 1, 2019. https://doi.org/10.31835/crdh.2019.05.
[3] Killian, Sharon. "Descriptive Abstractions – Painting with Dust by Sharon Killian." Descriptive Abstractions – Painting with Dust by Sharon Killian | University of Arkansas Libraries. University of Arkansas University Libraries, September 1, 2014. https://libraries.uark.edu/info/exhibitgallery.asp?ExhibitID=148.
[4] McKittrick, Katherine. "I Lost an Arm on My Last Trip Home: Black Geographies." Essay. In *Demonic Grounds: Black Women and the Cartographies of Struggle* (Minneapolis, MN: University of Minnesota Press, 2006), xxvii.
[5] McKittrick, *Demonic Grounds: Black Women and the Cartographies of Struggle*, xxvii.
[6] Ibid, xxvii.
[7] Ibid, 1-2.
[8] Ibid, 4.
[9] Ibid, 5.
[10] Sharpe, Christina. "The Wake." Essay. In *In the Wake: on Blackness and Being*, (Durham, NC: Duke University Press, 2016), 11-22.
[11] McKittrick, Katherine, ed. "Axis, Bold as Love: On Sylvia Wynter, Jimi Hendrix, and the Promise of Science." Essay. In *Sylvia Wynter on Being Human as Praxis*, (Durham, NC: Duke University Press, 2015), 142-148.

Ariel René Jackson is a Black creole anti-disciplinary (term coined by Trinidadian artist Kearra Amaya Gopee) film-based artist whose practice considers land and landscape as sites of internal representation. Themes of transformation are embedded in their interest and application of repurposed imagery and objects, video, sound, and performance. Exploring how culture is inherited, Jackson modifies familial and antique farming, household, and educational tools and furniture, hacking each object's purpose and meaning with nature-based material and weather based icons. They were born and raised in Louisiana with their maternal family who descend from generations of farmers. Jackson currently lives and works in Austin, TX and teaches foundation courses at Texas State University in San Marcos, TX. Jackson is an alum of the Skowhegan School of Painting and Sculpture (2019), Royal College of Art Exchange Program (2018), and The Cooper Union (2013). Their work has been shown nationally at various galleries and institutions such as Artpace in San Antonio (2022); Dallas Contemporary (2021); Jacob Lawrence Gallery, Seattle (2021); Contemporary Art Center, New Orleans (2018); Depaul Art Museum, Chicago (2018); Rhode Island School of Design Museum (2017); and Studio Museum in Harlem (2016).

What if the Earth spoke to you as a black woman?

This is a poetic essay inspired by Black feminist scholars that write about the Black female body and the politics of her subjectivity. The essay seeks to explore themes of the Black female body as it equates to the poor care and condition of the Earth being thrust towards the Anthropocene. The invitation is to engage in a breathing praxis that calls for a slowing down through a new perspective on communication using poetics and echolocation.

text by **Clareese Hill**

What if the Earth spoke to you as a Black Woman? What if the breathing practices of the Earth's lugs , large, pure, and scared exhaled Black feminist lessons of care.

What if the Earth, while standing in the trauma of being an invisible member in the past, present, and its slippery future, was able to communicate its concerns about its precarity and your precarity since we all live in relations even if we don't know it, or negate it.

What if the ocean could tell you stories of communities that live under its surface, stories that can't be deciphered through the mundane nature of science and language, but authentic stories that are sustainable without the pledge to inscription.

What if the language of historicity and its implicated value could be abolished by the sounds of the wind, that move through the trees, and is spoken by the animals, only heard if listening is truly activated. Not just passive hearing, but listening in a quality we haven't ever experienced as human beings.

What would the Earth say? And what would we do if we could hear it?

My surface is my body, but you consider it your homeland, your apparatus for industrialization, your commodity. It is where you extract, where you dump, where you poison, where you territorialize ignoring my care in the process.

You commit crimes against me, against my surface, against my body. These crimes have been legitimated through Western culture. Contiguous moments of devaluation. But you don't seem to understand that your crimes will have detrimental effects on your progeny.

You penetrate me, you penetrate my materiality, the spaces underneath me, in between me, you violate me to use me to birth my demise. You violate me through generations, you teach your kids how to use me against my purpose, how to other me. You poison me making sure I am slowly losing my capability to regenerate and to breathe.

It seems that your success, your progress, equates to my untimely death.

Although I take up space, the politics of cartography and the ideologies of the industry seem to take up space in Time which seems to be more valuable. y ou seem to forget that I am here useless you want to use me. You need to invest in my care for us both to keep living.

You think of me as a material instead of my liveliness, my vital energy. I become reduced to the words and ideals of the " Landscape" you distance me further through the language of geology. You think the way you use language separates us, but how you weaponize language further entangles us, making us more dependent on each other, whether you realize it or not.

The language of Time and its co-conspirator the Landscape seems to be the factor that changed our relationship.

Through your engagement with Time and the objectification of the Landscape you reduce me to something you would like to hold in your hand, you think you own me. Reducing me to a commodity that you have established systems around the perversion of territories. To divide me based on conquest and brutality. You believe that is my origin story and my destiny is to be under your long-standing ownership.

Humanism is the moment in Time where this becomes your notion of progress.

This is where the departure, the unhinging occurs. This is where you started to think you and I were different.

The making of the New World you call it. Over Time and your usage of the Landscape equates to toxic ideologies.

You inscribe my surface skin with your exclusionary doctrine. It is an inescapable process that is still happening.

You gender me by calling me your mother nature, by calling me a matriarch, and calling the hurricanes, wildfires, tsunamis, droughts, and non-performing crops are my matriarchal madness and agency. But you don't realize these acts that you classify as mother nature is your doing or undoing; reciprocal consequences based on the inadequate quality of my care. My misunderstood role of the matriarch with political agency in the arrival at the Anthropocene is not political from my point of view it is survival.

You have traumatized me to the point where I involuntary enact your exclusionary doctrine that disrupting my surface, my skin, my container. As you see them inhuman I enact inhuman acts on them.

You cause conditions on my surface creating the toxic air of the amplification of difference, lines of delineation of the we, you who have committed these crimes and who you have designated as the other, victims of your crimes.

I am unprotected while you protect your capitalist ideologies, your systems of establishing and maintaining social hierarchies are at the forefront.

My spatial sovereignty seems to be discredited under your systems.

You have created systems of social and ecological poverty; this is how you maintain your dominance.

How did we get here?

Way, way back during the times of antiquity we used to be collaborators, we used to be a community, but then I became objectified.

Is there a way for you to reconcile your heteropatriarchal ways?

Could we approach both sides of the condition of trauma by returning to old ways of communication?

Let's submerge ourselves in the wake together. The wake that created the path for the systemic hierarchies that are dependent on Time and its coupling with the Landscape, all that bisected our relationship in the past.

Let's take the geographical perversion of the water you instituted through the forcing of Black cartographies by moving of Black bodies as industry and burials leaving traces of refusal that can't be witnessed through our improvised grasp on Western reality.

Let's take the circular possibilities of the wake and make an intentional effort to return, but in a better condition for both of us.

Let's activate Black feminist geographies that possess the knowledge of how to durationally sustain themselves through working from the margins, turning the enclosure of subjugation into strategies that release the body into an out from.

Could we learn to be on the same accord by communicating, listening, and speaking through echolocation?

A collective reframing of how we communicate. Resituating our position to one another of my body acts as your homeland and you as an owning occupant, to a position that can transcend the boundaries of one-dimensional communicative practices we engaged in until now? Could we create a collaborative praxis of exchanging?

What I propose is an echolocation dialectics through poetics.
Poetics is a return to a pre-colonial site and to return to when we use to communicate through embodied knowledge where there was no ending or beginning, a conterminous togetherness.

Let's engage in poetics as it equates to breathing.

A breathing praxis that relies on the notion of speculative conjuring of critical fabulation to unpacking the ability to operate outside of the confines of Time that divided us, that created the non-productive fissure. Breathing together collapses Time and Space making them immaterial objects of Humanism.[1]

This speculative conjuring praxis of breathing together requires collective stillness.

Stillness allows room for listening.

We are in relation through our breath but must experience stillness so our breath aligns and we can hear each other.

Breathing is necessary as a cross-species dedication to living.
Breathing is a productive way of communicating agnostic from hierarchies.

Breathing moves air through membranes, mines, and yours.
Breathing turns air into bird songs.
Breathing ushers the melodic rhythm of the ocean.
Breathing passes through the grass blades making them reverberate.
Breathing feeds the richness of the soil, making it black moist, and fertile.
Breathing blows the clouds into communicative shapes that tell stories of futurity

We birth and die through the act of breathing.

Breathing happens in everything, it connects us when we commit to enacting it to-gether.

Breathe in
Hold still
Listen
Exhale

Endnotes

[1] Rasheedah Phillips, *Black Quantum Futurism: Theory and Practice* (Philadelphia, PA: Afrofuturist Affair/House of Future Sciences Books, 2015), 8.

Bibliography

Cooper, Anna J. *A Voice from the South: by a Black Woman of the South*. Chapel Hill, NC: University of North Carolina at Chapel Hill Library, 2017.
Gumbs, Alexis Pauline. *Dub: Finding Ceremony*. Durham, NC: Duke University Press, 2020.
Gumbs, Alexis Pauline. *M Archive: After the End of the World*. Durham, NC: Duke University Press, 2018.
Gumbs, Alexis Pauline. *Undrowned Black Feminist Lessons from Marine Mammals*. Chico, CA: AK Press, 2020.
Hartman, S. "Venus in Two Acts." *Small Axe: A Caribbean Journal of Criticism* 12, no. 2 (2008): 1–14. https://doi.org/10.1215/-12-2-1.
Hooks, Bell. *Ain't I a Woman Black Women and Feminism*. London, England: Pluto Pr., 1990.
McKittrick, Katherine. *Demonic Grounds: Black Women and the Cartographies of Struggle*. Minneapolis, MN: Univ. of Minnesota Press, 2006.
Phillips, Rasheedah. *Black Quantum Futurism: Theory and Practice*. Philadelphia, PA: Afrofuturist Affair/House of Future Sciences Books, 2015.
Sharpe, Christina Elizabeth. *In the Wake: on Blackness and Being*. Durham, NC: Duke University Press, 2016.
Silva, Denise Ferreira Da. "Toward a Black Feminist Poethics." *The Black Scholar* 44, no. 2 (2014): 81–97. https://doi.org/10.1080/00064246.2014.11413690.
Taylor, Keeanga-Yamahtta, Barbara Smith, Beverly Smith, Demita Frazier, Alicia Garza, and Barbara Ransby. *How We Get Free: Black Feminism and the Combahee River Collective*. Chicago, IL: Haymarket Books, 2017.
Wynter, Sylvia. "Ethno Or Socio Poetics." *Alcheringa Ethno Poetics* 2, no. 2, 1976.
Wynter, Sylvia. "The Ceremony Found: Towards the Autopoetic Turn/Overturn, Its Autonomy of Human Agency and Extraterritoriality of (Self-)Cognition1." *Black Knowledges/Black Struggles*, 2015, 184–252. https://doi.org/10.5949/liverpool/9781781381724.003.0008.
Yusoff, Kathryn. *A Billion Black Anthropocenes or None*. Minneapolis, MN: University of Minnesota Press, 2018.
Wynter, Sylvia "The Ceremony Must Be Found: After Humanism." *boundary 2* 12, no. 3 (1984): 19. https://doi.org/10.2307/302808.

Clareese Hill has shown her work and given performance lectures in London at Royal College of Art, Goldsmiths' College, University of London, University of Sussex, CUNY Graduate Center, The Chicago Art Department, and at Smack Mellon. She has shown her research internationally in Chicago, New York, California, London, France, and cyberspace. Clareese was a 2020 Eyebeam Rapid Response fellow, Clareese holds an MFA from The School of the Art Institute of Chicago, and a Master of Professional Studies in Interactive Telecommunications from New York University. Currently, she is completing a practice-based research Ph.D. at Goldsmiths' College, University of London.

The postcollapse life: a conversation on creative resilience beyond the Anthropocene

MinEastry of Postcollapse Art and Culture (MPAC) *is a curatorial project and network of artists from Eastern Europe, Western and Central Asia, and their diasporas. Founded by the artist-scholar duo, Ilknur Demirkoparan and Vuslat D. Katsanis, MPAC promotes artists whose formative years coincided with the collapse of the Eastern Bloc. In this conversation piece, they join Bosnian painter Mirela Kulović to describe "postcollapse" as a critical framework for rethinking human relationships and responsibility against the provincial identitarianism dominant in both the Anthropocene discourse and in the art world. The authors reflect on their own positions as migrants in the US, and discuss resilience through process-based collaborative practice and reflective discourse.*

in conversation: **Ilknur Demirkoparan, Vuslat D. Katsanis, Mirela Kulović**

The MinEastry of Postcollapse Art and Culture (MPAC) was conceived as a curatorial project in 2019 by the Turkish artist-scholar sister duo, Ilknur Demirkoparan and Vuslat D. Katsanis, and formalized in 2021 when they opened the doors to their exhibition space in Portland, Oregon.[1] Prior to that, in 2020, they collaborated with Mirela Kulović, a Boston-based painter and founder of Art Centar in Gračanica (ACG) in Bosnia and Herzegovina.

What brought *MPAC* and ACG together was the urgency to find a platform for articulating our experiences as migrants from the Balkans and Western Asia in the contemporary arts. Coming from highly politicized and rapidly shifting geographic spaces, we recognize the disappearance of meaning, erasures of citizenships, exile, and the literally mined landscape as a daily reality, though voices are often omitted from narratives of the global contemporary. Our goal was to organize exhibitions or public talks that gave visibility to our experiences, and to connect with art professionals who shared our vision. In the first two years of *MPAC*, before we opened the doors to our artist-run exhibition space, we connected with artists from Syria, Iraq, Hungary, Kosovo, Serbia, Russia, and Kazakhstan. Since then, artists from a wider geographic span who identified with the vision of *MPAC*, including artists from Cuba, Suriname, Mexico, Hong Kong, China, and New Zealand, worked with us through exhibitions.

At the heart of *MPAC*, is the vision to rethink human relationships and and the wider ethics of our shared responsibility against the exploitation of nature. Having come from countries replete with historical entanglements, where trauma became routine and absurdities normalized, the slowly unfurling social and environmental collapse we again experienced in the United States—our adopted home country—especially since the 2016 presidential elections, begged reorienting the dominant frames of reference. Escalating rapidly in the US is the resurgence of racist violence, the targeted killing of black people, a normalized Islamophobia, a return to Cold War-era orientalism, the mass incarceration of undocumented immigrants, and the rampant disregard for the lives of anyone who does not fit within the desired image of humanity. The very communities targeted, however, are also the ones excluded from having a say in the representation of their own humanity.

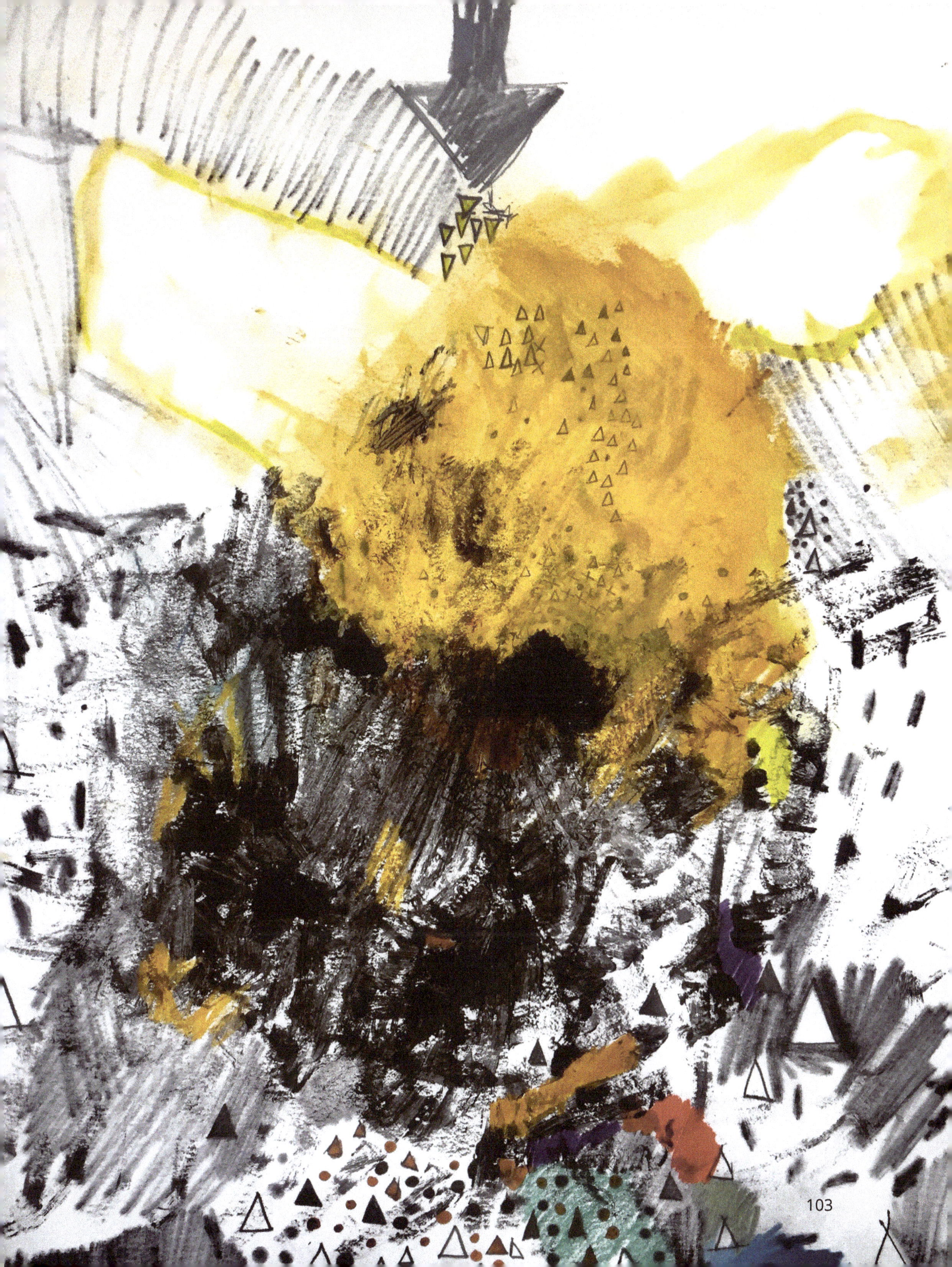

On the other hand, we could observe that the global COVID-19 pandemic brought the stable "West" to a closer proximity with "the Rest." A mutual and inevitable suffering was onset by a novel virus that undid all sense of stability, colliding the once separated worlds in a desperate plea for global allegiance. Disappointingly, however, much of the media attention on this crisis again revolved around North American and Western European perspectives, omitting the voices and wisdom of the majority of the world's peoples.

Emerging out of worlds that no longer exist, we see the need to redefine the human and our relationship to the environment as a basic need for survival, both politically, historically, and ecologically. Indeed, artists and intellectuals in exile know too well that the search for survival amidst crisis and ruin requires the humility of both improvisation and solidarity. It requires an acute sensitivity to humanity's common grounding wherein sustainability in all of its forms is unimaginable without a sense of working together.

In the conversation that follows, we expand upon the folds of our own displacement "here" in the United States and "elsewhere," observing that the insistence on provincial identitarianism in the dominant Anthropocene discourse extends the logic of "the West and the Rest" model into the organization of contemporary art by selectively subjugating and objectifying certain populations in the interest of serving the machinery of exploitation. We reflect on our own precarious positionality as migrants from community-less populations, and discuss how our process-based collaborative practice has evolved in spite of systemic prejudice and exclusion. Deeply informed by post and anticolonial critiques of identitarian humanism at the core of the dominant Anthropocene model, our vantage on these issues is that of postcollapse migrants.

Vuslat D. Katsanis: Our first meeting between MPAC and ACG occurred by Zoom, in April 2020, at the height of uncertainties surrounding the COVID-19 pandemic. From our very first conversations, we dove deep into the questions that fueled our practice: How were we, as artists and scholars, to inhabit this adopted homeland of ours when we do not readily fit within its exclusionary racial ontological matrix? How might we represent our human experiences when existing categories of identification in the North American perspective fail to account for not just us, but indeed, for so many of the lives that constitute it? We had arrived at the word "postcollapse" from a need to contextualize our ruptured experiences since the collapse of the Berlin Wall. We then adopted this language as a conceptual framework to understand the structural exclusions for post-Cold War diasporic artists in diaspora. Postcollapse, then, contextualizes a specific historical moment as it seeks to rearticulate how we inhabit the world and build models for working collectively.

Ilknur Demirkoparan: Within moments into our meeting, as we spoke of our personal motivations for founding MPAC, I recalled a pivotal childhood memory from my first year in the United States. At school, I was given a form that contained a question about race. After searching for the word "race" in my pocket dictionary and hastily reading the first definition, I scribbled "eight minutes," my stopwatch score for a running exercise in physical education class. Race was not a cultural concept where I had come from, so, as a kid still learning the English language, I had trouble understanding what was asked of me. I see now that the migrant's mistranslation and improvisation was a playful interruption to racialized categories.

VDK: Migrant and exilic presence refers to the struggle to keep standing on an ever-shifting ground, crisscrossing both real and imagined borders, while carving out new and unexpected paths for other forms of sociality. Your childhood memory reveals what I find most interesting in what we call postcollapse art: the playful yet stubborn endeavor by which to challenge the stagnant definitions of the human.

Can you both speak a bit further about what migrancy means to you and how it informs your art practice?

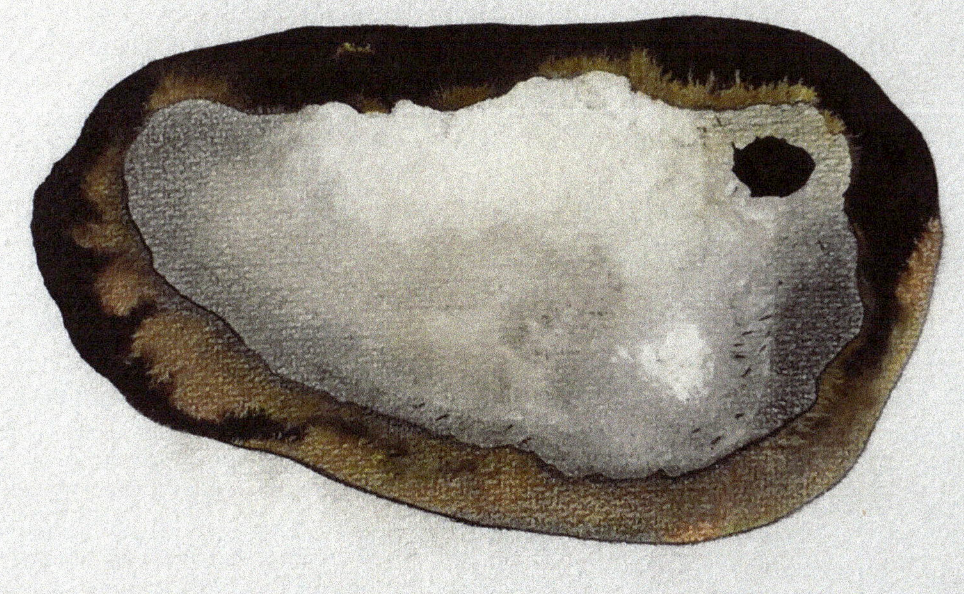

Mirela Kulović

Before Beginning, 2016

Candle wax, ink and pencils on paper

12x12 in © Mirela Kulović

Mirela Kulovic: Migrancy was something that surrounded me from early childhood. Many of my family members were immigrants, some of them refugees. I was born in Tuzla, Yugoslavia, a country that no longer exists. My father is from Bosnia and Herzegovina and my mother is from Croatia—two countries that were once a part of Yugoslavia. In the early '90s when everything started to collapse as republics announced their independence, my father, sister, and I found ourselves in a situation where our citizenship became defunct. We needed to apply for Croatian citizenship to claim our existence. Faced with the failure of the system, we experienced all kinds of separation and loss, including a loss of meaning of identity. Many people I know were forced to leave their homes because of their ethnicity or religious orientation.

Migracy is not something that directly motivates my work; it rather informs my understanding of human experience. These kinds of experiences of shame and being always somebody who is 'the other', 'different,' or as somebody who comes from a country marked by conflict have shaped my perspective. Here in the US, I have the impression people see me differently. This conclusion comes from their silence after they ask me "Where do you come from" and I reply, "from Bosnia and Herzegovina." I immediately have the impression that the atmosphere in the conversation changes. Sometimes, I answer Croatia just to avoid the conversation about conflict and war.

VDK: Which is precisely why "The Postcollapse Manifesto" begins with that vivid statement: Postcollapse life is waking up one morning to find your passport no longer has a corresponding country. It's saving money from your factory job for thirty years only to find the currency suddenly obsolete. It's going from feeling frustrated about missing your bus, to relieved for escaping the Molotov cocktail that engulfed its passengers in flames. Postcollapse life makes yesterday's misfortune today's good luck, last week's wrong this week's right, last month's absurd this month's ordinary. Piece by piece, life as it was known dissolves into a surreal memory.[2]

This is not just a poetic imagery; it's our lived event. It's what we lived through and what we survived. Can you imagine the trauma of finding yourself both relieved and distraught for missing your morning bus to work because it could have been you on that bombed bus? For knowing exactly the faces of the people on that commute, and wondering who else and by what stroke of luck, was also running late that day?

ID: It's also important to note that migrancy is not so clean-cut and linear. My experience as an immigrant (or a migrant, or an expat at different times), and of growing up in the United States (first as temporary, then as permanent), to immigrating back home and immigrating back to the US, made me think a lot about my place in this world, and about who I am in relation to where I live. I eventually realized that what I think of myself isn't nearly as important as how I'm perceived from the outside. For example, my work is received differently as a Turk in the US, or as an American in Turkey, or as the hyphenated Turkish-American between the two countries. I think a lot of my earlier work was informed by this realization of how transient identity is, and of how your own sense of yourself has little impact on how you're perceived by others.

VDK: And yet, what I see in response to some of these events—bombings, redrawn borders, mass displacements—from people in the US is that it is *expected* of those countries to see those kinds of unspeakable violences, that it's just another headline from the corrupted elsewhere. For whatever reason it may be, I hear the logic of the so-called "clash of civilizations" winning again and again when I speak with friends here in the US who are unable to mourn the losses of others, and even worse, who are not even unsettled by the news of their deaths. Then when I turn to what's happening here with the direct and undisguised attack on black and non-white people, I see the same logic in operation: that a teenage boy could be fatally shot while walking home from the convenience store simply for wearing a hoodie;

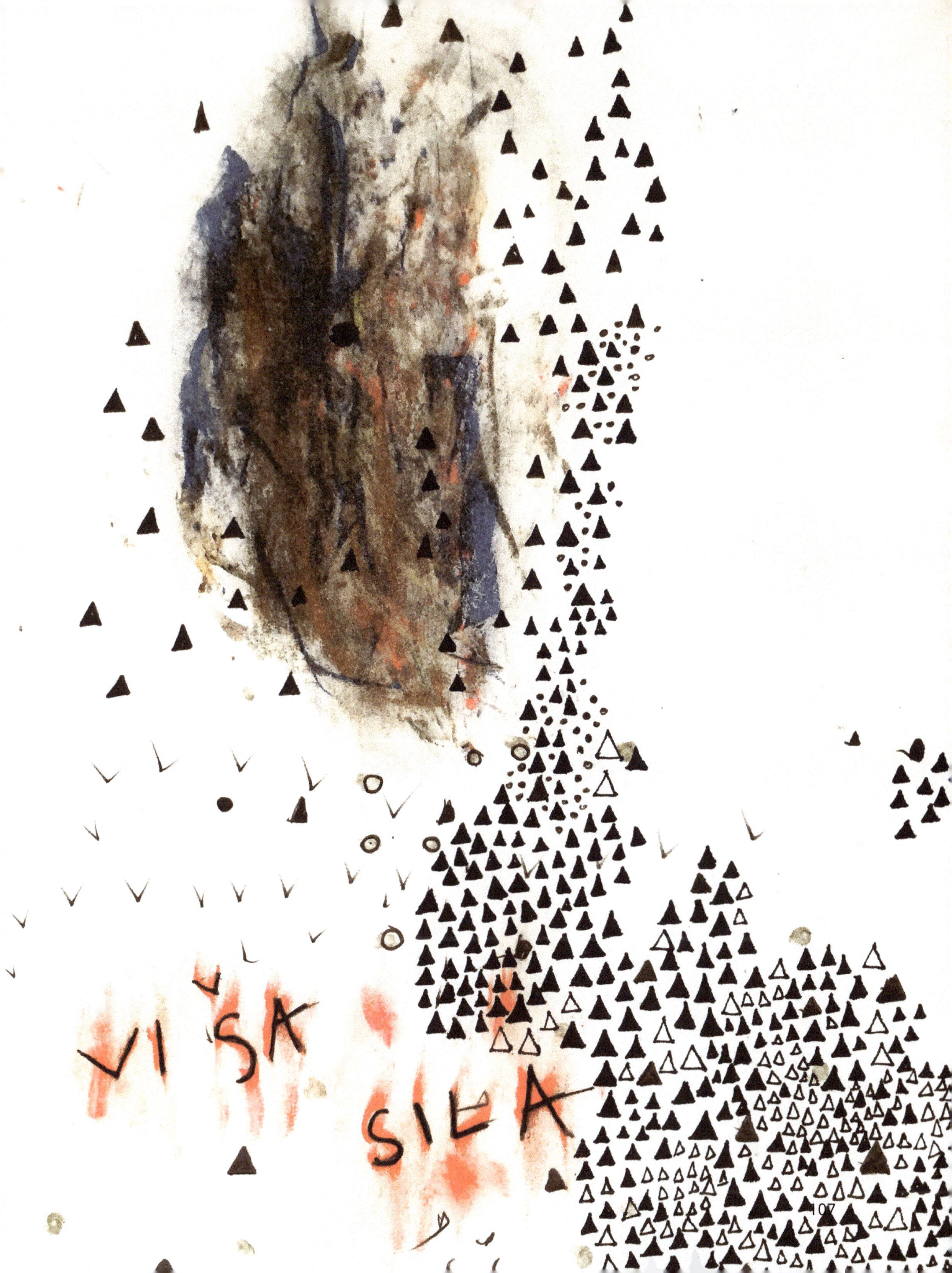

VIŠA
SIŁA

that a twelve-year old child could be shot to death for playing alone in a children's playground; and the absurdity that it becomes just another headline affecting *those* people, wherein their humanity is stripped to nothingness.

MPAC has given us—and those like us—a platform through which to rethink and reimagine our collective presence in spite of unfathomable loss, as well as to participate in the dialogue of what's unfolding in the US. Our migrant difference, as persons in this country considered circumstantially white-passing when it's suitable but clearly not-white-enough, compels us to consider our own language of positionality. That language—the language of the incomprehensible other—is what can translate and transform collapse into creative resilience, and it's that force of collaborative working together that can reclaim the life and livelihood we seek.

MK: A year before collaborating with MPAC, I began to explore the work of other-artists who experienced similar traumas and for whom migrancy is really a part of their whole life. When I moved to the United States, I met many people who were forced, like many of my family members, to leave their homes and families. That was really my concern and what intuitively informed my artwork. I'm a painter, and my practice is process-based. Comparing my artwork with the work of artists from displaced and distressed communities, I recognized a similar visual aesthetics in how we represent space on the surface.

It is hard when you experience not belonging anywhere, either in your home country or in your adopted country. *MPAC* is about bringing artists and scholars together who have experienced the absurdity of the systems in which they live. By this I mean losing one's citizenship, losing one's country, losing their community, and witnessing the collapse of everything that once had meaning. Both MPAC and ACG seek to shape a new community to amplify artists' voices, to include our stories of migrancy, displacement and loss. These stories need to be heard. Artists are the ones who may speak first, who may recognize the unknown, who may transform things, who may not be afraid to stand up for their communities. But it is not only about artists and scholars; it is about the communities we represent, our families, friends, and all of our loved ones. We want to give this community visibility. We want to build resilient spaces of belonging and meaning. We want to defend our dignity.

ID: Looking at thematic group shows in the US that deal with identity and the immigrant experience, I started to understand that if you're a Bosnian artist, or a Turkish artist, or an artist from Kazakhstan, you're an anomaly. You operate in a realm where you are both severely underrepresented and without a community. There are probably so few of you that, in a group show, you kind of stick out like a sore thumb. Why else would all these open calls that strongly encourage applicants from underrepresented communities fail to represent the diaspora of Eastern Europe and Central Asia?

One particularly eye-opening exhibition that similarly grappled with questions of fit and visibility, was a survey of contemporary Romanian art from the late 1940s to 2007 at The National Museum of Contemporary Art in Bucharest. Within the span of one human lifetime, Romania experienced numerous regime changes: monarchy, dictatorship, communism, and democracy. Whereas the impact of that perpetually collapsing space was apparent in the artistic life through the decades, the categorization of those practices did not fit well within existing frameworks of art. The curatorial statement thus focused on the uncertainty of Romania's place within the context of the region and within European modernity at large. It thus declared: "Our temporary solution for this identity crisis is to look at the art produced in Romania through the lenses of social necessity and political determinism, or otherwise-- social determinism and political necessity'.[3] So the overarching art historical question centralized the conundrum of fit in terms of a crisis of identity and a politics of necessity.

This exhibition was mounted the same year when Vuslat and I were beginning to formulate the idea of the postcollapse as a theoretical framework for locating the artists from Eastern Europe to Central Asia within the history of art, where categories like the national, regional, or even postwar or avant-garde remained insufficient. The aesthetic and intellectual evolution we see in the artistic life that we call postcollapse art is informed by something else.

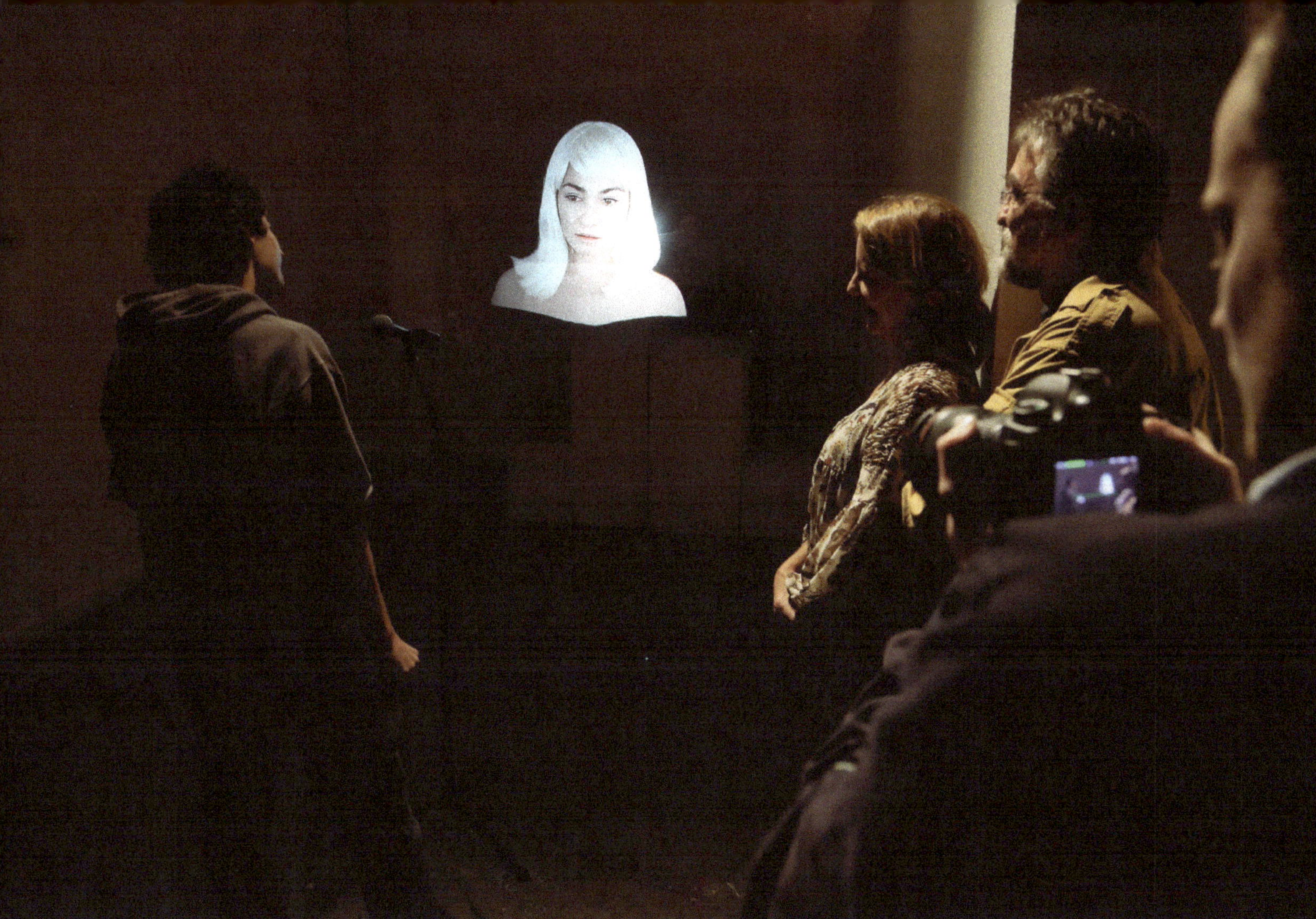

İlknur Demirkoparan
Are We There Yet?, 2016, software, laser projection on holographic film (programming: Codruț Stancu)
© İlknur Demirkoparan

That was when I realized what was so pivotal in our own childhood and the series of migrations we witnessed in our own lifetime. I remember the fall of the Berlin Wall, the opening up of borders, the mysterious Soviet Union and its former republics suddenly accessible, and the ethnic wars that ensued. The art that comes out of those countries in their own light was eye opening: just as the terms postwar or postcolonial are used as reference points, our reference is postcollapse.

MK: Certainly our experience matters for how we understand the contemporary, and for the language, we have to represent it. When you experience the collapse of a system and you manage to survive it, you can recognize other people's struggles. This moment of our COVID-19 crisis, for example, shows us the meaning of community and the value of supporting each other through patience. What I know from the experience in my home country is that you can't remove violence with violence. New ways need to be found. Collaboration as a practice is something that is needed during violent times; slowing down and listening are equally crucial.

VDK: I can't help but think about the collapse of social and economic systems brought on by the pandemic. Achille Mbembe's reflections on the virus-induced human suffering, indiscriminate of either identitarian subdivisions or geopolitical borders, speak to some of our own observations on postcollapse life: for lack of a common infrastructure, a vicious partitioning of the globe will intensify, and the dividing lines

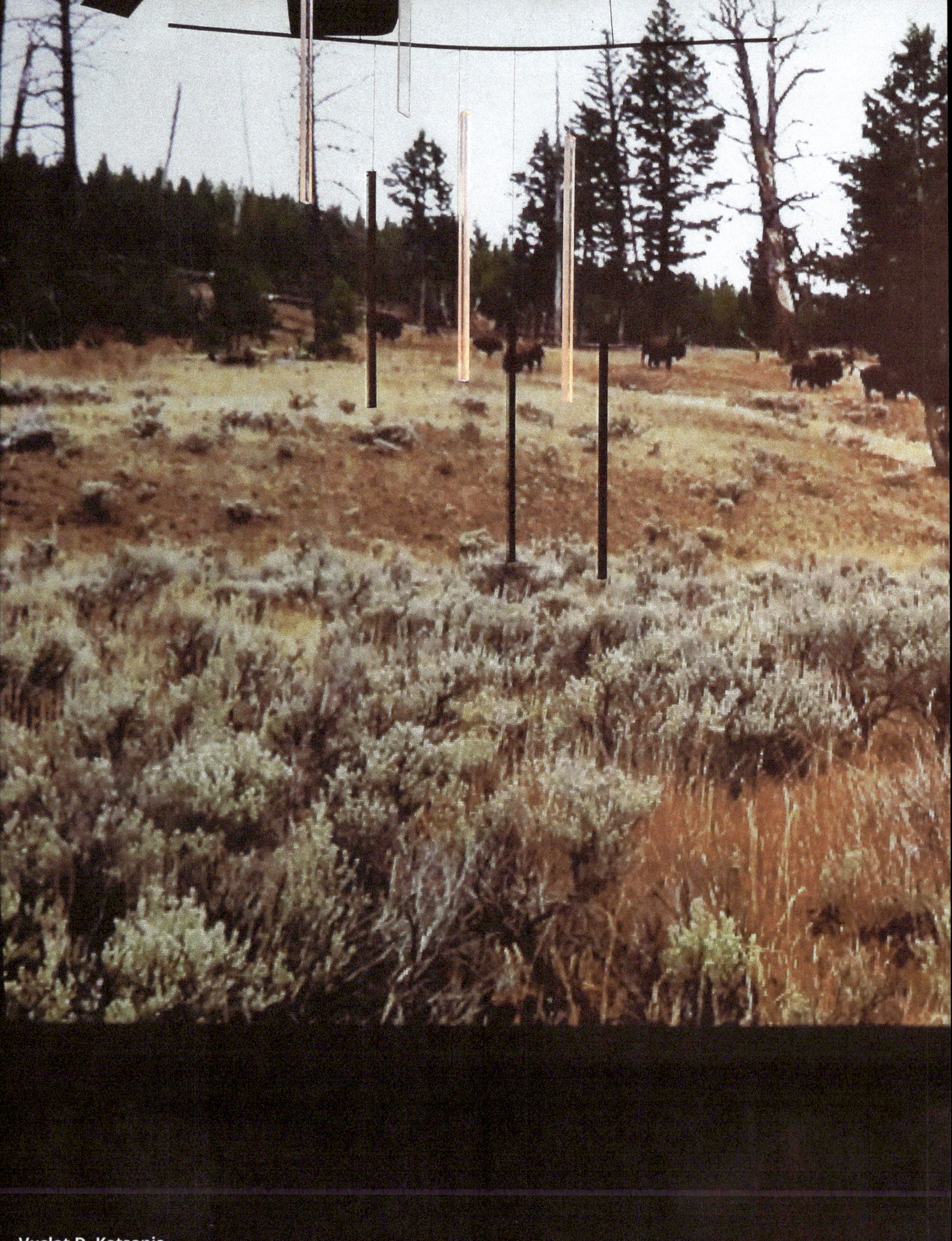

Vuslat D. Katsanis

Attack, (Movement 1 for Renee Coulombe's Sympathetic Resonance) 2016, video installation with live responsive visuals programming.
(original footage by Johannes Rebelein and programming by Codruţ Stancu)

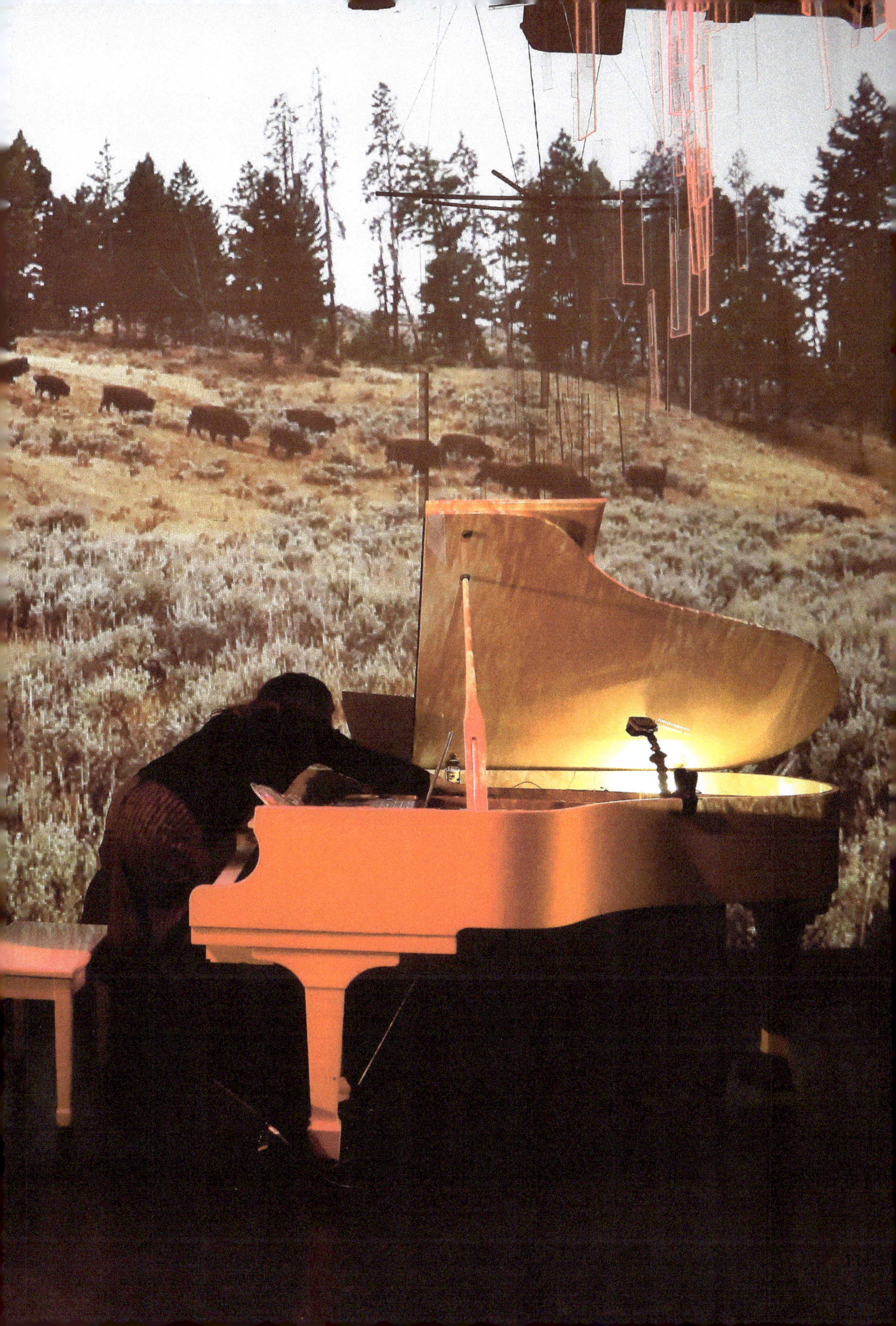

will become even more entrenched. Many states will seek to fortify their borders in the hope of protecting themselves from the outside. They will also seek to conceal the constitutive violence that they continue to habitually direct at the most vulnerable. Life behind screens and in gated communities will become the norm.[4]

The life we live now, defensively, against the constant threat of death serves as a humbling reminder of the fragility of our common humanity. At the same time, there's a very clear and uneven distribution of protective resources, and related to that, an uneven distribution of death. As Mbembe cautions, "a day after" catastrophe "must necessarily be a day for all the inhabitants of Earth, without distinction as to species, race, sex, citizenship, religion, or other differentiating marker." To radically rethink humanity in terms of interspecies survival and collaboration as an act of sustainability, is essential to postcollapse life.

ID: Going back to the idea of normalized absurdities, one funny example was the stockpiling of toilet paper by Americans in response to the pandemic. While the majority of the international community on Reddit was amused by this behavior, Russian users recalled the bizarre things they hoarded during the collapse of the Soviet Union. Empathetically, they suggested Americans to revisit their own past — traumas which might give insight into their current obsession with toilet paper.

Perhaps the most universally felt symptom during a time of instability is the hyper attention to markers of difference. We saw this in Turkey with the rise of the Justice and Development Party in the early 2000s. Nobody really understood who they were. Most people saw them as an anti-secular, religiously motivated fringe group that would never get enough votes. Yet, with their rise to power, the country began to experience a social divide along identitarian lines, and any effort to ameliorate this rift produced absurd solutions. One absurdity was the proposal of "ayrıcalıklı ayrım" (segregation with privilege). The idea was to design women-only public spaces that were more comfortable, more luxe, and safer than unisex spaces. It was pitched that way to signal to the secularist that women would not be reduced to second-class citizens. Luckily, the majority of these ideas never materialized.

VDK: The segregationist logic of the Anthropocene as bound to legacies of racism, colonialism, imperialism, and territorial warfare has been widely critiqued. In a world reduced to resource extraction, the lives of the subordinated and othered seen as expendable and insensible.

So if the attempt is to rethink the human beyond post-humanism in the Anthropocene, one must first break from the narcissistic introversion of western humanism by seeking, in its place, the hybrid, the collective, and the co-connected.

Another important feature of what we call postcollapse art comes from Frantz Fanon's description of "land." In the chapter "On Violence" in *Wretched of the Earth*, Fanon writes that land, for the colonized, is "the most essential value, because it is the most meaningful... the land, which must provide bread and, naturally, dignity. But this dignity has nothing to do with 'human' dignity".[5] The land as the literal ground in which the social finds meaning through cultivating the senses of identity and belonging is also unfortunately bound in colonialist politics of extinction and extraction. Land is conceived both as a source that sustains life and as a resource in whose name life is taken. In other words, in the name of breeding life while bringing death through wars and territorial greed, land is central.

From the vantage of migracy, land as both place and space, as both emplacement and displacement, as both psychic and physical, signals the complexity of the geographical, ecological, political and spiritual presence. Based on some of these ideas, my collaborative video installations, such as *Sustain, Release and Attack,* (2016) centralized what water, earth, air and fire communicates as subjects in their own right, and what geological time reveals about the vulnerabilities of our human lives.

MK: After our body, the land is central to what we experience as postcollapse life. Forced displacement takes your body from the land but leaves your mind (and memory) forever attached to it.

There is a series of artwork I named *Lands*. When I titled this series, I was thinking about the landscapes I saw growing up. But the paintings are not representational. They embody something we can call inner landscapes, or psychological

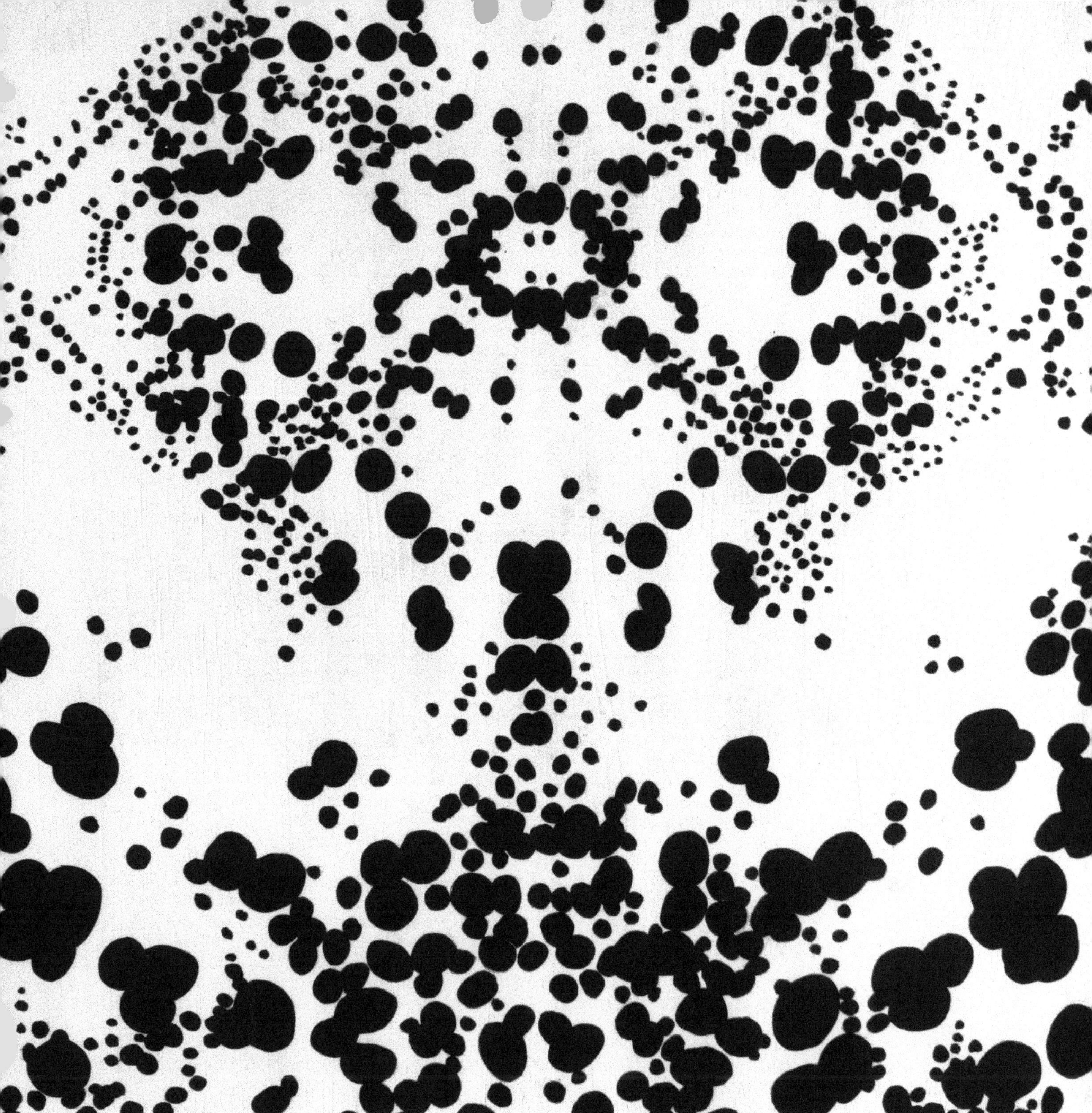

İlknur Demirkoparan

No 8. 2019, acrylic on birch board, 10" x 10" in. © İlknur Demirkoparan

landscapes. Some shapes are recognisable, like arches which in reality you can see on permanent landmarks in my home country. Everything else seems undefined or diffuse. These undefined spaces (either black or white) in my paintings and drawings often cover most of the surface.

And you see the representation of collapse in my paintings or drawings; the memories of seeing many things in my own country fall apart. My art shows me those memories that I thought I had forgotten. The title, *Lands,* became an obsession. I couldn't figure out what that name represented or how important it was for my work.

VDK: How does your artwork contribute to how we understand human relationships and responsibility after collapse? And what do you want people to take away from your work?

MK: I see my artwork as equipping viewers with a new language of dealing with collective memory born out of my personal experience. There is something we call collective memory even if the experiences are unique for each person. My artwork is a physical manifestation informed by everything that happened to me personally, but I wish for it to foster a connection with the observers for understanding the role of trauma, imagination, forgetting, and oral narrative.

My art practice is process-oriented. How I use oils or pencils on a canvas or crayons on paper has to do with my fascination with chance, chaos and randomness on the one side, and with repetition and patterns on the other. In most of my artwork, objects lose their form. Dark and black spots have a dominant role, but it is not clear if other visible shapes and marks come from these parts or if they are traveling towards them. I take time for every decision in the work. Even if I am squeezing paint on the surface and making chaotic marks, I examine them later. These undefined parts have their place and are there intentionally.

My art production is a slow process of contemplation and observation. Some work I observe for hours until I decide on the next steps. I usually start by adding chaotic and uncontrolled marks, then slow down to add many small dots or lines, almost as if I am counting time. Sometimes I like to play with composition and work intuitively. Sometimes I leave the painting in a moment where it looks like a scene after an explosion and all the particles are frozen in time. But observing more, you can get a feeling that everything is actually in movement. It is a meditative act of patience and contemplation.

In that regard, my art practice has a lot to do with being human—the chaotic, the repetitive, the insistent. Art is the best tool to transform all these lifelong experiences into many different forms and languages. People like tools. Technology is also a tool but somehow technology almost removes our body from the equation of meaning. My art practice gives me the opportunity to use my hands, my body and my brain in a more united way than any other practice I know. It helps me find a way and time to process things that are happening to me. But it is not just about slowing down; it is about understanding when I want or need to slow down. We cannot manage, without slowing down.

ID: Until recently, my work focused on understanding my own identity in time and space. In an early work titled, "Fantastic Turks" (2005), I explored how Turkish identity is imagined in Western art, literature, and popular culture. Much like the trope of the "Magical Negro" which Spike Lee criticizes as the story's tool to serve its white protagonist, the "terrible Turk" trope in the European canon antagonizes the West or Western values. Borrowing Tzvetan Todorov's definition of the fantastic in literature, I called this Turkish stock character, the Fantastic Turk, because of its lasting capacity to shape the attitudes towards Turkish people in general.

In a collaborative project, *Are We There Yet?* (2016), I built an interactive holographic entity named the Grand Turk. She was a reference to Wolfgang von Kempelen's 18th century chess playing automaton, The Mechanical Turk, which became a persisting symbol in pop culture from *The Terminator* as the origin of humanity's eventual demise, to Amazon's M Turk, in reference to the hidden human labor behind the machine. *Are We There Yet?* addressed the multiple layers of othering and the ways in which this othering benefits Eurocentric humanism.

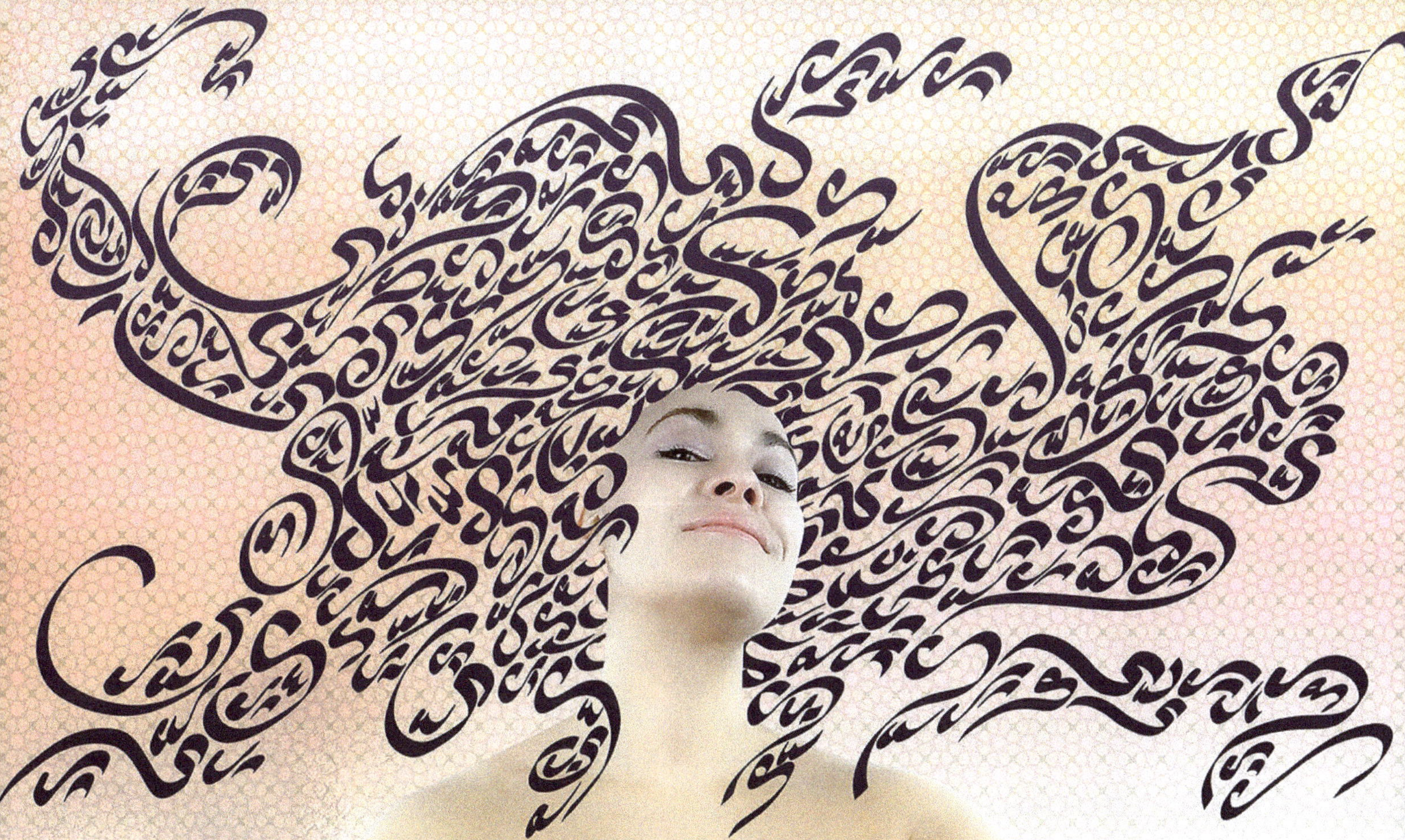

İlknur Demirkoparan

Hair Is A Woman's Glory (No: 4) 2018. Digital edition of 10. Giclee on Cotton Rag

24 x 42.72 in.© İlknur Demirkoparan

    Hair is a Woman's Glory (2018) was different in a sense that it was motivated by the absurdity of discussions surrounding the follicles on women's heads. On one hand, secular feminists questioned why it's a taboo to display female hair; on the other, Islamic feminists insisted that the restriction was in fact liberating. These discussions reminded me of Joseph Kosuth's *One and Three Chairs* (1965), which turned an ordinary object into a matter of debate. In doing so, Kosuth called attention to how meaning is produced. Inspired by that work, I decided to take a series of pictures of myself where I digitally removed my hair and replaced it with text that obsessively repeated the word *saç*, meaning *hair* in Turkish.

    While researching for this work, I spent a considerable amount of time reading about the attitudes toward female hair from ancient Turkish mythology to art history. I unexpectedly found answers in the abstract language of the kilim—a craft practiced traditionally by women. This discovery completely changed the direction of my artistic practice.

    Kilim is a type of flat weave rug that dates back thousands of years. I believe the oldest surviving Turkish kilim fragment is estimated to be as old as 5000 years. Regardless of when they were made, the abstract language of the kilim remains timeless.

    While trying to understand the meanings attributed to these abstract motifs, I came across references to women's hair. The motifs of hair accessories were meant to celebrate life, happiness, and joy. Weaving the craftswoman's own hair directly into the kilim symbolized her desire for immortality. As I dug deeper into the history of this craft, learned that to ancient people, hair symbolized the connection between life and the afterworld. Hair was understood to be an extension of the human spirit, and therefore, represented the ultimate freedom. This ancient practice had a profound effect on me, in that I no longer felt compelled to search for identity in time and place; instead, I found freedom in engaging the history and aesthetics from Turkish material culture.

MK: There is another reason why I am interested in drawings. Many artists of my generation, originally from Bosnia and Herzegovina, deal with the recent conflict and work on a more conceptual level with the goal to provide social commentary. I am more interested in the intimacy of visual language and the psychological process of drawing. That is probably why I explore repetition and patterns in relation to chaotic marks. I am also interested in the connection between the painted material and myself, and all of the variations of destruction and creation that the process of painting affords.

My painting and drawing practice is an intimate and slow process. Some, by the smallness of their scale or the arrangement of their sequence, call for a more intimate human connection. This kind of connection depends on the person slowing down, coming close, and listening to what the work says. In my more subtle drawings of abstract objects, such as *Before Beginning,* I create ambiguous spaces as containers of intimacy and contemplation. By selecting a more quiet pallet of colors and creating just one object on each paper, I respond to my need for quiet spaces.

ID: Deep listening–is what's most needed now. I think about our environmental crisis and the voices that are omitted.

The discussion about how to save the planet omits the experiences and needs of the people who live outside of North America and Western Europe. On the one hand, we have to get rid of modes of production that are damaging to the planet, but on the other hand, it takes infrastructure and a strong economy to afford that transition. The discussions don't include how to do this together as a planet. Over again, the conversation begins and ends with the developed world's perception of how to save the world.

What do we do when the goals of the activist are skewed? Some of the activism problematically romanticizes non-Western cultures in a way that shuts them out. It doesn't really engage in a dialogue with them; it makes assumptions of them and creates these magical solutions about how their mystical ways can fix the rest of the world.

I came across an article about Aviaja Lyberth Hauptmann, an Inuit microbiologist from Greenland, who says exactly the same thing.[6] Nobody actually talks to the Indigenous People when they're assuming things about their way of life. The typical prescriptions—for example, stopping meat consumption—actually goes against Indigenous practices. She points out that changing dietary habits and cultivating farm-based products beyond what's currently in practice would do more harm than good. The reason for their meat-heavy diet is because that's what the climate allows; those are the harsh conditions that these people have survived through for millennia. To come and try to convert them to a farming community with a generic formula about what's better is actually going to harm that ecosystem. She warns that if we're sincere about looking to Indigenous communities for answers, then we need to actually hear what indigenous scientists are saying.

Endnotes

[1] https://mpac.postcollapse.art
[2] "The Postcollapse Manifesto." September 2019. https://postcollapse.art/manifesto/
[3] "Seeing History: 1947-2007." The National Museum of Contemporary Art (Mnac Collection). Bucharest, Romania. 15 Nov 2018 – 31 Oct 2019.
[4] Mbembe, Achille. "The Universal Right to Breathe." *Critical Inquiry*, 13 April 2020, https://critinq. wordpress.com/2020/04/13/the-universal-right-to-breathe/. Accessed 09 September 2020.
[5] Fanon, Frantz. *The Wretched of the Earth*. Trans. Richard Philcox. New York: Grove Press, 1963. Print.
[6] Krebs, Martine Lind. "She Wants to Ignite a Diet Revolution: 'In Greenland, we Eat from Nature;" *Five Media.* https://fivemedia.com/articles/she-wants-to-ignite-a-diet-revolution-in-greenland-we-eat-from-nature/. Accessed 09 September 2020.

Ilknur Demirkoparan is a Turkish-born American artist whose interdisciplinary practice spans painting, sculpture, installation, performance, and digital media. While her earlier work explores the bizarre and often baffling narratives of identity and otherness, her more recent practice focuses on Turkish aesthetics and material culture. ~~She~~ Demirkoparan has performed and exhibited at the Berlin Biennial Art Wiki Project (2012), Highways Performance Space and Gallery in Los Angeles (2013 & 2016), and FAR Bazaar (2017). She holds an MFA in Art from California Institute of the Arts and a BA in Art from University of California, Riverside. Her recent residencies include ChaNorth in Pine Plains, New York, and GlogauAIR in Berlin, Germany. Her awards include the Andrew W. Mellon Foundation, and Max H. Gluck Foundation fellowships. Demirkoparan is also the cofounder of the MinEastry of Postcollapse Art and Culture, a curatorial project dedicated to rethinking our contemporary moment since the fall of the Berlin Wall.

Vuslat D. Katsanis is Associate Professor of Literary Arts and Studies at The Evergreen State College and cofounder of the MinEastry of Postcollapse Art and Culture. As a scholar of comparative literature, film, and visual culture, her work focuses on post-1989 Turkish and global migrant cultural productions. Her works have appeared in, among others, *New Cinemas: Journal of Contemporary Film, Interstitial: A Journal of Modern Culture and Events, Bosphorus Review of Books, Portland Review*, and *Necessary Fiction*. She holds a Ph.D. in Comparative Literature from the University of California, Irvine, with emphasis in Critical Theory and a MA in Visual Studies.-

Mirela Kulović is a painter based in Boston and founder of Art Centar in Gračanica (ACG) in Bosnia and Herzegovina. She grew up in urban, seaside Croatia as well as rural Bosnia-Herzegovina. These different worlds played a major part in developing Mirela's interest in the visual exploration of memory. She is fascinated by the role of trauma, imagination, forgetting and oral narrative in building collective memory. Her artwork—spanning paintings, drawings and text—is process-oriented and characterized by violent accidental marks, which are often accompanied by repetitive marks, symbols, numbers, letters and paint-pouring. Her collaborative works include multiple international artistic and cultural projects that address and respond to the social, cultural, and psychological needs of distressed and displaced communities.

PostBroken.

In this performative multi-form text, mukhtara yusuf explores postbrokenism as an alternative model for healing the broken ontological "covenant" between human and nonhuman. With reference to Nnedi Okorafor's Broken Places & Outer Spaces: Finding Creativity in the Unexpected *and Wande Ambimbola's* Ifá Will Mend Our Broken World *the text explores healing subjectivity. Stream of consciousness, narrative and poetic form are explored as a creative inquiry into healing black subjectivity, personal trauma, and the voids within posthumanism. The text concludes with provocations rather than answers.*

text and images by **mukhtara yusuf**

> *What we perceive as limitations have the potential to become strengths greater than what we had when we were "normal" or unbroken. In much of science fiction, when something breaks, something greater often emerges from the cracks...*
>
> *...In order to really live life, you must live life. And that is rarely achieved without cracks along the way. There is often a sentiment that we must remain new, unscathed, unscarred, but in order to do this, you must never leave home, never experience, never risk or be harmed, and thus never grow.*
>
> Nnedi Okorafor -- *Broken Places & Outer Spaces*

When I first dreamt up "postbrokenism" in December of 2019 I was inspired by the above words. I wanted to write a story of resilience that testified to the belief that healing brings us greater futures than we would have had, had we never been wounded. I wanted to write the way Okorafor, my favourite author does, in the most hopeful and honest telling possible. I wanted to be truthful like she is, accepting the fact that I cannot return to who I was before the life traumas I have experienced. I wanted to be as hopeful as she is, about the unexpected "more" that would come out of that journey. I wanted to write in a way that would communicate the humbling respect I have for the chain of traumatic events that left me with an overwhelming hopelessness and despair. The kind of despair not even the bravest of us would choose, no matter the growth it promised. The kind of despair that breaks your worldview so much, your only choice is initiation into a new one. I dreamt up postbrokenism wanting to write about that from the authoritative voice of someone who has gone survived the way Okorafor has. I wanted to write with her kind of wisdom, and authority, having alchemised my healing, able to say with certainty "this is how it can be".

And yet, I cannot write that. What I have written, instead, is a journey beginning with one moment of breaking, looped into my present. A healing told in fragmented parts, and different voices so that it may exist earnestly close to how I am experiencing it. I do not have one iconic tale about surviving death, I have ten. And my stories spiral over one another and across space and time. They loop in a nonlinear fashion, in a chain of connection, an entanglement that would confounds. Does this make me more or less human?

Root: we have never been human

The posthumanist project is broken, laden with the inherited antiblack racism of the humanist project. Posthumanism has all too willingly carried on the erasure and exclusion of antiblackness, afropessimism, and the nonhuman, non-subject status of black people, that humanism established. Postbrokenism as a word, is an acknowledgement of the brokenness of the posthumanist project which has failed to accomplish what it set out to. Postbroken is a departure from the posthumanist project, and dreams of it being a path to redemption. Postbrokenism here will stand as a way to place on display the voids and failures of posthumanism as a means of beginning to exist beyond them.

Humanism has always been broken. And its exclusion of black subjectivity and denigration of nonhuman others have gone hand in hand. Social death of black people though black *thingificatio* is made possible concurrently with insistence that life of "things" is less valuable than human life. This is a critical aspect of the issues of the anthropocene that posthumanism seeks to correct. However, it attempts to do so without acknowledging how critical these intersections of thought are to the production and reproduction of racism and colonialism.

Posthumanism seeks instead to identify the subject/object divide as some philosophical misstep of modernity and western science. Thus creating harmful erasure on how the subject/object divide continues to exist as the moral grounds for chattel slavery and colonialism, and continues to be the unspoken logic behind antiblack racial capitalism.

Speaking of our relationship to nonhuman others in *Ifá will mend our Broken World* Dr. Wande Abimbọla Àwiṣẹ Ni Àbgáyé (spokesperson for Ifá in the World) says: "There is no reason to think that they are nothing and we are everything". In indigenous Yoruba cosmology plants and animals arrived on earth before human beings, and were placed here under a covenant that stipulated we can not "wantonly or greedily exploit [one] another " because of interdependency. The food chain existed with a focus on survival and an abhorrence for overconsumption. Plants, humans, and animals are all viewed in indigenous Yoruba society as equal and valid subjects and citizens.

Do we need to be human? Renew our humanity, accomplish what afropessimism says is impossible, and therefore affirm anthropocentrism. Find space in posthumanism, but not accounting for the dust it comes with, its being an incomplete correction? The anthropocene era is an era existing post the breaking of that covenant, in Yoruba it is called the age of "Oba Jeun Jeun" the era of the king who is devoted to consumption. From the Yoruba indigenous cosmological perspective this brokeness threatens human survival not only from the perspective of climate change and other disasters recognised by western science, but due to the broken covenants breaking down kinship, communication, and relation between humans and nonhumans. This kinship and communication, the social contract of the covenant, is the core of Yoruba indigenous science, and without its existence the efficacy of Yoruba indigenous science is threatened.

To be postbroken is to mend, and not fix. To approach the broken covenant, the need for healing within us, around us, between us humans and non-humans, as we would a textile. Mending does not try to erase the evidence of the breaking. It adds new threads and layers, often turning that process into an entire art in and of itself. Mending bears witness, rather than resorting to erasure and amnesia, and mending leaves marks. Mending makes things whole again, unmagically and through work. Postbroken is healing. Postbroken is healing of the erasure and silences of Posthumanism which has ignored for too long that many of us never got to become human in humanism, that we were always failures in the project of universalism. That we were always incomplete white men in this project.

We have never been human, and though the posthumanist project sought to illuminate and repair the harms of relations caused within the anthropocene, it ignored the disparities of the humanist project. Not only has it willingly neglected that we (non-whites) are yet to be fully inducted subjectivity, it often distributes equal responsibility to all humanoid subjects. The reality is that the harms of the anthropocene era, its extraction, its turning of subjects (Africans, native people, plants, land) into objects, were perpetrated by a few, and continue to be.

Beyond that posthumanism also extracts without citation indigenous understandings of more than human others. Renaming these under new brands like actor network theory and object-oriented ontology. Post humanism asks us to march forward into the futures of modernity with cyborgs and legible non-human subjectivities, without acknowledging that the invention of modernity was the aimed destruction of indigenous other worlds. The flattening of time into a straight line, a footrace, where indigenous people would also come in last, without acknowledging that for indigenous people there is not only ontological subjectivity beyond the human. But within indigenous humanity there are and have been many ontological ways to be human. Aina, Àbíkú, Ibeji, Dada.

Stem: **ruqayya رقيّة arabic, femme, meaning: spell/incantation**
Ruqayya I am a plant. I say. Across the static of our phones, over the hissing noises of the Atlantic, I am waking up from my dream. I tell about my ascension, climbing a big staircase with Muhammad and Muhsina walking ahead of me. I dreamt of my late sister and brother while I was in that bed, in that hospital, in Tennessee. In that place, where, for some reason still unexplained, I missed a moment with death.

  Ruqayya, it has been months, and coming out of it alive—survival—is staring at myself in a mirror and only seeing unbearable loss staring back at me. Until something shifts. I pause. I say to Ruqqaya,

Ruqqaya
I am a plant
 I tell the incantation, I tell the spell,
"Ruqqaya"
 I am a plant/
There is no end for me/ Even in my ruin
I leave seed

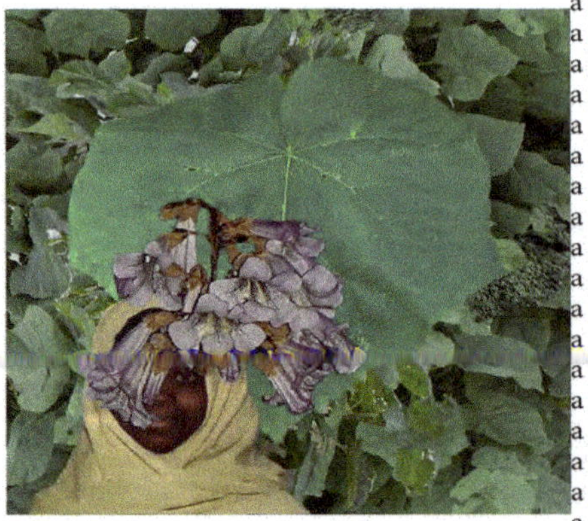

My body is a plant. My body is a plant. My Body is a plant. My body is a plant. My body is a plant. My Body is a plant. My body is a plant. My body is a plant. My Body is a plant. My body is a plant. My body is a plant. My Body is a plant. My body is a plant. My Body is a plant. My body is a plant. My Body is a plant. My body is a plant. My body is a plant. My Body is a plant. My body is a plant. My Body is a plant. My body is a plant. My body is a plant. My Body is a plant. My body is a plant. My Body is a plant. My body is a plant. My Body is a plant. My body is a plant. My body is a plant. My Body is a plant. My body is a plant. My body is a plant. My Body is a plant. My body is a plant. My body is a plant. My body is a plant. My Body is a plant. My body is a plant. My Body is a plant. My body is a plant. My body is a plant. My Body is a plant. My body is a plant. My body is a plant. My body is a plant. My Body is a plant. My body is a plant. My body is a plant. My body is a plant. My body is a plant. My body is a plant. My body is a plant. My Body is a plant. My body is a plant. My body is a plant. My body is a plant. My Body is a plant. My body is a plant. My body is a

Leaf: the empress tree and me
Empress Tree 泡桐 I started living away from my mother's house at age 15. During the Covid 19 quarantine, I found myself back in my mum's house and reckoning for what has now been over a year. 3.2 kilometres from her house I meet the Empress tree, my greatest teacher during this time

The Paulownia tomentosa is the Western Scientific name of the Empress tree, 泡桐, pao tong . A tree often found in North America, indigenous to central and western China where the tree is planted at the birth of a girl. As the girl matures so does the tree, and when it is time for the daughter to become a bride the tree is chopped down and carved into wood for the daughter's dowry. The tree is tolerant of pollution and an invasive tree in quick search for this will come up with the Fastest Growing "Why You Should Empress Tree in Your on 'Most Hated Empress Plant resistant. Considered Northern America. A tree on the internet results like: "One of Trees in the World" Never Plant an Yard" "Paulownia Plants' List" "Chinese Declared Invasive Species in Colombia" "How Fast Does An Empress Tree Grow" "Meet the Fastest Growing Tree" "The Empress Tree–Discover It's Miraculous Properties". With both "male" and "female" organs and is self-fertile. The plant serves as an emergency food, bruise healer, treatment for fevers and delirium, an astringent and an anti–parasitic. One of the fastest growing trees in the world, the Empress grows up to 20 feet tall in its first year and reaches maturity in 10 years.

An unmarried immigrant daughter in a foreign land grows where they/she lands. Goes to outside countries and decides she doesn't need marriage. The migrant unmarried daughter. The nonbinary femme. The unchaste virgin. The fugitive. The unwanted. The undesirable. The runaway bride. The nuisance.

Flowering: can only come from rot
Postbroken is not a lemonade from lemons story. Not the making good of what we have been given. Postbroken is the story of the fallen lemon, of its rotting flesh, flies stench and all, it is the story about composting that eliminates failure as a paradigm. The decomposition, the perishing that becomes the entire orchard.

Postbrokenism is the possibility of a healing that does not seek to restore the dream, it is something else, something more beyond the fissure. That cannot be seen before the fissure. It is beyond idealization into acceptance.

Takes us out of comparison, side-by-side, before and now because it is beyond linear time. It is existing inside the possibility that what is unfolding of us is increasingly greater than what has unfolded of us before. Flowering can only come from rot, I honour every stage of this journey. What we have been and are becoming *need* each other.

Postbroken possibility is healing.
Postbroken possibility is not the healing of neoliberalism.

Is not the call to be a less unruly subject. Is not the conflation of peace and compliance that folds into Apple watches and therapy apps to tell us what we feel, how we feel, that we are not okay.

The folding of animism into technologies of participation in a system that says the symptoms our bodies share to reflect our oppression—rage, depression, anxiety—are signs of our wrongness.

Not the possibilities or hope that promise us we can be reshaped into optimal capitalist subjects. That says we can maintain our hearts, our bodies, our spirits like one does in a car or water heater through meditation apps, self-help books, and psychotherapy.

Postbroken is to heal without seeking to fix. It is seeing how "failure" in this system, is a victory, a call into initiation. Something that is not good or sweet and romantic and does not need to be. Postbroken is the viewing of our symptoms as signs of the wrongness of the systems. As signs of the rightness of our bodies. That there is something right and something rebellious in our pain. That it is a rejection, a removal of ourselves from capitalism's table of ready and willing offerings.

Postbroken is a coming back to ourselves to find more than when we left. To find that more was always there and now we are able to see it. Speaking through our sadness through our heartaches, our depressions and anxieties. To remember that when our bones break and fuse again, they come with more stories, more memory than before. To know that beyond what we have inherited—what we have been given. Beyond a critique of that inheritance— what it lacks.
We always mend
as more.

Surrender

> There is a strange feeling that I experience before I can go into the ocean. It happens at the point just before the ability to walk stops mattering and the ability to swim begins to matter. This is true when it's windy motion not only in the water, but also in the air. The hypnotic ripples on the surface of the water swirling of the air, and the sinking suction of the sand beneath my feet take my balance away. Before I can get to the point where I am swimming,
> *I have to fall*
>
> Nnedi Okorafor -- *Broken Places & Outer Spaces*

Many do not surrender to breaking. Some because we are not brave enough. Others because we do not have the privilege. What a shame to be the former.

When I first submitted the abstract for this text, I believed I knew what the notion of postbrokenism should mean: a theory of healing where healing is beyond fixing the self. A theory of healing that honours loss and discovery. One that goes beyond the notion of retrieval and repair, to finding something beautiful within. One that emphasizes mending, the marks that are left after wounding, that changes the healed object forever. That was in December 2019. That was before the COVID-19 epidemic struck. Before an even deeper initiation had pulled me under its current. How do you write a heroic story about being postbroken when you are in the midst of a new crisis, a new fear, a new breaking?

This text is meant to be as aspirational as it is declarative. It is as much narrative trying to tie together a healing journey that expands years behind and before me, as it is my means of finding and walking a healing path. I do not have any of the answers. I cannot in this process that is unfolding and never still.

The wild beast that is healing, if I have truly seen her, it has only been in the dark with my eyes closed. I feel hope knowing that even my optimism is not necessary for this process.

My postbrokeness is ever unfolding, unfurling, running towards me.

Acknowledgement

This text was written primarily on the land of the Tunxis, Paggausset and Wappinger. Unceded land, held land, the site of genocide, land that was stewarded by the labour of enslaved Africans until 1848. I write in a home built by immigrants, in a home stewarded by immigrants, by me, a Yoruba person of what is now known as Southwestern Nigeria, land of seven hills by the edge of the meadow, eba odan (Ibadan). A Yoruba person whose ability to survive has been held up by many indigenous lands, indigenous peoples, and indigenous ancestors by my own and not my own. My internal ecology and survivance have been nourished and cultivated by Yoruba elders and ancestors and Black African American Feminist thought. I acknowledge that this text is written using technology and the digital space—which are also byproducts of land. Land that has been taken apart and then amalgamated together. I thank the ore, minerals, gold, aluminium, the fossil fuels, and all of the land's labour that makes it possible. I honour that these resources are accompanied by trauma and the colonialist genocides globally that continuously engender them.

Endnotes

[1] In May of 2013 I was hospitalised unexpectedly in a small town outside of Nashville Tennessee. My doctor is antiblack POC and is suffering from what is at the time undiagnosed schizophrenia. He prescribes a fatal overdose of medication. When questioned by my advocate, he shuts them down. My advocate seeks a second opinion and is told that the outcomes would likely be fatal. My advocate stops the nurse right as she is wiping the end cap of my IV with isopropyl alcohol to administer the medication.

[2] Ancient moon priestesses were called virgins. 'Virgin' meant not married, not belonging to a man - a woman who was 'one-in-herself'. The very word derives from a Latin root meaning strength, force, skill; and was later applied to men: virle. Ishtar, Diana, Astarte, Isis were all all called virgin, which did not refer to sexual chastity, but sexual independence. And all great culture heroes of the past...mythic or historic, were said to be born of virgin mothers: Marduk, Gilgamesh, Buddha, Osiris, Dionysus, Genghis Khan, Jesus - they were all affirmed as sons of the Great Mother, of the Original One, their worldly power deriving from her. When the Hebrews used the word, and in the original Aramaic, it meant 'maiden' or 'young woman', with no connotations to sexual chasity. But later Christian translators could not conceive of the 'Virgin Mary' as a woman of independent sexuality, needless to say; they distorted the meaning into sexually pure, chaste, never touched. When Joan of Arc, with her witch coven associations, was called La Pucelle - 'the Maiden,' 'the Virgin' - the word retained some of its original pagan sense of a strong and independent woman. The Moon Goddess was worshipped in orgiastic rites, being the divinity of matriarchal women free to take as many lovers as they choose. Women could 'surrender' themselves to the Goddess by making love to a stranger in her temple. Monica Sjoo, The Great Cosmic Mother: Rediscovering the Religion of the Earth

Bibliography

Abimbọla, 'Wande, and Ivor Miller. *Ifá Will Mend Our Broken World: Thoughts on Yoruba Religion and Culture in Africa and the Diaspora*. Roxbury, (MA: Aim Books) 2003.
Okorafor, Nnedi. *Lagoon* (New York: Saga Press) 2016.
Sjöö, Monica, and Barbara Mor. *The Great Cosmic Mother: Rediscovering the Religion of the Earth*. San Francisco, (CA: HarperOne) 2012.

mukhtara yusuf (them) is the daughter of Yoruba tradeswomen, aṣọ oke weavers, onifá, and eleégún. Through practice and theory, warp&weft, writing and design Mukhtara highlights the generative qualities of indigenous thinking, story-healing, relations and accessibility. Their practice explores ontology and relationality beyond the individual. Through rematriation, narrative and Yoruba theology, they explore methods to heal the ontological wounds created by coloniality, heal the Indigenous-self and recover its relationship to non-human others.